MARRIAGE MEANS ENCOUNTER

MARRIAGE MEANS ENCOUNTER

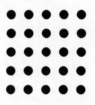

Edited by

GEORGE ROLEDER

Mt. San Antonio College

WM. C. BROWN COMPANY PUBLISHERS
DUBUQUE, IOWA

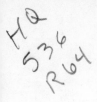

This book is dedicated to my parents on their fiftieth wedding anniversary. Theirs has been a lifetime of successful encounters.

Why This Book
xiii

AREA 1
ENCOUNTER IN PREMARITAL SEX

My Life with Women
3

Richard Armour recalls the tragic comedy of his childhood introduction to women, sex, and marriage.

The American Dating Game: Heterosexual Stage
7

Frank Cox describes the plight and behavior of adolescents biologically prepared and socially propelled toward sexual encounter long before society permits its complete expression.

I Love Him ... But Do I Like Him?
15

Daniel Sugarman and Rollie Hochstein (Seventeen) claim that modern marriages based on love work out no better than older marriages based on arrangement by parents. Suggestions for improving chances of success are offered.

Forms of Sex Knowledge
22

Ian Fraser reports findings of a seven-year interaction with adolescents in Scotland. Gaps in sex information are noted.

Some Concluding Comments on Premarital Sex
29

Robert Bell shows how it may be possible to predict the emerging sexual codes of the young by studying the "wrongs" of adults.

It's Not Who You Know in Rock Circles Anymore
36

Lucinda Franks (UPI) updates the movement of musical star worshippers from old-fashioned swoon to the real thing: sex.

The Harrad Experiment   *Novelist Robert Rimmer relates the*
38   *arrangements in an (imagined) ex-*
perimental college where males and
females live as roommates and keep
required diaries of their sex adjust-
ment.

"No!"   *This editorial (Decision) advocates in*
43   *definite terms the non-sex approach*
to premarital relations and gives
samples of how it is handled.

AREA 2
ENCOUNTER IN MARITAL SEX

Sex Experts Discuss Future   *Pamela Reeves (UPI) reports the*
47   *at-odds conversations of Masters,*
Watts, Fort, Hunt, Calderone,
and Simon.

What Goes on in His Head   *Tom Congdon (Glamour) relates his*
When You're Pregnant?   *personal experiences with pregnancy*
49   *from a husband's point of view. Re-*
actions of panic, frustration, joy, and
relief are documented.

Who Makes the Babies?   *Stanford biologists Paul Ehrlich and*
57   *John Holdren (Saturday Review)*
explain why being able to afford
large families is not an acceptable
reason for having them.

Group Sex   *Gordon Bermant (Psychology Today)*
60   *reviews a current book by a par-*
ticipant in sexually deviant groups
practicing as "swingers."

The Report of the Commission   *Excerpts from the findings include*
on Obscenity and Pornography   *the effects of explicit sexual materials,*
63   *need for sex education, and legislative*
recommendations. Also printed are
sections of a report by three dissent-
ing members who challenge the
motives, methods, and conclusions
of the majority.

AREA 3
ENCOUNTER IN MARITAL ROLES

Division of Labor in Two-Income Families 93 — *Robert Blood, Jr., reports research to show what happens to housekeeping and child-rearing tasks when the wife goes out to work.*

Mother Went to Work ... and Father Stayed Home 99 — *Jorie Lueloff (Woman's Day) details how a switch in economic roles saved a marriage and gave the mates new understanding of each other's feelings.*

Why Working Mothers Have Happier Children 108 — *Psychiatrist Bruno Bettelheim (Ladies' Home Journal) examines the female's conflict in trying to be both a good mother and a happy woman.*

Fatherhood and the Emerging Family 113 — *Leonard Benson asks how the wage-earner can still be a man if his traditional status as breadwinner is undermined by the modern welfare ethic. Research includes comparison with Russian, Israeli Kibbutzim, and Canadian family life.*

AREA 4
ENCOUNTER IN PARENTHOOD

Why Are Children So Unreasonable? 123 — *Betty Canary (NEA) records what happened when her young son began thinking as he had been taught to think.*

Can I Practice What I Preach? 125 — *Helen Jean Burn (McCall's) describes the effect in her home when her (white) daughter began dating a black.*

Helping Children Grow Up Sexually—How? When? By Whom? 132 — *Eleanore Luckey (Children) reviews the race toward sex education in public schools amidst confusion resulting from the wide range of sexual behavior and values existing in this country.*

Spare the Rod, Use Behavior Mod
142

Roger McIntire (Psychology Today)
illustrates how techniques of condi-
tioning were used by parents and
professionals to shape the desired
behavior of family members.

Why Parents Should Take
a Firm Stand
147

Bruno Bettelheim (Ladies' Home
Journal) *suggests through conver-*
sations with mothers the relationship
between making choices and devel-
opment of a healthy personality.

AREA 5
ENCOUNTER IN THE NEW MARRIAGE

A Valentine's Guide to
the "New" Woman
155

Women's Liberation spokeswoman
Sandra Shevey (Family Weekly) *out-*
lines the correct approach to courting
the liberated woman.

Today's Marriage or the New
Marriage—Which Way for You?
158

Herbert Otto contrasts today's mar-
riage and the aims being practiced
by a new class of Americans—
the actualizers.

Practicing Marriage Without
a License
160

Betty Liddick (Los Angeles Times)
reports on her visits in homes of
unmarried couples living together as
though married. Financial, legal,
moral, and psychological implications
are discussed by current authorities.

The Intimate Network of Families
as a New Structure
177

Frederick Stoller argues that neigh-
borhood families must organize to
save themselves from the damaging
effects of isolation. He shows how to
create a clan.

Cold Mountain Farm
181

Joyce Gardener shares intimate expe-
riences of members in a group family
commune, struggling with each other,
with drifters, and with the public.

AREA 6
ENCOUNTER IN MARITAL FAILURE

The Scope of Successful Marriage
193

Judson and Mary Landis describe marriage as a powerful force whose interactions move persons either toward the alluring marriage ideal or toward personal destruction.

Professionals View Their
Failing Marriage
195

Herbert Otto reveals his notes on conversations with divorced friends.

A Child's Eye View of a
Failing Marriage
198

Psychiatrist J. Louise Despert reports in detail the effects of parents' discord and divorce on their child and suggests ways to help children throughout the stages of divorce in the family.

Children Who Hate
213

Fritz Redl and David Wineman describe the sources which produced the most hateful children with whom they had ever worked.

Thousands Finding Marital Relief
in "No Fault" Divorce
215

Reporter Jack Fox (UPI) illustrates the effect of recent changes in California divorce laws.

The Double Cross
217

George Roleder provides a two-part survey which can alert dating and married pairs to attractive but troublesome personality trait matches.

Index
227

Marriage Means Encounter was compiled for those who suspect that living together in love does not come naturally.

This collection of articles is designed for those who are hoping to find happiness in their present or future marriage, and are willing to work at it—reading, thinking, discussing, experimenting.

The aim of this book is to expose six areas of encounter which are common to all marriages regardless of type, nationality, class, or religion. These six areas are (1) premarital sex, (2) marital sex, (3) marital roles, (4) parenthood, (5) the new marriage, and (6) marital failure. Areas of encounter are arranged in the chronological order of a family life cycle. Articles within each area follow a sequence which first introduces the elements of the encounter, followed by articles which illustrate crucial personal relations between courting couples, members of the family, or between members and the public. An annotated table of contents will help you select the information which best fits your interest or need.

The goal in selection of articles was to find writers who had reported an actual experience with one of these vital encounters. Some have written as participating members. Others have reported as sociologists and psychologists. Still others have shared their experiences through professional journalists. Thus there is scholarly research. There is also dialogue. There is even humor, for much of marriage is enjoyable, and a book of readings about marriage ought to reflect that fact.

Reading the stories of courtship and marriage printed here can help your important habit of watching and wondering, which goes on constantly and will continue throughout your married life. Here you merely take a slower, longer, more inclusive and organized look at other people's experiences. There should come a sharpened sense of what you will need to do to make your marriage (whatever arrangement you choose) a growing source of happiness for you and your family.

Students of marriage and family courses continue to surprise me. In reading their reports and hearing them talk with each other, I am impressed with their seriousness about doing a good job—as good as or better than the marriage which produced them. Many of the articles chosen for this book were first read and recommended by them, for which I am grateful. If you are one of those serious ones, continue to work hard. We need your success. Your happiness will also be ours.

Special thanks must go to my wife Betty, whose "encounter" was with our closed study door while this project was underway. Thanks, also, to Cindy, Nancy, and Amy, who keep me realistic about family life. For professional guidance I am indebted to Bob Nash, a knowledgeable and patient editor.

GEORGE ROLEDER

AREA 1

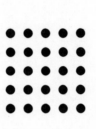

ENCOUNTER IN
PREMARITAL SEX

MY LIFE WITH WOMEN

Richard Armour

Until I was eight years old, I had no thought of getting married. Though small for my age, I was the best marble player in our block, with a large bag of aggies and immies that I had won while playing for keeps. My mind was on marbles, not women, and there seemed no reason for any change, especially when I was doing so well.

It is not that I was unaware of sex, or at least of the difference between the sexes. There was a blonde next door who was seven and a half, going on eight, and she was always coming over to our house and hanging around. I knew what she was after: my marbles. Once, to get rid of her, I gave her a couple of dobies, but that must have given her the idea she was making progress and might get some aggies out of me if she kept at it.

But that's all she ever got, just those dobies. I might have given her more, if I had liked her, but I didn't. She was too fat. And she picked her nose.

However, it was from this girl next door, the first blonde in my life, that I learned about the difference between the sexes. It was very simple. Boys can play marbles and girls can't. This girl used to beg me to show her how, and I did, but she could never learn. There was something wrong with her aim, or she didn't have any muscle in her thumb, or something.

One day I let her have it. "The trouble with you," I told her, "is that you are a girl."

This hit her pretty hard. For a while she just stood there, picking her nose. Then she started bawling and ran home.

The sad part about it was that after she had had a good cry, and her mother had washed her face, which really needed it, she came back over to our house as if nothing had happened. The way I disliked that girl, it's a wonder I wasn't finished with women for life. Certainly she contributed to my decision, when I was eight years old, never to marry.

Then I fell in love with Miss Webster, and everything changed.

Miss Webster was my third-grade teacher and all I had ever hoped for in a woman. She had a soft, sweet voice. Her eyes crinkled when she smiled. She smelled good. And she could write on the board without making the chalk squeak.

One day when I came home from school, I broke the news to my mother, who was in the kitchen making cookies.

"I'm going to marry Miss Webster," I said.

"That's nice," my mother said, not the least surprised. It was almost as if she already knew. Could Miss Webster have told her? And yet I hadn't told Miss Webster myself.

"And we're going to have two children, both boys," I said.

"That's fine," my mother said. "Now you can scrape the bowl and lick the spoon."

All the time I was scraping the bowl and licking the spoon, I was thinking of Miss Webster. We were going to be very happy together. I would look after her and give her everything she wanted, and she could just stay home and make cookies.

A short time afterward, I disclosed my plans to one of my friends during recess while we were swinging on the monkey bars.

"I'm going to marry Miss Webster," I said.

"So am I," he said.

This came as a surprise to me. I was even more surprised to learn, after a little asking around, that every boy in the class planned to marry Miss Webster. I was not greatly disturbed, however, since I had an advantage over most of the others. We were seated alphabetically, and I sat in the front row. I was much closer to Miss Webster than boys like Jack Williams and Eddy Zorn. Besides, Miss Webster obviously liked me. Who else got to clap erasers twice a week?

But I had competition more serious than my classmates. One day I saw Miss Webster go by in a sporty car with the top down. She smiled and waved at me. I waved back but I couldn't smile. A man was driving the car, and he had one hand on the steering wheel and the other around Miss Webster. After waving at me, Miss Webster said something to the man, and he turned and looked back at me and laughed.

As the car drove on and disappeared around a corner, I had a feeling that I was losing Miss Webster. For the first time it occurred to me that she might marry someone else, someone who owned a car and was old enough to drive it.

I was right about Miss Webster. Just before the end of the school year, when I should have been excited about summer vacation and being promoted to fourth grade, I got the bad news. Though I had rather expected it, I was pretty depressed for several days.

"I am not going to teach after this year," Miss Webster told our class. "I am getting married." The girls cried, they were so happy, and the boys would have cried too, if they had not been boys. As it was, they just looked miserable.

It was the first time I had ever been beaten out by a rival, and I took it hard. Miss Webster had led me on and then let me down. But she wasn't as much to blame as the man in the car. I hated him. A couple of times I imagined myself fighting a duel with him, the winner to get Miss Webster. One time it was with swords and one time it was with pistols, and I won both times. But I couldn't go on imagining forever, and when I wasn't imagining I knew I had lost Miss Webster for good.

When I came home from school and told my mother Miss Webster was getting married, she sympathized with me.

"I know how you feel," she said. "But I've always thought she was a little old for you."

Then she told me that Miss Webster was twenty-two, and by the time I was twenty-two she would be thirty-six. By the time I was thirty-six she would be fifty.

"A woman can be older than her husband," she said, "but she shouldn't be too much older. I'm three years older than your father, and that's about enough."

"Why?" I asked.

"Well, it just is," she said, and seemed to think this a satisfactory answer. It was all I could get out of her.

By the time I was eight years old, I had learned a good deal about women. From the girl next door I learned that the ones who are always after you are the ones you don't want. From Miss Webster I learned that the ones you want are always the wrong age or something, and then somebody comes and carries them off anyhow.

It was discouraging enough to lose Miss Webster, but that wasn't all. A boy moved into the neighborhood who could knuckle better than I could, and he won all of my aggies and most of my immies.

It was a bad year for me.

After that unfortunate experience with Miss Webster, I thought I was through with women. This was only partly because I had been beaten out by a rival suitor. It was also because, about the same time, I was given a bicycle by my parents, who thought I needed cheering up. I got so busy riding that bicycle and oiling it and polishing it that for a while I forgot about women entirely. You just can't think about women when you are pedaling hard and ringing your bell and being chased by a dog.

But this didn't last long. I was barely nine when Carl Hawkins, who was ten and big for his age, told me some things about Lucille Briggs, who was also ten and big for her age (they were all big for their age but me), that started me thinking. My first reaction was disbelief.

"You're making it up," I said to Carl.

"No, I'm not," Carl said. "Cross my heart."

According to Carl, Lucille had come over to his house one morning when she knew his mother and father were away, and she had done some really peculiar things. She had done them in a clothes closet into which she had taken Carl after locking the closet door. It was hot and stuffy in there and the light wasn't any too good, but Carl swore he could see perfectly well and this was the way it was.

I asked Carl to tell me the whole thing over again because I wasn't sure I had got it straight, and he did, gladly.

Well, I was really amazed. Momentarily, I forgot about my bicycle. I kept thinking about Lucille, in that closet with the door locked. I wondered what I would do if Lucille, who lived in the middle of the next block, ever came down to my house and did these things.

Once, when my parents were away, Lucille came over to our house and I fully expected her to head straight for our hall closet and pull me in there with her and lock the door. I was frightened and confused, and I tried to remember everything Carl had told me. But Lucille only wanted to get a bowl her mother had lent my mother. She went out to the kitchen, right past the closet, and came back to the front door, past the closet again, and all she said to me was, "My mother said that if your mother kept the bowl much longer she'd think she owned it."

When Lucille left, carrying the bowl, I was relieved and disappointed, about half and half. After all, I was only nine and she was ten. Besides, as I have said, I was small for my age. I was lucky I had an older friend like Carl, who would tell me everything.

For the next couple of years, Carl kept me posted. As soon as he learned anything, he let me know. For instance, he got hold of a book called *How Babies Are Born,* and we went over to his garage and climbed up a ladder into a storage place and put the book on top of an old trunk and turned the pages. We especially studied the drawings, which were easier to understand than the writing.

"I see now," I said. "I could never quite figure it out before."

"I've been trying to tell you," Carl said. "I've known about it ever since that time Lucille came over to our house."

Carl was twelve now, and according to the book he was old enough to become a father. Just thinking about it made him feel pretty important. As for me, I had a year to go.

THE AMERICAN DATING GAME

The Heterosexual Stage

FRANK D. COX

The normal heterosexual stage in our culture begins with puberty. The onset of puberty occurs, on the average, at about 12 years of age for the female and about 14 years of age in the male. At this time the child becomes adult biologically (able to reproduce the species) and for the first time the male-female relationship takes on an overtly sexual nature. This fourth stage, under normal conditions, will last throughout adulthood until sexual potency begins to decline in the later years. The early years of dating and mate selection are a sub-stage of full adulthood that will be discussed under the name "The Sexual Stress Period."

It is a stress period because biology has prepared the child for normal adult sexual behavior (intercourse), and yet our society traditionally denies and tries to repress this readiness by placing restrictive rules and taboos on early sexual behavior. This stress period lasts until the child marries, for it is in marriage that our culture allows one to engage freely in sexual activities. The median age for marriage is decreasing. In 1962, the average bride was just over 20 years of age, while her groom was about 22½ years of age. The average age of marriage in most of the western countries is 24 years for women and 27 years for men (this too is decreasing).[1] Thus, in the United States there is an average span of eight years during which our society acts in opposition to the biological urges of the young adult. Interestingly enough, this span includes the period of highest virility for the male; the late teens.[2]*

There are two logical methods by which to reduce the length of this stress period. Either the average age of marriage can be reduced still further or the gang stage can be prolonged. Many of the more primi-

From Frank D. Cox, *Youth, Marriage and the Seductive Society*, rev. ed. (Dubuque, Ia.: Wm. C. Brown Company Publishers, 1968), pp. 21-28. Reprinted by permission.

*Our society has created an inconsistent set of rules for the adolescent in many other areas as well as in sexuality. Ruch terms this period the "not quite age," not quite adult, not quite children, not quite sure of themselves. For example, a young man between 18 and 21 is called upon to bear arms for his country and yet has not the right of vote nor, in fact, may he buy a beer in many states. [EDITOR'S NOTE: Since the appearance of the author's original article, the voting privilege has been extended to 18-year-olds. The matter of buying alcoholic beverages is still being debated.]

tive societies as well as some of the eastern societies practice child marriage which completely eradicates the American sexual stress period. In
addition, some cultures, such as the Polynesians, are highly permissive
in allowing early sexual experimentation, thus also avoiding a prolonged
period of conflict and restrictive social folkways. In fact, an anthropo-
logical study by Murdock found that of 250 societies throughout the
world, some 70% permit sexual experimentation before marriage. In the
nuclear western-type family, the first solution, reducing the average age
of marriage, has many things against it which will be discussed in greater
detail in the chapter, "The Young Marriage."

The second method, prolonging the gang stage, can only reduce the
stress period by at most a few years since one cannot postpone or reverse
the biological process of puberty. One can, however, slow down the
rate of male-female interaction. This is the system used by the middle
and upper classes of most western European countries. The girls and
boys are kept more segregated than in the United States. Many more
of the schools are segregated according to sex. Early adult behavior,
such as the use of makeup, dating, etc., is strongly discouraged. The
middle-class European girl of 15 or 16 is, on the average, most similar
to the American girl of 11 or 12. She still participates mainly with her
gang of girlfriends. Her behavior toward boys is one of early teasing
and flirtation with little if any prolonged contact. What dating there is
will usually be on a group basis. It should be noted, however, that the
system is being influenced by the American culture and this description
of the European middle-class girl is gradually being modified with time.

The American system, unfortunately, does nothing to slow the early
heterosexual contact of its youth. In fact, just the opposite is the case.
The society works to encourage early heterosexual contact. Many elementary schools promote coeducational dances and parties. Often parents worry that their child will not become popular and so pressure
their children into developing an early interest in the opposite sex. Make-
up, more adult fashions including bras for 10-year-olds (size AAA,
termed "air cups" by the author), increased sophistication through close
contact with mass media,[3] etc., all tend to speed the transition from the
gang stage to the adult heterosexual stage.

Time magazine ran an article about this problem which began with
a series of brief descriptions of the pre-teens. One description read as
follows:

In Los Angeles, Bill's parents gave him his first "sit-down" dinner and dance
(live music) for his tenth birthday. Tuxedoed boys escorted dates who wore
corsages. One boy showered too much attention on another's date. "I had to

talk with him and remind him he brought his own little date," explained Bill's mother.[4]

In this same article a professor of family relations at Pennsylvania State University is quoted as saying,

"By the time these children have reached their teens, they have pretty well covered the field, and are ready for nothing less than marriage."[5]

More recently, *Esquire* magazine ran as its cover article, "Life-styles: The Micro-bopper," which discussed the growing sophistication of the 9- to 13-year-olds (pre-teens). Included among the numerous anecdotal stories were the following statistics:

. . . one percent of all bras as well as girdles are sold to this age group, in 1966, more than 5000 girls under 14 years of age had babies, 425 boys under 14 were arrested for rape, and there were 1214 arrests among the pre-teens for embezzlement and fraud, forgery and counterfeiting.[6]

Although such statistics are sensationalistic, they represent a growing trend toward earlier sophistication and adult-like behavior on the part of our children. It would seem from such articles that our culture is more inclined to increase pressure on the youth rather than allowing them time to make a gradual transition to adulthood.*

Compounding still more the conflict over emerging sexuality during the stress period is the extended opportunity that a young couple in modern society has to be alone together. The automobile has not only revolutionized transportation and contributed to the highly mobile American way of life but it has also revolutionized early sexual experimentation for the youth. The automobile for the teen-age boy is more than mere transportation, it is an extension of his ego. It becomes as much a part of himself as his physical stature. He will be known and admired, or not, by the car he drives. His ability to attract girls will be greatly influenced by his auto. And most pertinent to this discussion, the mobile bedroom characteristic of his automobile will increase greatly the pressure of the stress period. He can be alone with his girl at almost any time and in almost any place he chooses. By escaping the company of others, group control and influence are lessened. There is no one that might report a breach of the established social mores. The feeling of anonymity and distance from the social system is increased. In essence, the young couple are thrown completely onto their own resources in

---

*A good deal of this pressure comes from American business. America is a country of young persons. 47% of the population is now under 25 years of age and the proportion is increasing. Thus, the children and youth represent a vast market potential and are actively cultivated by business. See chap. 7.

determining just what their behavior will be. In the end, they alone will make the decision as to the type of sexual behavior in which they will engage before marriage. The auto, probably more than any other single influence, has wrought a change in premarital sexual behavior among the young.* One researcher terms this change, "The glandular crisis of a parked car."[7]

Let us follow a young American couple through an extended period of dating and observe how the American dating game is played. Remember the weakness of generality when it is applied to actual rather than ideal behavior and do not consider the actions about to be described as descriptive of any particular young couple. The couple we will observe is a nice, well-reared, clean-cut pair of American youth. Everything about their relationship has been done in the socially prescribed manner. They are in no way bad or promiscuous or delinquent. They are simply good middle-class, young American teenagers. We will take a developmental approach to their dating behavior. Let us start, then, when they were first allowed to begin dating. This age will vary greatly with each family but, in general, it has gradually become younger so that dating at 11 and 12, especially for the girl, is not as unusual as it once was. Let us further assume that the boy has just reached the age of legal driving and is able to talk his father out of the family auto for his date.

The young man has known the girl superficially for some time since they both attend the same school and have met previously at various school functions. Although it requires courage, he finally asks if she can accompany him to a movie on the coming Saturday night. A movie is usually a safe first date for the young adolescent since it requires so little interaction with one's date. Both the boy and girl receive an O.K. from their own parents. It may even be that the parents contact one another although this is increasingly unusual. At the appointed time on Saturday night, the young man proudly arrives at the wheel of the family auto. Although she has been ready for some time, she is discreetly "not ready." This serves a twofold purpose: she does not appear over-eager (her mother has told her to play hard-to-get) and secondly, it gives the parents a few moments in which to look over the boy and discuss the evening's rules with him; mainly the proposed time of return. At the psychologically correct moment she makes her entry and together they depart.

*An Idaho study reported in *Life* magazine some years ago showed that not a single straight A student owned a car and only 15% of the B students owned one. But 41% of the C students had cars and 71% of the D students. And among the flunkers, a spectacular 83% owned cars.

The darkened theatre actually becomes the location of the first confrontation. The young man strongly feels the pressure of his friends, and the anonymous larger group of peers loosely defined as "the boys." According to the mores, enough of the double standard remains so that it is he who must take the initiative. And, indeed, to feel masculine and proud among "the boys," the young man is obligated to at least try some type of physical contact with the girl. Thus, as he sits watching the movie, the first of many conflicts concerning sexuality begins to take form. He notices that her hands are lying one inch in his direction upon her lap. Perhaps this is a clue. Should he attempt to hold her hand? If she vigorously rejects this advance, everyone in the row might notice and his embarrassment will be acute. If, on the other hand, she accepts, how will he be able to withdraw his hand from hers when it becomes sweaty and begins to cramp without her taking it as some kind of rejection? This little game is obviously at a very early and naïve level.

The fascinating and unique characteristics of the American dating game is what one may term "escalation." In other words, dissolution of this first level minor conflict does not end the problem. If the girl accepts his first advance, then the pressure he feels to prove himself to "the boys" actually increases since the whole procedure is designed to test just how far he can go toward overt sexuality with the girl. Granted, much of this pressure may be unconscious for the boy, yet he feels the need to prove himself. Naturally, the further the boy moves, the more pride he will feel when bragging to his friends of his prowess with the girls. Thus, once he has taken her hand, he must now look to the slightly greater problem of attempting to place his arm around her. The rewards are obviously greater but so are the risks. If she vigorously rejects his attempt, the whole movie house will notice (at least it will seem this way to him). If she accepts, there is always the ensuing cramped shoulder to look forward to as well as the necessity of facing the new escalation level and all of its ensuing conflicts and insecurities. The girl is having conflicts too because she does not want to lose her reputation and yet at the same time she does like the boy and thus does not want him to think her a prude in which case he may not ask her for another date.

The American dating game evolves into a game of offense versus defense, and in the course of history a defense has never won a war. With each step toward sexual intercourse taken by the boy, the girl will have to retreat and reintegrate her new behavior into her value system. Since her value system will in all probability already be vague and nebulous because of the swift changing and pragmatic character of the American society, the continuing pressure upon her will cause great confusion and insecurity.* By this age, it will be the peer group that wields the greatest influence and both she and the boy will be highly susceptible to the argument that everyone else engages in such behavior. Her own insecurity will be her worst enemy.

Thus escalation brings physical relations from the naïve level described to necking, petting, petting to orgasm, and finally to intercourse in an increasing number of cases. The rapidity of the escalation depends upon the inner security of each member of the couple and the length of time and exclusiveness with which they date one another. The more insecure the young persons the more they will seek security in conforming to what they believe the peer group is doing. Time is obviously an important factor. To place highly vigorous young adults who like one another together for long periods of time without supervision is obviously going to lead to sexual activity.

In the last analysis, as stated before, it is the couple alone that is forced to make the decision as to how far they will go. At this point there begins a strange (almost schizophrenic-like) unrealistic game called "sex-not-sex" and it is usually the girl who makes up the rules. Since she must control how far the boy goes, she must have some operational definition of what sexual behavior is. She knows that actual intercourse is sex, but she is unsure of how to categorize all the other behavior; kissing, necking, and various degrees of petting in which she gradually indulges. If she can categorize kissing as "non-sex," she can kiss as much as she likes and need feel no threat or guilt. If, on the other hand, because of upbringing, she categorizes it as "sex," she will then have conflict, and guilt will arise when she engages in such behavior.

When one asks a cross section of young American women what they define as sexual behavior, there is no one agreed-upon answer. One girl may become upset and in a state of conflict when she feels passion upon kissing. Another girl may be able to indulge in mutual masturbation with little if any conflict because she has defined all but actual intercourse as "non-sex." In reality, in the broadest sense, intimate physical contact of any kind between male and female is sexual behavior. It can be, and indeed should be, the foreplay to sexual intercourse.

The boy is not only pressured by his peers into making advances toward the girl but he also feels this necessity because he cannot judge where any one particular girl will draw the line. Thus, he is insecure

---

*One of the most susceptible periods for the girl insofar as premarital sex is concerned is after she and her steady boy friend have broken up over sexual problems and then go back together again. Her fear of losing him makes her acquiesce to his demands as a way of holding him.

in her presence until he knows the rules whereby she is willing to play the game.

Because of the type of dynamics herein described, the young adult stress period becomes centered on sex to the exclusion of most other things. Even a final solution to escalation problems, sexual intercourse, does not end the preoccupation with sex.* Indeed it often serves to exaggerate it even more as we shall discuss in the chapter on premarital intercourse. It might be noted that boy-girl relationships tend to be much more relaxed and comfortable in societies where the attitude toward sex is more realistic than in our own. Cultures that allow early sexual experimentation do not find the young peoples' relationships centered in sex. Sex is allowed to take a more natural place and the need to be preoccupied with it is absent. Many young American soldiers find themselves more comfortable with foreign girls where sex is more open and honest. If a girl looks inviting and acts the role, she is usually available. He need not continually concern himself with whether each girl he meets will play the game differently. In this context, then, premarital sexual experimentation is more natural than prolonged and frustrating petting in which so many of our young American middle-class couples indulge.

Further compounding the problems of this period has been the increasing tendency to pair off at an early age and "go steady." There is little doubt that this tendency has increased since World War II, but the exact rules and manifestations of it vary greatly from one locale to another. The phenomenon tends to add pressure to the sexual conflicts experienced by the young couple. Their contact is much more frequent, and because there is little distraction by dating others, their relationship becomes more quickly intimate. As a result, a great deal of possessiveness manifests itself in jealous behavior. The American boy tends to regard any attention or compliments paid to his steady as insulting and usually restricts her social interactions to himself. Actually, in a more mature relationship, attention and compliments to one's girl or boy friend can be taken as a compliment to oneself. It is flattering to be out with a person whom others regard as attractive. This, of course, demands a certain amount of security in both partners as well as within the relationship itself.

---

*If one agrees with Terman that only 20% of marital adjustment depends upon sexual compatibility, the American dating couple who preoccupy themselves with sex miss out on testing the other 80% of their future marital relationship.
Lewis Terman, *Psychological Factors in Marital Happiness* (N.Y. McGraw-Hill, 1938).

For example, among most middle-class European young adults, general social interaction with numerous persons of the opposite sex is preferred to tying oneself too tightly to just one. At a dance each male is expected to dance with at least every other female sitting at his table. It is regarded as highly impolite if he does not. This serves to reduce the level of emotional attachment to an easier level for the young adult to handle.

There are several other disadvantages to "going steady." One of these is the loss of individual freedom. Another is the reduction of opposite sex contacts and practice interactions. This latter results in a narrowed frame of reference from which to select one's future mate. These two disadvantages will be further discussed in the chapter, "The Honeymoon Is Over." There are also arguments in favor of going steady. In the main, these arguments justify it by pointing to the beneficial interpersonal relations practice that can come from a deeper, longer-lasting relationship. It is true that this is an advantage, but upon examination of all of the results of going steady, it seems that the disadvantages far outweigh the advantages.

In summary, the American Dating Game is generally characterized by an exaggerated emphasis on sex, a tendency to narrow one's field through the technique of "going steady," resulting in greater possessiveness and jealousy which serves to heighten even further the emotionality of the relationship. Because of these dynamics and the rapidly changing value structure of the modern American society, premarital intercourse is increasing.

REFERENCES

1. Demographic Yearbook UN, 1965.
2. Alfred Kinsey, Wardell Pomeroy, Clyde Martin, *Sexual Behavior in the Human Male*, Philadelphia: W. B. Saunders Co., 1948.
3. George Murdock, "Sexual Behavior: What Is Acceptable?" *Journal of Social Hygiene* 36: 1950, pp. 1-31.
4. Marshall McLuhan Q. Flore, *The Medium Is the Message: An Inventory of Effects.* New York: Random House, 1967.
5. *Time* Magazine: "The Pre-Teens," April 20, 1962, p. 68.
6. *Ibid.*, Carlfred B. Broderick.
7. Saul Braun, "Life-Styles: The Micro-bopper," *Esquire*, Vol. LXIX, No. 3, March, 1968.
8. Vermard Eller, "Old Morality of MAD Magazine Praised," An interview article by John Dart in the *Los Angeles Times*, Jan. 1, 1968.

I LOVE HIM . . . BUT DO I LIKE HIM?

Daniel A. Sugarman and Rollie Hochstein

It is estimated that 1,500,000 women will be married for the first time this year. Half of them will be under twenty! Hopefully these young brides will be ready to take their vows. If you are one of these planners, ask yourself a bold question: "Do I like the man I love?"

Love life begins shortly after birth with the attachment of a baby to the mother-nurse who feeds and cuddles her. Typically a father joins the circle of love—as admirer, protector, playmate and authority. By degrees a child's love reaches outward toward brothers and sisters, pets, perhaps teachers and classmates, hometown, flag and country. Literature, art, music, even nature offer emotional outlets for the adolescent. These kinds of love are preludes to love's most powerful aspect: sexual desire. And a girl's responses to the various manifestations of love from childhood onward may foreshadow her reactions to her own burgeoning sexual urges.

Falling in love—like the taste of apple pie—is hard to describe. It's sudden, strong, compulsive, largely irrational. Often it's frightening, as is any explosive emotion. A girl may feel tongue-tied, limp, almost helpless near the boy she loves. A wildly beating heart, a squeaky voice, trembling and breathlessness may make it nearly impossible for her to act natural in his presence.

A phone call, a word of encouragement, a smile or a touch brings on a sense of elation. In fact a thriving love affair acts for most people as a powerful, primitive tonic; it actually stimulates physical and emotional health. Conversely, a strained or threatened relationship induces depression, so it is no wonder that teen-agers with their ins and outs of love often seem moody and volatile. Nor is it surprising that reason frequently flies out the window when love walks in the door. It's impossible to be totally objective in dealing with people, but when romance is involved we are likely to drift far away from reality. Falling in love is admittedly more a matter of emotion than of rational choice.

Most girls believe that romantic love is the only proper basis for marriage and that marriage is the natural outgrowth of romance. Neither idea is necessarily true.

Love as a basis for marriage is a fairly recent historical concept. Dating from the ancient Greeks and Hebrews, the institution of marriage has served a variety of personal and social functions: the maintenance of property or power, status, companionship, the protection of children, affection, the sharing of work, the continuity of a culture. The satisfaction of sexual needs was usually not a prime objective.

In primitive societies marriages were arranged by a clan chieftain. In the Middle Ages the church took over as marital arbiter. Until this century, even in the United States, most marriages were family decisions and had little to do with the bride's wishes. In many parts of the world still today, brides are selected for "suitability"—based on social standing, blood lines, money, capability, child-bearing potential. All of this may seem alien, even horrifying to you, given the love-laced society we live in. However, there is no evidence that a marriage for love works out any better than does a marriage of convenience or a marriage by arrangement.

This is not to suggest that your parents take over your love life, but merely that you leaven your romantic tendencies with common sense. It generally isn't hard to fall in love, but it's not always easy to understand why a girl falls for a particular boy. One explanation is that her psychological eye may glimpse a quality in a man that she feels is lacking in her own personality. All of us, consciously or not, have certain crevices in our personalities, gaps between what we are and what we would like to be. Naturally we want to bridge these gaps in some way. Thus a shy, inarticulate girl may fall in love with an extrovert whose easy conversation compensates for her reticence. A dependent girl may be attracted to protective men. A competent, confident girl may lean toward men who seem to crave mothering or need to be drawn out of their shells.

A girl's taste in boys changes as she matures. Commonly a girl in her early teens develops a crush on a pop singer or TV star or a man teacher—someone safely unattainable. By her midteens, when fantasies begin to give way to reality, she may be drawn to boys who compensate her for her own supposed lacks. A boy who is confident, good-looking, popular and successful in school "lends" these qualities to the girl he goes out with; her love for him is an extension of self-love.

A girl's relationship with her father strongly influences her love choices. A concerned and loving father who communicates his approval and admiration helps a daughter to feel desirable and to approach young men with confidence. Often a girl is attracted to boys who resemble her father in looks and manner. But when the father's influence has been nonexistent or harsh, detached or subordinated to a dominating mother, a girl may look for qualities that she missed at home. An authoritative older man is often extremely appealing to a girl who feels an unsatisfied need for fathering. When she begins dating, the boys who attract her are often older than she, usually serious and strongly determined. Such a girl needs a man "to look up to."

Social and cultural environment play a part. Most girls tend to fall in love with boys who are acceptable to their friends. Every group has its own ideal: the hunter-warrior, the man-about-town, the go-getter, the all-around man, the athlete, the aesthete, the intellectual. Consider the range of American movie idols of the past twenty years: from the sophisticated Cary Grant to tough-guy Humphrey Bogart to the clean-cut all-American boy like Tab Hunter, and more recently to the sensitive, lost young man typified by Dustin Hoffman. A popular image may be adopted by a community or a school, and your taste will undoubtedly be affected by whoever is currently in with your particular group.

Moreover most young girls, whose experience is limited to family, school and community, tend to choose someone of a similar social, ethnic and economic background when they first fall in love with a real boy as distinct from a faraway idol. Proximity and parental pressures foster this reaction because common backgrounds and interests do of course make for easy company. In the larger society of college and the business world, the "man market" is more varied and a girl's interests may well broaden accordingly.

Although your own good sense should point you toward a boy of responsible character who cares about you and whose company you enjoy, many extraneous influences may also be present to some degree in every case of young love. They could and often do lead to trouble. For example, when a girl's love life is primarily an outlet for unresolved personality problems, she is certain to make unsound choices. Status-seeking, revenge, rebellion and sublimation often masquerade as love—seldom with healthy effects.

One girl I know uses her love life to express anger at her socially involved mother and her traveling, business-conscious father. She felt neglected, and when she began to date she unconsciously gravitated to boys who were grossly unacceptable to her parents—boys who were troublesome in class, rowdy, unkempt. She took great pleasure in producing a pot-smoking dropout one night when her parents were entertaining business friends and several times showed up at the country club with beaded, booted hippies. This is not to say that dropouts and hippies can't be lovable; the point is that this girl chose her companions more for shock value than for her own interest in them. Only when she sorts out her own problems will she be ready to find real love.

What about sex? While it's doubtful that man-woman love can exist without an element of physical attraction, it is certain that physical attraction alone is not enough to sustain love. Nor is love an inevitable outgrowth of a warm friendship. Admiration or sympathy or gratitude or great compatibility can feel a lot like love; but in love, as distinct from geometry, the whole is indeed greater than the sum of its parts. A girl who is not deeply aware of *herself* may get seriously mixed up.

Once you're convinced that you're really in love, a new question arises: does marriage necessarily follow? Our culture seems to take this progression for granted. Actually romance—for all its dash and delight—can lead to extremely difficult marriages. With its yearning for immediacy, perfection and mystery, intense romantic love can seldom survive the humdrum of daily marital routines. The realities of budgeting money, keeping house, raising children and catching viruses are not romantic. As familiarity sets in, many a romantic feels cheated and eventually persuades herself not that her standards are unrealistic but that she made the wrong choice.

Maturity and compatibility are not guaranteed by the marriage certificate. Only after the rice is swept away does the real work begin. The myth of the "one true love" has pushed many a girl into a miserable marriage. Love alone is just not enough—especially for people under twenty who have not settled into any particular life style.

Let us suppose that you are in your late teens and are thinking of marrying. Undoubtedly you've grown a lot in the past five years. But have you grown enough? Can you make the inevitable transition from romance and mystery to acceptance of a man with all his doubts and weaknesses? Can he accept you, both literally and figuratively, without make-up? Mature love is predicated on a deep mutual respect that is capable of weathering lean times. "Falling in love" has nothing to do with "for better or for worse . . . in sickness and in health." The wedding vows express the distinction well.

Of all the institutions yet devised by the many and varied societies of the world, marriage has proved the most universal and the most durable. The high divorce rate in America today is not so much an indictment of marriage as an argument against marrying too quickly. While one out of two teen-age marriages fails, divorce odds drop with every year of a girl's age up to the mid-twenties. Of course, there are no figures on the marriages that endure in misery only because of religious, social, ethical or financial obstructions to divorce.

Therefore, before you marry, make sure that you know what it's all about. Children can play house but it takes men and women to make households. Ask yourself these questions.

1. Can I be myself when I'm with him?

Dating is a great opportunity to discover what boys are like. There is a danger, however, of confusing a good date with a good mate, of overdoing the how-to-get-along-with-boys routine.

Most boys have a dream girl in their mind's eye and you may try to alter yourself accordingly. Bent on pleasing, you may bend yourself into a shape you hardly recognize. Losing your identity is too much of a sacrifice for you to sustain either your own self-respect or, in the long run, a man's interest.

His assertiveness and his independence of spirit may impress you in the beginning as fascinating masculine traits. His ridiculing of your friends or his quest for a life style apart from the "phony values" of his or your parents may sound adventurous; it may turn out to be merely uncomfortable.

The quiet girl who falls for a lively swinger may assume an unaccustomed animation, play down her own interest in books and music, pretend wild enthusiasm for sports. She may change from Peter Pan collars to psychedelic prints and jangling jewelry. Presently she doesn't know who she is anymore. Such a pliable character tends to be dull to other people, unsatisfying to herself.

2. Do I accept him as he is?

If you need a hero, you will never be satisfied with a real-life boy. If you begin to find fault and prescribe remedies the moment you have him hooked, it won't work. He is too serious; he's too deeply involved in lab work; he spends too much time tinkering. He is irresponsible; he doesn't call when he says he will; he is usually late; he doesn't dress properly. These are things to think about ahead of time rather than saying to yourself, "I'll straighten him out when we're married."

The best single indicator of a person's future performance is his past record. If you want to know what kind of husband your beau will be, take a look at what he is right now. A reforming woman simply becomes a nagging wife. Personalities do change, but only from the inside out and not because somebody else insists on revisions. Try to be sure, before you take him seriously, that whatever faults your man may have, they're the kind you can live with.

3. Can I grow in this union?

Only physical growth stops; intellectual, emotional and social growth continue throughout life. People thrive in an atmosphere of interest and approval.

In the first rapture of attraction, it is easy to listen for hours to a man if he talks mostly about his favorite subject: himself. Later, when the infatuation wears off, you can be hurt by his evident lack of reciprocal interest in you.

A boy who continually puts you down or cuts you off is not likely to turn into a man who will help you grow. But a boy who will encourage you to cultivate your own interests, who will console you when things go badly and who will applaud when things go well is the boy who will let you fulfill yourself. When he disagrees with you or is angry at you, he will say so frankly. But he will neither compete nor domineer.

4. Can he grow too?

Boys mature more slowly than girls. The two-year lag doesn't even out until the late teens or early twenties. Though individuals vary widely, in most teen-age romances it's the girl who has the edge on maturity. It's the girl then who should keep things casual until the boy is seasoned enough to know what he wants.

In our mobile society, a man can climb socially, financially, intellectually as far as his ability and ambition will take him. A girl who marries an ambitious man should be ready to climb with him. It means providing an atmosphere in which he can work, entertaining his friends, even changing friends as tastes mature. The plight of a man who married too young a girl who was either unable or unwilling to keep up with him is indeed sad. Attempts to restrict his friendships, his interests and his achievements suggest insecurity. A possessive, demanding, clinging girl can—and very often does—keep a good man down.

5. Have we passed the time test?

You may now be dating and possibly wearing the ring of the boy you believe you truly love. But stand back a little and ask yourself: "Will I feel the same in two years?"

The only honest answer can be, "I don't know." Nobody can foresee the future, but if you're under twenty, the odds heavily favor change. Better wait out those two years and see how you feel. Give your love a chance to weather before you tighten its knots.

6. Can we afford to get married?

It is possible to live on love, milk and peanut butter sandwiches. You may be prepared to share a single room and decorate this haven with orange-crate furniture and cheese-grater lampshades. You may be a financial whiz at managing money. But there is always the possibility that one of you will get sick or that something will happen to the car or that you will get pregnant unexpectedly. Unless you both hold paying jobs, you will probably be living on very little, and an emergency can be ruinous. Furthermore, the joys of struggling tend to wear thin after a while, especially if friends are having fun you can't afford.

You may have the option of living with your parents or his—or else accepting financial support. Either could be feasible or unbearable, depending on the circumstances. If your parents tend to treat you as a child, the fact that they're paying your way can only reinforce their conviction that they are still entitled to controlling interest. If you're all living under one roof, the temptation to interfere might be even greater.

Your husband's pride is another factor to consider. Will it diminish his feeling of manliness if you support him through his studies? Will a heavy sense of obligation to his family or yours weigh him down? Before you marry on love alone, you should be sure of the answers to these questions.

7. Do we agree on the important things?

Lovers need not agree on everything; we'd worry if they did. Republicans marry Democrats; atheists marry churchgoers; athletes marry eggheads—often quite successfully. What matters is that you tolerate, even appreciate one another's viewpoints.

Differences are healthy as long as they are not central to the marriage. On issues of mutual concern to you as a couple, however, there should be agreement. If he wants a family and you won't hear of it, then you've got a big problem—one that should be settled ahead of time. Likewise, each of you can hold individual religious beliefs, but how will the children be raised? What about a city boy and a country girl or vice versa? What if a girl dreams of settling down into conventional community routine while a boy wants adventure? What if a girl wants a career and a boy insists she be a full-time homemaker? These matters should be thoroughly explored before marriage.

Recently I noticed a young couple wearing his-and-her sweat shirts. His said "Master"; hers said "Slave." I did not find it amusing because it symbolized the sadness in many a so-called love affair. I'd be happier to see a couple in shirts that said "Partner." Only two self-reliant, independent people who come together willingly, hopefully, tenderly and in mutual respect can really know what love is.

FORMS OF SEX KNOWLEDGE

IAN M. FRASER

"We need to do two things: arm young people with knowledge, and stand at their side." Here, in a nutshell, is the responsibility which adults are called upon to discharge.

The reactions of some young people might be, "We want to make our own mistakes." However shortsighted an attitude this might be, however likely to land them in trouble, it should not divert adult society from its duty. Any generation with experience of life has an obligation to make the benefits of that experience available to a younger generation. The action may be welcomed or rebuffed. The soundings we took showed that young people were eager for such a sharing, longing that adults would take them into their confidence and talk straight about how they had found life. Our main evidence suggests that what may be given by experience to inexperience will be welcomed—if it is given sensitively and modestly, and if there is a readiness on the part of older people to listen as well as speak.

There is no intention by what is said in this chapter to take from people the right to make their own decisions. The intention is rather conveyed in the words of the report on the 1964 consultation: "What is essentially needed is that people should be as responsible as possible in the judgments they make, by being equipped with knowledge regarding every factor which comes into the relationship between the sexes." Young men and women can only mature and become fully adult if they handle their responsibilities. No human authority has a right to take these over and lay down for human beings what they must do. To equip with knowledge is not to invade privacy but simply to provide means whereby judgments can be imaginative and instructive.

Knowledge of physical facts is wanting. Strange as it may seem, the venereologist and the obstetrician in the company testified that sexually

From Ian M. Fraser, *Sex as gift*, (London: SCM Press Ltd., 1967; American edition, Philadelphia: Fortress Press, 1967), pages 26-33. Reprinted by permission.

This book is based on a seven-year series of consultations on sex and sex education with adolescents at Scottish Churches' House in Dunblane, Scotland. Frequent references to the "Schofield Report" refer to "The Sexual Behavior of Young People," which is considered a "Little Kinsey" among the British.

experienced young people who come into their care are often substantially ignorant of the physical facts.

Those who stop short of full penetration in intercourse—who play safe, as they think—quite fail to reckon with the motility and length of life of sperms. There seems to be no awareness that V.D. can cause infertility. The myth that kissing can lead to a baby is, suprisingly, still around. The more dangerous myth that "keeping it for marriage" brings with it a risk to fertility, health, satisfactory performance or adequate parenthood later on—that for genuine manhood and womanhood chastity has to be got rid of—still holds where it suits people to hold it, or where the ignorance of some opens them to exploitation by others. There is no shred of medical evidence to support it. It needs to be shown up for the eyewash it is.

Basic information about physical parts and functions should be given, as a right, to those whose lives it affects. In a survey of sexual attitudes and habits in certain colleges in the U.S.A., the source of knowledge which was said to give most help was pornographic photographs. People wanted to know what happened and how it happened.[1]

Knowledge of differences of male and female make-up must also be provided.

Girls are often unaware of how quickly boys can be aroused (for instance by provocative dress); boys, how deep it goes once a girl is aroused. Thus in the same association the boy may be looking for physical sensation, the girl for lasting relationship.[2] They need to grow together in understanding if they are not going to hurt one another deeply. In an article on the B.C.C. report *Sex and Morality*, Monica Furlong wrote:

I listened not long ago to a girl reduced to the verge of suicide by repeated sexual relationships with men, none of whom had ever bothered to penetrate beyond an attractive body to the very lost and frightened person inside. They had been seeking sex, she had been seeking love.[3]

Shame and fear are more readily induced in girls than in boys. This is understandable, she is left to "hold the baby"; and she has an inborn awareness of her responsibility for the future welfare of the race.[4]

With some boys, girls need to take into account an attitude of male superiority, a knock-'em-off-and-chalk-'em-up approach. A technique is regularly applied. You put on an act of concerned love, soften up your victim, get her where you want her, take your pickings and then cut clear to be rid of consequences. There are well-worn gambits for breaking down resistance. "If you really love me you will . . ." The word "wait" is a thoroughly adequate one to finish such a sentence. "If you won't have it with me, that shows you are frigid." This is a cutting, heartless charge. The best answer is to laugh in the speaker's face and to tell him that he has been taking old wives' tales for gospel. This answer has the double virtue of being true and of turning the tables psychologically.

A dual morality is still powerfully in evidence.[5] There are boys who look for someone who keeps herself for marriage, but themselves take chances with others on the way. There are girls who keep themselves for their future husbands, but want that future partner to be experienced. How many of them ever face the fact that this takes for granted the existence of an assortment of girls, who are simply used and discarded?

Of course, girls are seducers as well as boys. Those of either sex who are put under pressure by the entreaties of the "steady" should be aware of the close relationship between giving in easily, and losing respect. You don't hold another person by being accommodating all the way. If your resistance at important points means the break-up of a relationship, then respect for the person, which is part of real love, must be missing in it. As likely a consequence as any of "easy come" would be the attitude "If I get in so easily, what guarantee do I have that others won't?" As likely a consequence of "so far and no further" would be deepened admiration.

The young of both sexes need to know another thing about their sexual make-up. Once the body is awakened sexually it develops an appetite. Sexual passion can act like a drug. The incidental can only too readily slide into the occasional, and the occasional into the habitual. Young women in particular need to be aware of the longing for a child which follows after a certain degree of intercourse. Men are usually quite ignorant that this craving follows on the other. Women who have a dim awareness of it can be taken by surprise to find how powerful it is.

Knowledge of the operation of the will and of the emotions is essential. Giving in in small ways may produce a situation in which one's main intention has been nibbled away to such an extent that, when the crisis comes, it turns out to have been quite undermined. Bodily rhythms and emotional tides tend to sweep people past points they rationally fixed beforehand as stopping points. Medical students and nurses, for instance, may be made over-confident by their knowledge. Where their wills and emotions are not equally educated and mature, they are as likely to be caught as others. Characteristic remarks of those interviewed were: "Thought flew out of the window"; "I had decided where to stop but found I was caught up."[6] Thus knowledge of contraceptives and of V.D. risk, as well as knowledge of the physical facts, can be made quite ineffective if the will and the emotions are not in control.

Knowledge of possible human consequences needs to be furnished. These must be taken into account in any relationship which would claim to be responsible.

Furtive and hasty sexual encounters may result in a revulsion, a fear of the sex act, a tendency to frigidity. On the other hand, sexual appetite might be aroused powerfully—and then, if one partner cools off and moves off, each may have a craving for physical satisfaction which he or she is tempted to indulge wherever and from whomever they may get it.

The experience of rejection has a quite different depth to it once sexual union has taken place.

There is a third-party risk—a child may be conceived. The rising rate of illegitimacy, coinciding with knowledge of and availability of contraceptives on a scale never known previously in history, is a powerful reminder that there are still no absolutely foolproof ways of preventing conception. To give a third person the poorest of starts in life is human tragedy and sin. Consider the options: the backstreet abortionist with the risk he brings to the possibility of having other children, and the risk of causing the death of the mother. The way of adoption—experience of which may mature a young unmarried mother, or cause brooding and bitterness which deeply affects her personality. A forced marriage, which can mean torture for two people and for whatever further children they may produce. How fortunate it is when the option is open of a marriage entered into of free and willing choice, even if it comes earlier than intended. It can provide the security which the prematurely conceived child needs from birth.

How-far-to-go knowledge is very much asked for. Those concerned with youth organizations begged that such knowledge should be provided. "How can I keep my boy friend without letting him go too far?" "Why should I keep off my girl—if I don't give her what a woman wants, someone else will be only too ready to oblige." There is a conspiracy in the church to say a code exists, a useful collection of "dos" and "don'ts," to help at this point; but, as has been said, no one can quote it. At one point the consultative group tried out a "Guidelines for Conduct" flier, almost fruitlessly,[7] on relevant church committees. It invited acceptance, rejection, amendment, alternatives, to certain green, amber and red lights which young people appeared to recognize almost instinctively when they remained in control of a situation. There was holding hands, kissing, and some caressing over clothes, which seemed thoroughly acceptable when a relationship was being established. Caressing under clothes brought up an amber light: it could be fairly innocent and pleasurable, or as genital massaging it could set the pulses racing and stimulate the body to crave deeper contact. The lights turned red with the placing of sexual organs directly against one another. This often brought people very close to or into intercourse (interviewers preparing material for the *Schofield Report* were at times not clear whether what had taken place was intercourse or simply apposition[8]). The sub-chapter of the *Schofield Report* entitled "Five Stages of Sex"[9] bears an interesting resemblance to the main points at which, we suggested, how-far-to-go knowledge was needed by young people. The points may prove of value in guiding others. Girls showed a marked reluctance to move from kissing and caressing over clothes (considered romantic) to caressing under clothes (considered to invite to sex play).[10]

Knowledge of the situation which exists at present is important. The idea is abroad that "everybody is doing it"—sleeping around, getting rid of virginity as soon as possible. Those who speak about a sharp decline in moral standards aid and abet this. The fact is, that until the Schofield Report came out, no adequate statistics were available regarding the sexual attitudes and habits of young people, and we have no statistical evidence to indicate how moral standards today compare with those of other ages. The report makes it clear that two-thirds of the boys and three-quarters of the girls interviewed had no premarital sex intercourse at any point.[11] It was rightly pointed out that there is enough teenage premarital intercourse to show that it is not a minority problem confined to few deviants. But young people should realize that those who refrain from intercourse are anything but exceptions. The Schofield Report showed that young people interviewed thought that their acquaintances were having much more sexual experience than was indeed the case.[12] People boast of sexual exploits accomplished only in the mind. The impression of general laxity needs to be punctured by the arrow of well-checked statistics.

It should be stated that medical opinion, sought in the process of consultation, was unanimous that sexual intercourse which is premature is unnecessary and probably quite damaging.

The knowledge which is imparted should contain such an awareness of the mystery of human persons and the variety of situations in which they find themselves as to make the hearers sensitive, unwilling to prejudge. Our sexuality is an invitation to ventures in relationship. In venturing, people may be caught up in tangled situations for which there is no simple moral road out. Or they may establish relationships which society would not tolerate as regular, which have a quality about them which is not simply to be written off. Any Christian ethic simply registers the point to which people in some part of the world have been brought as they have sought to work out their relationships in obedience and thanksgiving to God. This ethic presents a challenge to dubious relationships. But also, wherever quality is found in relationships which do not keep in step with such an ethic, the ethic itself comes under challenge and may need to be revised or reinterpreted. The ethical task of a pilgrim people moving through history, taking one step of obedience at a time, will be both to crystallize the lessons of history for their instruction, and to keep themselves continually open to new insights. People who know where they stand and where others should stand, through a confidence that they know just where Christ stands in this matter, have missed the point that he is alive and continually prodding men to a new doing of the truth. The harsh application of ethical laws (wrenching wives from families in the time of Ezra,[13] or in Africa today[14]) should give us pause about other relationships which place a question against hard and set ethical attitudes.

REFERENCES

1. See *Sex Histories of American College Men*. Drs. P. and E. Kronhausen (Ballantine Books) pp. 43-46.
2. *Schofield Report*, p. 248.
3. *Scottish Daily Mail*, October 18th, 1966.
4. It could be (though there is no proof of this) that in a society where free sexual association was acceptable these feelings of guilt and fear might diminish or disappear. That this would be a good thing must not be assumed. A sense of shame and guilt reminds people that there are precious things which can be betrayed. Provided it is not morbid, it marks an awareness of human dignity.
5. *Schofield Report*, p. 248.
6. Dr. Freeth's report (see also Appendix, pp. 76 f).
7. It initiated some work, which one denomination, the Salvation Army, is still continuing. But there was no direct dealing with what was, admittedly, a "hot potato."
8. Page 32.
9. Pages 39-49.
10. Page 30.
11. Page 248.
12. *Schofield Report*, ch. 10 and p. 227.
13. Ezra, chs. 9 and 10.
14. "The big copper-magnate who exploits 40,000 underpaid, badly-housed labourers is a good church member. But the polygamist who remains faith-

ful to his wives, all working peacefully together for the good of the family, is not allowed to join the church. His wives are also excluded, and even his children; the church refuses to baptize them at all—even later on in their lifetime—unless the man sends all his wives away except one. What is to happen to those wives who are sent away and to their children separated from the affection of the family in these rapidly changing societies? They can only become prostitutes and outcasts who are hostile to the church." The *Ecumenical Review*, Autumn 1963, p. 74.

Additional Note

When this book was at the proof stage, my attention was drawn to developments which could have a startling effect on contraception possibilities for the near future—provided only that enough money should be forthcoming for the remaining research work required.

These concern:
1. A male anti-fertility pill (at present there are side-effects if alcohol is taken);
2. Anti-nidation methods, to prevent the implantation of the fertilized egg in the uterine tissues (effective in animals; but dosage and long-term effects for humans not yet satisfactorily estimated);
3. Anti-embryo methods, which could make the present discussion on abortion substantially irrelevant (so far tested only in animals; a small but possible risk remains of the embryo not being killed but badly damaged).

Should some of these materialize, it will be even clearer that the only course open to responsible adults is to help young people to be themselves responsible in their relationships, and as mature as knowledge and thought can make them. Traditional sanctions related to conception will have disappeared.

At the technical level, an article by G. Pincus in the Ciba Foundation Symposium on "Pre-Implantation Stages of Pregnancy" (ed. Wolstenholme and O'Connor, J. A. Churchill Ltd., London, 1965) and the Oliver Bird Annual Lectures might be consulted.

Less highly technical is G. R. Venning's *Advances in Reproductive Physiology*, Vol. I (ed. McLaren, Academic Press, 1966). The work of A.S. Parkes is also to be commended to those who want the essential information more popularly presented.

SOME CONCLUDING COMMENTS ON PREMARITAL SEX

ROBERT R. BELL

In this book we have examined a number of social forces that have influenced premarital sexual values and behavior. It seems clear that American society is characterized by confusion, contradiction and hypocrisy in the general area of sex. The result is a tug and pull on the individual and especially on the girl as to what is "right" in the area of sexual intimacy. As Hunt points out, the young woman is pulled in two directions at the same time, "one way by residual Victorianism and left-over Puritan ideals, the other way by contemporary hedonism and the emphasis on the healthful fulfilment of love."[16] This conflict of values has been well described by Reiss who suggests that the American society is like a man whose past way of life has been challenged.

He cannot ignore the challenge, for the challenge originates within himself. Yet he is so strongly tied to the past that he is not certain that he wants to or is able to change. This is a portrait of internal conflict—this is the setting in regard to our sexual standards in America today.[17]

Yet, there are opposite views as to the importance of premarital sex presented by different behavioral scientists. For example, the sociologist Pitirim Sorokin says that while the new sex freedom is only one factor it is significant "in the drift toward social revolution and political disorder, toward international conflict, toward a general decline of creativity, and irremediable decay of our society." Sorokin goes on to state that "the sex factors and the accompanying disorganization of the family are among the most important contributions to these pathological phenomena."[18] According to Sorokin, there are few problems or evils in the

Abridged from Robert R. Bell, *Premarital Sex in a Changing Society,* © 1966 by Prentice-Hall, Inc., Englewood Cliffs, New Jersey, a spectrum book, pages 166-172. Reprinted by permission.

16. Morton M. Hunt, *Her Infinite Variety* (New York: Harper & Row, Publishers, 1962), pp. 70-71.

17. Ira L. Reiss, *Premarital Sexual Standards in America* (New York: Free Press of Glencoe, 1960), p. 69.

18. Pitirim A. Sorokin, "The American Sex Revolution," in Edwin Schur, ed. *The Family and The Sexual Revolution* (Bloomington: Indiana University Press, 1964), pp. 153-54.

world today that cannot be linked to the changes in American sexual values and behavior.

A very different interpretation from that of Sorokin of sex in the American society is presented by the psychologist Albert Ellis. He writes that

maybe, if we were willing to devote millions of dollars and years of research effort to devising a set of courtship customs and mores which were specifically designed to lead to exceptionally low level premarital, marital, and postmarital sex satisfaction for both males and females, we could actually devise a more sexually sabotaging set of dating procedures than we now have. Maybe.[19]

As with Sorokin, it is doubtful that many behavior scientists would agree with Ellis' extreme interpretation of the present state of sex within the setting of overall society.

To further illustrate the contradictory views about sex, we may quote Howard Whitman who states that the sexual relationship is the ultimate interpersonal intimacy. "Without marriage it (sex) rests on no foundation, and to the extent that it is thus shaky and uncertain it also is unsatisfying."[20] Whitman represents a common phenomenon, the moralist who pretends to be objective, but who has only one aim—to sell a particular brand of morality. Given the views of Sorokin, Ellis and Whitman as illustrations, it is no wonder that reading the sexual "authorities" in America often results in great confusion for the many who turn to them for some insight or understanding about sex in general and premarital sex in particular.

It should be recognized that premarital sex is often used as a convenient scapegoat for the "explaining" of many personal and social "evils" thought to exist in America. Also, being against premarital sexual intimacy is as safe as being against sin and evil. Rarely does one encounter any argument for premarital sexual intercourse presented with anywhere near the strength of value commitment as found with those who argue against it. If one did argue for even some premarital sexual freedom, he would have to gather an overwhelming body of evidence in his support and would still be subject to severe moral criticism. On the other hand, many who argue against premarital sexual freedom do so with little objective concern with evidence and usually receive social approval for their traditional stand. This leads to a difficult problem of assessing the significance of values and behavior when there are sharp differences

19. Albert Ellis, *The American Sexual Tragedy* (New York: Twayne Publishers, 1954), p. 66.
20. Howard Whitman, *The Sex Age* (New York: Charter Books, 1962), p. 203.

in what is required as reasonable evidence. No doubt some readers of this book will assume that because we critically examined some of the views supporting premarital chastity that we are against chastity. Nevertheless, the purpose of this book is the examination of available evidence without either being for or against premarital chastity.

Given the present knowledge about premarital sexual values and behavior, what general conclusions can be drawn? First, since approximately the period following World War I there is no evidence that the frequency of premarital coitus has increased. Second, values have been altered at least to the extent that many girls accept premarital coitus if there is an emotional involvement with the partner and some commitment by him to marriage in the future. Third, and of particular importance to the traditional values of premarital chastity, is the increasing body of knowledge about the relationships of premarital coitus to marital coitus as well as overall marital adjustment. Ehrmann points out that

premarital chastity shows only a slightly greater statistical relationship to subsequent general marital adjustment than does premarital unchastity. Furthermore, many other variables (such as childhood happiness, happiness of parents, lack of conflict with mother and father, attitude toward sex, parental discipline, and others) have been found to have a far greater relationship to marital adjustment than do premarital coitus or abstinence.[21]

Fourth, premarital values and behavior are significantly influenced by differences in social class, education, race and religion. This suggests that general values and behavior are modified by certain social forces related to important differences within society.

Our analysis of the available conceptual and empirical studies of premarital sexual intimacy clearly indicates the need for far more comprehensive analysis. An expanded approach would contribute to a better understanding of sex in general and its implications for the family, and also to a better analysis of society in general. There needs to be an increasing conceptual and empirical approach to sex as related to different life stages. What are the relationships of different premarital sexual patterns related to marital and postmarital sex? Or what are the relationships of different premarital or marital sexual patterns to the adult's view of what is appropriate for his own children? A broader and more comprehensive approach would not only lead to a better understanding of sexual activity in general but would also contribute to a

21. Winston W. Ehrmann, "Premarital Sexual Intercourse," in Albert Ellis and Albert Abarbanel, eds., The Encyclopedia of Sexual Behavior (New York: Hawthorn Books, Inc., 1961), p. 867.

better understanding of the family and its significance for all types of sexual intimacy.

The most valuable and fruitful conceptual approach to the study of premarital sexual values has been made by Ira L. Reiss and it is hoped that others will move in the direction of study indicated by his work. In behavioral research, since the Kinsey studies, there have been no comprehensive studies of sexual behavior in the United States. More sexual research is needed with a focus both on what is common to Americans and on what is different. This should increasingly be the contribution of sociologists. At the same time there is a need for more social-psychological analyses into premarital sexual values and behavior, leading to a better understanding of the relationship between the individual and the various social forces that act upon him.

PREMARITAL SEX IN THE FUTURE

We will conclude this final chapter by making some tentative projections about premarital sexual values and behavior in the future. Projections or predictions about social behavior must be based on an understanding of the present situation within a historical context; even so, there is always the possibility that at some time in the future new and unanticipated social forces may bring about changes in values or behavior very different from what appear to be logical projections given our present state of knowledge.

A further problem in making projections about the future direction of premarital sexual behavior is that at present conditions are changing and the American society is characterized by such a variety of views that many different patterns for the future are possible. Furthermore, the complexity of social change means that changes in regard to sex are intertwined with more broad and general patterns of social change; we have tried to show that changes in premarital sexual values and behavior have come about because of many kinds of social change. Sometimes social change may be of a sort that many Americans approve and they would not want to give up those changes even though they may not like related changes that developed with reference to sex. That is, sometimes desired social change contributes to other changes not desired by many. For example, the social change of greater female equality, while resulting in a great reduction of discrimination against women in education and occupations, has led to a liberalization in sexual attitudes which is very disturbing to a large part of the population.

Many Americans tend to see the emerging codes of premarital sexual intimacy as if they existed separate from the more general social values.

It may be that for many adults there is a tendency to be sensitive to what they feel are the "wrongs" of young people without recognizing that the values of young people are often influenced by the "wrongs" of the adult world. That premarital sexual behavior often goes contrary to the values that adults assume for young people should not be surprising, for the adult world itself is characterized by many contradictions between stated values and actual behavior. As Max Lerner points out, it is "difficult to make the ideal of honor persuasive in college sports when it is not applied to business, labor, and politics. It is hard to preach homilies to young people who have witnessed the triumph of shams in their communities and homes."[22] In fact, one might argue that young people are strongly influenced in their behavior by the adult world—they have been successfully socialized to develop and pursue patterns of hypocrisy.

We have suggested that the new patterns of premarital sexual values and behavior were not initiated by the present younger generation, but are a further development of change at least partially instigated by their parents' generation. What is most important is that over the last two generations new codes of premarital sexual conduct have emerged and that, as Reiss points out, they have been fashioned for the first time by the young people themselves.[23] Parents should recognize that they contributed to the emerging patterns when they were young people and contributed later as parents by accepting related patterns for their children. Most parents, in accepting the idea that young people should choose their marriage mates, accept by implication a certain amount of independence for young people in deciding how they will behave sexually in their dating and courtship.[24]

Probably the most important single factor with regard to present premarital sexual values has been the alteration of the traditional double standard:

For the first time in thousands of years we have sexual standards which tend to unify rather than divide men and women. Especially in permissiveness with affection, coitus is no longer forbidden, and the motivation to deceive the opposite sex in order to obtain pleasure is greatly reduced.[25]

The same general point has been made by Lewinsohn, who writes that "women who enter on marriage with knowledge behind them are partners from the first, sexually or otherwise, and not subjects. What has

22. Max Lerner, *America as a Civilization* (New York: Simon and Schuster, Inc., 1957), p. 673.
23. Reiss, *op. cit.*, p. 246.
24. *Ibid.*, p. 246.
25. *Ibid.*, p. 245.

been realized here is a part of the emancipation of women, and not the least important one."[26]

Given the values of increasing equality between the sexes, the available evidence points clearly to increased sexual permissiveness among the young before marriage. Several reasons are suggested by Reiss for the increase in premarital sexual permissiveness. First is an increase in abstainers who nevertheless accept heavy petting. This group can maintain their virginity until marriage but still become highly experienced sexually prior to marriage. Second, Reiss suggests there will be continued modification of the double standard, permitting coitus for women who are in love while still allowing men coitus at any time. The fact that many women want sexually experienced men indicates their implicit approval of males having extended premarital coital experience. Third, an increase is likely in the pattern of permissiveness with affection. If there is an emotional commitment and some stability to the relationship then intimacy probably will be more acceptable to both males and females. Fourth, the permissiveness-with-affection patterns of college students will become more common as a greater percentage of young people go on to college.

It seems logical to assume that the pattern of permissiveness-with-affection will continue into the future. However, at the present time there is little evidence to suggest that in the future premarital coitus without affection will become more common. This will probably be true even though evidence suggests that at least for the male there is still a good deal of body-centered sexual behavior.

But such behavior most often takes place in a double-standard setting wherein only the male's behavior is viewed as acceptable. It is relatively rare to find such behavior occurring, *and* being accepted, as right for *both* the male and female, as is the case in permissiveness without affection.[27]

Unless some new and unforeseen social forces emerge we would project that premarital coitus within the setting of permissiveness-with-affection will increasingly be the accepted pattern for larger numbers of young people. This is not to say that all young people will accept the pattern and certainly not that there will be any great verbal acceptance of this pattern from the adult world. What is of great importance is that many of the patterns of conduct among the young are not directly controlled by social institutions reflecting adult values. We have argued

26. Richard Lewinsohn, *A History of Sexual Customs* (New York: Harper & Row, Publishers, 1958), p. 400.
27. Reiss, *Premarital Sexual Standards in America, op. cit.,* p. 119.

that the direct influence of religious institutions has been greatly weakened in this area, and there is no present evidence that religion is moving back as a major force over the premarital sexual values and behavior of the young. On the most general level, the movement in the American society seems to be toward greater sexual freedom.

IT'S NOT WHO YOU KNOW IN ROCK CIRCLES ANYMORE

Lucinda L. Franks

London (UPI)—Being up is so good it will last you a kind of eternity and that's a bit of luck because once you're up there's nowhere to go but down.

That's groupie philosophy.

For the groupie—the camp followers in today's rock scene—up means getting the top member of the top pop group into bed. And the lowest kind of down is to end up back in the audience—where it all started.

In the early '60s, all any ordinary female rock fan could expect out of a concert was good listening and maybe an autographed picture. But then the Beatles came along and they were from Liverpool, not Mayfair, and they drank their beer at the local. Things changed for the young star-worshippers and they found that the new bands which followed in the tradition of the Liverpool four were as available as the boys back home.

So began the groupies—armies of working and middle-class girls in their teens who were no longer satisfied sitting on the other side of the stage, ripping their handkerchiefs and undergoing emotional swoons. They wanted the real thing. They immersed themselves in the hip-pop culture, following groups from gig to gig, aspiring to "pull" or sleep with a bigger and better star next time.

The groupie scene today is not much different than it was back when it started in the ecstasy of the Beatle era. There is a reservoir of new pop groups and they are followed by new generations of girls who will do anything to be part of the underworld of superstars.

For the groupie who doesn't work, day begins in midafternoon. Then a light meal and a clean-up. If there's a gig on and you want to pull a guy, there's the getting ready. Groupies are mavericks—their sexual and social mores would never be found among the straights—but they aren't hippies. They care about looking flash. So they paste on eyeshadow from cheekbone to brow, don freaky clothes—rug skirts, floppy hats, thin beaded blouses—and have their hair style changed periodically.

Then maybe you pill up to make sure of a good time. Uppers and downers, pills that make you dreamy, pills that make you think you

Reprinted from the Ontario-Upland *Daily Report* by permission of the editor and UPI.

can compile a lexicon of undiscovered ideas. Usually its just a swallow-
ful of liquid cannibis prescribed as a tranquillizer—if you can find the
right doctor.

The gig may be anywhere—a hall, a church basement—depending
how big the group is. The junior groupies hang around the stage door
but if you've been around, you usually know the group and sit to the
side of the stage.

The band begins and the groupie mind explodes in a world of senses
—of crushed velvet trousers, steel strings, and scattering lights. The groupie
bounces, writhes, and tears to the beat, to the sirens-sound of the words,
and afterwards, she makes it with the boy who has made the music.

"You dig the sound, you dig what the guy is doing with the sound
and that's enough," said Brenda, 18, a tiny redhead who has been on
the scene for about a year. "He doesn't have to be good-looking."

Or even nice. Groupies, especially beginners, are treated like dirt.
They might keep a guy for three weeks or three hours but they don't
mind. Making it with a big group member is, more than anything, a
status symbol.

What counts about being a groupie is that it makes you count. Without it, life would be a nine-to-five as a typist, ham rolls in front of the
telly, and the occasional flick with Harold, the office runner. Without it
there would be no highs or lows, no changes and colors, and maybe life
would be just one gray working-class morning.

Jenni Fabian, a girl in her early twenties who lived with the group
"Family" and who won some fame of her own with her book "Groupie,"
talks about how it felt when she made the scene.

"It wasn't that I minded being part of the audience, I just hadn't
known any better," she said. "Now I had the privilege of the dressing
rooms, I also seemed to have a new identity."

The life of a groupie is not easy and a low pain threshold is not an
asset. The health risks are obvious.

"To make that scene you have to be hard and calculating. You can't
let yourself get hung-up or lose your cool. After all it's a game, it's a
career," Brenda said.

"Sometimes you feel brought down and used. But then you're using
people too," she said.

Human ruin is not uncommon on the scene. Those who travel up
through the groupie hierarchy—from road manager, to personal manager,
and finally to lead guitarist—often fall rapidly.

There comes the day, inevitably, when no one wants her any more.
That's down, and sometimes it gets pretty far down.

THE HARRAD EXPERIMENT

ROBERT H. RIMMER

FROM THE JOURNAL OF STANLEY COLE

September, the First Year

So this is Harrad College . . . ye Gods! How did I ever get myself
in this place? My friends back in Public School 133 would call it mad.
Strictly mad . . . or just plain kook.

Following instructions from the Tenhausens, all students at Harrad
are expected to keep a journal . . . strictly private stuff of their reactions.
Phil Tenhausen is a nice guy, a little owlish behind those glasses, and
his wife Margaret . . . wow! Since when did Ph.D.'s come in such nice
packages?

This morning we got the big indoctrination lecture in the Little
Theatre, a new modernistic building located across the quadrangle from
the Harrad dormitories.

"You are entering a new phase of your life, quite at variance, not
only from your past emotional life, but from what present day society
calls the norm," Phil Tenhausen told us. "After this meeting I'd like
all of you to pick up spiral bound notebooks at the bookstore, and use
these to keep a journal of the emotional and intellectual history of your
days at Harrad. Write down who you are, your joys, your fears, your
reactions to your roommate, your reactions to the Harrad Experiment.
These journals do not have to be works of art. They are your private
place to blow off steam. As time goes by we think they will be particularly helpful to you in assessing your growth, and the meanings and purposes of your life. While we don't make it compulsory, we do hope
that someday before graduation, or after you graduate, you will turn your
journals over to Harrad to be used, not only for improving our program,
but also as guideposts as to what we have achieved or failed to achieve
for you."

So, okay, Phil and Margaret, I am writing! Hunched over her desk
is Sheila Grove, my roommate . . . a girl. A girl . . . with breasts, and a

Abridged from Robert H. Rimmer, *The Harrad Experiment* (Los Angeles: Sherbourne
Press, Inc., 1966), pp. 11-18. Reprinted by permission.

fanny, and a pussy, trapped with me! While I knew it was going to happen, I can't quite believe it. Some of the time Sheila is writing . . . when I look in her direction . . . but mostly she's staring out the window. The sun has almost disappeared, just a few rays catching at the upper branches of the elm trees that tower over all the grounds and seem to hide this building and the Carnsworth gardens. Maybe Sheila and I are lost in some magic forest, and outside the world has stopped.

Back to this morning. I might as well write down what Phil said. Who knows? Someday a thousand years from now if some one discovers this journal I may go down in history as the man who chronicled an upheaval in the male and female relationship. Phil's words!

Phil sat informally on the edge of the stage as he talked to us. "The purpose of this meeting is to get you into the Harrad groove. Many of you, in coming weeks, are going to wonder if the groove is a rut and if we actually know what we are doing, or if we have a definite program at all. Admittedly, some of our approaches in this first year are tenuous. You are in the enviable position of creating a new approach to life with us. If it doesn't work with this group, the project will probably be abandoned. Both as a group and as individuals you have the possibility of making our pipe dream come true or puncturing it rudely. After studying your scholastic aptitude scores and your various achievement tests, I can tell you that Margaret and I are more than a little frightened. I doubt if anywhere in the world there is an equivalent group of a hundred students who have a scholastic ability equal to this group. How this pairs with your emotional development remains to be seen.

"Tonight, without guidance and without preparation, you will begin to live in close proximity to a member of the opposite sex. At the beginning, you'll have to make your own adjustments to this situation. Next week our required course in 'Human Values' will meet daily five times a week, here in the Little Theatre, directly after dinner, from 7:00-8:00 P.M. We may later shift this to an afternoon schedule, depending on how your courses at the various colleges and universities in this area jibe with an afternoon time slot.

"Right after this meeting you will pick up your appointments, which have been arranged with the various colleges that you will attend. For the remainder of the week you are going to be busy with your prime responsibility of developing your own personal program of study. Practically all of you will be taking advanced placement courses, but in no case should you overextend yourself. The course in Human Values, which is the only required course at Harrad, is a stiff one. At the same time you will be expected to maintain in your other scholastic studies the same high standards that have permitted you to participate in this unique project. If any of you have the idea that your four years at Harrad will be an indolent sexual picnic, you had better resign now. The thought has actually occurred to us that you will be so busy we are not even sure you'll have time for sex."

Phil waited for the laughter to subside, and then continued. "Now, the problem of transportation. Realizing that we are a commuter based college, we have permitted all students who have automobiles to bring them to Harrad. We have forty-six cars available for one hundred students. Working cooperatively, we should be able to pool transportation and get everyone to classes on time. By Saturday we will announce carpool arrangements.

"By this time you may have met your roommates. Margaret and I expect yowls of protest from some of you; first, because there have been no formal introductions. Keep in mind that if you were attending a regular college and living in a dormitory you would meet your roommate of the same sex without formality. We feel that this is the easiest way for rapid adjustment. Second, some of you may wonder how and on what basis you were selected for roommates. Let me tell you that Margaret and I, through our intense documentation on each of you, probably know more about you than you know about yourself. In a sense, at least temporarily, the faculty of Harrad is a composite parent choosing one possible mate for you, and doing this with more knowledge of you as a person than you yourself or your parents have. If you question our choice, we ask that you bear with it through the first semester. Many ideas you now have are going to change rapidly. However, we want you to know that there is no rigidity in any aspect of our program. It will be possible for students unable to make an adjustment to form their own splinter groups, and room alone, or if available, live with a member of their own sex. We are betting this won't happen, but we are not overlooking the possibility that it might.

"Because of your overall intellectual capacities, I assume you are all well aware of the hows and wherefores of human conception. But after this conference, you will all please pick up a copy of *The History of Contraception*, by Norman Himes, at the bookstore. This is a very detailed study from the earliest known history of man's attempts to prevent birth. While the book is about six hundred pages long, we expect you will read it within the next week and be ready to discuss it in our first conferences in Human Values.

"Ultimately, we expect you will have normal sexual relations with your roommate, therefore we want to reiterate a basic concept of Harrad. Heterosexual relations among strangers are very nonsatisfying relationships. Even though you may be living in close proximity, we actually assume that a love requirement (in a wider sense which will become clearer to you as the year progresses) will occur concomitantly or prior to any actual sexual relationship. Again, this is a personal matter and we simply want to make you aware of the pitfalls. With the present day knowledge of birth control methods available to you, and with the complete knowledge that we will give you of their use, there is no need for any of you to have fear of unwanted children.

"Moreover, we believe that until you finish Harrad College, you are all, without exception, too young to enter a monogamous family relationship. In a sense, you are the vanguard of future generations who, we believe because of the world population growth or explosion, as the press calls it, will be required by law to limit your progeny. The act of sexual intercourse will, if human beings are to survive, be an act largely of pleasure and emotional depth, and not one devoted to irresponsible procreation.

"We are fortunate in having attached to the staff of Harrad, Tom and Sandy Jelson, and Doctor Anson Fanner. Dr. Fanner does not live on the grounds of Harrad. He is an M.D. whose practice is in Cambridge. Dr. Fanner will discuss contraceptive techniques with you as a group and will be available for individual consultation with your roommate for specific methods to fit your own emotional needs and personalities.

"Tom and Sandy Jelson are a nationally famous husband and wife team who are in charge of our Physical Education program. They are also thoroughly familiar with contraceptive techniques.

"One of our responsibilities at Harrad is to maintain a sound mind in a sound body. Because we have accepted you in good health, we plan to keep you that way. One hour of Physical Education is compulsory daily. The hour you choose, or you and your roommate choose together, is up to you. In our long experience in dealing with high I.Q. students, we do not believe we can put Phys. Ed. on an honor system. We are fortunate in having on the Harrad grounds a fine gymnasium with a large indoor swimming pool. The pool and the gym will be open from 8 A.M. to 5 P.M. daily. Each student will have a time card assigned to him and must punch in and out daily. A minimum of one hour daily five days a week will be expected, and the only excuses will be on the basis of ill health or for female students during the time of their monthly period. Incidentally, Mrs. Jelson will maintain for each female student a complete record of their periods. This record will not only help students avoid obviously fertile periods in their sexual contacts, but will also quickly reveal any female who is overdue. Naturally, we hope this won't happen, but if it should, we have limited arrangements for married students. Of course, if all of you decide that you must immediately have children, then the Harrad Experiment will come to a rapid conclusion. The next four years of your life is not the time to have children. It is the time to prepare yourself for a responsible marriage.

"One other aspect of the Physical Education program will tie in with our seminar in Human Values. All sports, exercise, and swimming in the pool will be done in the nude."

Phil stopped talking, and grinned at the gasp of disapproval from the female students. "My lecture is over. For those who are shocked, I can only say that we are not nudists, *per se*. Nudism as a society or a way of life would be inconvenient. But we must face the fact that man took to clothing to keep warm and for personal adornment. You will find the gym well heated in the winter, and you'll be very comfortable without clothes. From a psychological aspect, we feel that it will prove extremely healthy for you to view each other calmly and objectively as naked human beings."

That was Phil's lecture. Actually there was a lot more, but if I keep going I'll fill this notebook in a couple of days.

I wonder what Sheila is thinking about? I'll bet she's scared to death. All the kids were raving and kidding at dinner, but Sheila didn't have much to say. We've been in the room for over an hour and she hasn't said two words. It's eight o'clock. Within a few hours one of us has got to make the move to go to bed. I'm not going first. I'm going to sweat her out. I'll bet a dollar no man . . . boy? . . . has ever seen Sheila in her birthday suit.

How did such a prim broad ever get herself into such a predicament? Maybe her mother thought this was the only way she'd ever get a man. Well, you're elected, Stanley Kolasukas. Yeah, elected; but you don't have to take office. Nothing in the Harrad rule book says you have to go to bed with your roommate. How the devil did they ever pick us for roommates, anyway? The only thing that I can figure that we have in common is that we are both the silent type.

Well, it's my luck. There's fifty other girls enrolled in this mad paradise. Some of them are really stacked, and I get Miss Prim-Dim for my one and only. Maybe she wouldn't be so bad if she wore a little lipstick. I wonder what's under that droopy sweater? It wouldn't fit tight on an elephant. She has a nice face, though . . . big sad brown eyes. Hell's bells, why get myself in a stew over a dame? I'm not really convinced, anyway, that this mad Utopian idea of living with a girl will ever work.

NO!

An Editorial

The best and safest answer, we believe, for a girl to give a young man when he makes what she considers an improper advance is "No!" This can be done simply by forming the lips into an oval, placing the tongue at the roof of the mouth, and exhaling with a short, sharp sound. This method has no substitute.

But there are many ways of saying "No"—ways which can be used to help the boy understand the meaning of character and integrity; ways which will teach him more about the kind of person with whom he is dealing. The response a girl makes is not only her protective armor; it is also her Christian witness. Virtue is a girl's prized possession, and the committed life includes a challenge to protect it and so to insure one's future under God.

We have asked a young member of our editorial staff, Mark Eastman, to prepare some practical suggestions that might prove useful to our younger readers who are looking for help in this area. Mr. Eastman has conferred with his colleagues of both sexes, and has come up with these thoughts:

"To help her date understand that she's a virgin and isn't about to go all the way with the first good-looking guy who comes along (or with anybody else before marriage), she will have to explain how she feels. We are offering a few ideas a girl might use in talking with her date. She would take this stand not only as a way of cooling his forward behavior but as a way of showing him that she's a Christian.

" 'I've heard of other guys and girls going as far as they can without getting in trouble, but the way I look at it, it comes down to obeying God or not obeying him.'

" 'I like you a lot and I really like your folks. I sure would feel crummy if we did something that would get back to them and hurt them.'

" 'Some day I'm going to get married and then sex will be full and meaningful and complete, the way God intended it to be. I'm sure not going to louse things up now.'

Editorial appearing in *Decision,* vol. 10, no. 6, June 1969. Copyright © 1969 by The Billy Graham Evangelistic Assoc., Minneapolis. Reprinted by permission.

" 'I want you to know that no matter how much you mean to me, my relationship with Jesus Christ will always come first.'

" 'I've learned from the Bible that my body is the temple of the Holy Spirit. I don't want anyone tampering with it.'

" 'I think you'll like and respect me much more if our relationship stays the way it is now. Anyway, I'll take that chance.'

" 'I'm much more interested in you as a total person than as just a physical body. I really hope you think the same about me.'

" 'You think we're alone out here. Well, Jesus Christ is right here with us. I've resolved never to go anywhere or do anything that would make me embarrassed to have him along.'

" 'You know, I heard a sermon the other day in which the pastor said that so many guys today are just running around looking for a body. They don't care what a girl thinks; they don't even care if she *can* think!'

" 'Hey, why don't we get something to eat?' "

Our mail may bring us letters accusing us of a "double standard" because in this editorial we are addressing ourselves to only one sex. However, we asked these young people to deal with a specific problem. The Gospel gun is not a blunderbuss. If you like what you have just read, we can ask them to take up other problems. The generation coming up needs help, and we intend to give it to the utmost of our ability.

AREA 2

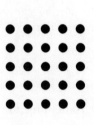

ENCOUNTER IN
MARITAL SEX

SEX EXPERTS DISCUSS FUTURE

Pamela Reeves

Chicago (UPI)—Casting an eye to his own bare pate, sex researcher Dr. William Masters accused "the bald-headed generation" of refusing to recognize sex as a natural body function. The young, he said, are coming along better.

Masters, 55, coauthor with his wife, Virginia Johnson, of "Human Sexual Response" and "Human Sexual Inadequacy," appeared Thursday on a six-member panel to discuss "The Future of Sex."

It was sponsored by Playboy.

"We of the bald-headed generation have never treated sex as a natural function," Masters said, but just as a baby begins to breathe, its sexual organs begin to function, and both actions come naturally later on.

The catch, he said, is that a person "can hold his breath a short time, his bowels a longer time, but sex has the unique facility of delay, of denial."

"It is the only natural function that has been denied."

As a consequence, we know a lot more about breathing than we do about sex.

"We don't know the vaguest thing about human sexuality," Masters said. "We're all guessing, and sometimes even guessing wildly."

Masters said young persons, however "are moving to some concept of naturalness." He pins hope on "their lack of inhibition, relative to my generation."

As he envisions it, there's no reason that men and women can't function sexually in their 80s and 90s. Dissemination of information, once we learn more, will change things, he said.

Some of the other panelists took a lighter view of the problem than did Masters. Pop philosopher Alan Watts said he entirely agreed with the researcher, "But I think he's too serious about it."

"There's nothing more boring than a nudist camp," Watts said. "All life is based on conceal and reveal. Therefore if you don't have a game in sex, it ceases to be interesting."

Reprinted from the Ontario-Upland *Daily Report* by permission of the editor and UPI.

(In a parenthetical aside to the 200-member audience, Watts noted that all the panelists had made a good deal of money from the game.)

Dr. Joel Fort, 41, an author and lecturer, disagreed with Watts. "I think sex can stand on it's own, let's say two feet, if we have the dimension of love," he said.

"I don't think the future of sex depends on concealment. As the basis of love and mutual equality, sex will survive and flourish," he said. "That's what the goal should be."

Author Morton Hunt said he thinks healthy people laugh about sex, but it's the kind of laughter "that is not the antithesis of seriousness."

"We're full of criticism about how bad we Americans are at sex," he said, "I think it would be better to say, 'By George, we're coming along. There may be something better, but at least we're moving.'"

The only woman panelist, Dr. Mary Calderone, cofounder of the Sex Information and Education Council of the United States, accused fellow panelist Dr. William Simon of male chauvinism.

But she said women achieved far more from 1915 to 1965 in all areas than they have since the women's liberation movement got strong.

Simon, coeditor of *Sexual Deviance and the Sexual Scene*, denied he was picking on Mrs. Calderone, and he said, "the aims of women's liberation must be realized." Then he turned the conversation to lust, and said there wasn't a man in the room who hadn't felt it "and sometimes been tortured by it."

"What about women?" Mrs. Calderone asked.

"Hopefully, we'll get you there," he replied.

"Lots of us are already there," she answered. "Where are you?"

WHAT GOES ON IN HIS HEAD
WHEN YOU'RE PREGNANT?

Tom Congdon

"The trouble with all the books about childbirth," my wife said one evening several months after our first child was born, "is that they tell you everything except how to put up with your husband."

I asked her what she meant.

"Nothing personal," she said. "It's just that your behavior throughout this whole thing was incredible. Not bad, just incredible. Every woman I know who's had her first baby says that husbands turn peculiar during pregnancy. It really makes you wonder what goes on in men's heads."

It wasn't until years later, after much thought and many conversations with other fathers, that I gathered a notion of what does in fact go through men's minds when their wives are bearing. My wife, I might add, was right: women don't have a clue as to what their husbands are feeling. The manuals that expectant mothers read are written from the woman's point of view, never the man's. There is natural childbirth, of course, the system in which husbands take part in the birthing, and it's all very well and good; I went through it myself for our second baby with happy results. But even natural childbirth is a totally female-centered routine, with the husband serving as acolyte and coxswain and spectator while the woman does her unique thing. No expert I know of has paid much attention to the fact that though childbearing is physically a female enterprise, psychologically it is fully 50 percent male.

To begin, let me suggest that for a young new husband, the day his wife tells him she is pregnant is the day it dawns on him that this— and not his wedding day—is really the end of his bachelorhood. Until there is a baby on the way, the footloose part of a man can pretend that this isn't a marriage he's got himself involved in, it's just the latest in his string of love affairs. No matter how much he loves his wife and no matter how much, on one level, he desires a baby, there is something in the situation that whispers to him: "Locked in forever."

That "locked-in" feeling can sometimes cause a young husband to resist the new situation. And this, in turn, can be distressing for his wife, who had assumed he would be just as happy about the baby as she.

From *Glamour* Magazine, December 1970. Reprinted by permission. (The author is a senior editor with Doubleday & Company, Inc. Publishers.)

When my wife first got pregnant we'd been married only three months. When she gave me the news I found myself insisting that we couldn't have a baby. We'd just put all our money—$7,000—into buying a ramshackle townhouse in a terrible slum. We had no choice but to live in the place, I pointed out, and no choice but to do the renovation ourselves. I needed her as a workman, I said; she couldn't quit on me. And how, I asked, could we bring a nice new baby into a former tenement that still had rats and rotten walls?

I pressed her so hard that she glumly agreed that we could ask the gynecologist if he would "help" us, if there was anything he could "do." We drove to his office one evening and sat in the car, trying to get up the courage to go in and make our request. But we never did find the courage. We went back home to our slum and went along with the inevitable. My wife managed to keep working with me on the renovation all through her pregnancy (one neighbor, watching my wife burn old paint off the front door, said: "Lady, you're the only pregnant blowtorcher I ever saw"), and by the time the baby came, we had finished some rooms for it and I had thoroughly finished with bachelorhood.

The "locked-in" feeling, however, is a hidden factor, where it exists at all. Perhaps for many men it is at most just a fleeting reaction, quickly controlled and dismissed. And of course there are factors acting in the opposite direction, impelling a man to become a father. The usual ones include the very obvious desire to be a father and to have a child with the woman one loves. Less obvious but almost as strong is a man's desire to confirm his fertility. For a man, on some level of consciousness, the ability to conceive is closely related to his sense of personal power. If he can't make a baby, it reflects on his entire capacity to act. I'm not saying this is a sensible or a wholesome attitude, but I do believe it is a prevalent one.

Fueling this anxiety is a set of sub-anxieties so bizarre as to seem ridiculous to a woman. For example, there is the memory of the time when he was fourteen years old and a baseball hit him in the testicles; the pain was so bad that surely, he half believes, the blow must have sterilized him. And what about that attack of mumps? And there are those Portnoian suspicions that despite the gingerly reassurances offered by the Boy Scout Handbook, masturbation really isn't good for you and may even be bad for you—and maybe, he thinks, he used up his sperm quota before he even got married. Or what if . . . (Masters and Johnson, the sex researchers, would understand; they have statistically documented the male's concern about the brevity of his sexual apparatus) . . . what if his penis is too short to effect the transport? When a man and wife learn they are going to have their first child, the husband's first reaction may be joy or panic, but his second reaction is likely to be relief.

The third reaction, somewhat delayed, will be exasperation, because there are few things as exasperating as living with a pregnant woman. In the beginning, she may be sick, and most husbands are no good at coping with a normally sturdy wife who suddenly gives out. A husband tries to be sympathetic, but after a few days he has to fake it. What he really wants is for her to get up off her bed and start making breakfast.

And then when she stops being sick she starts being hyperhealthy. Nature programs her hormones to give her that famous pregnant-woman glow and also to send her off into that little dreamland For Prospective Mothers Only, where no disturbing thought may intrude. But nature doesn't do a thing for the prospective father. Nothing is programming his hormones to make him tranquil, to insulate him from reality. While his wife becomes daily more serene he becomes daily more frantic. He's all alone with the stark thoughts any sane person has when approaching one of life's great confrontations.

Such as, what if the birthing goes wrong? What if the baby is born defective or injured? What if his wife dies? (The statistics on death-in-childbirth suddenly seem menacing.) The possibility that his wife could die as a result of his desire to make love; the fact that she runs the whole risk herself—these are fears that scratch at the edges of consciousness, contributing to that air of unease that distinguishes the prospective father. And there are anxieties of a lesser order. Is it true that having a baby deteriorates a woman's figure—spoils the resiliency of her breasts, slackens the vagina and God knows what else? Not that it matters all that much, except that it does matter to a man.

And what about sex during pregnancy? A man expects certain things of his wife, including a continuous supply of meals, a continuous supply of fresh underwear and a fairly continuous supply of sex. Suddenly he is faced with the prospect of a period of abstinence. Even new husbands know that it's all right to make love during pregnancy, but some think that the permissible period is only the first few months. Once the woman's belly begins to swell they grow nervous; and nervousness is the enemy of good sex. In truth, there *is* something vaguely redundant about making love to a pregnant woman, something akin to carrying coals to Newcastle. And there *is* something about maneuvering around that belly, especially since one is always aware that there's a small person inside it. Hence the strange thoughts that flit through the mind during intercourse. Invariably, though very briefly, it would occur to me that my penis might poke the placenta. Once I confessed this absurdity to another father, and he replied that he was somewhat inhibited during sex with his pregnant wife by the occasional lunatic fantasy that the baby might bite him.

I hasten to add that there are nice things about sex during pregnancy. As is often observed, many women are in some ways more attractive when pregnant. Their skin may be fresher, their coloring higher, their breasts fuller and firmer. And there is the obvious fact that for most new husbands, sex with a pregnant woman is a novelty, and novelty in sex can be pleasant. Piet Hanema, hero of John Updike's novel *Couples*, enjoyed loving Foxy most when she was pregnant. On the other hand, Foxy was someone else's wife, and he didn't have to put up with all the routine aggravations of living with a pregnant woman. And when Foxy got too pregnant, Piet had other women to turn to.

The other-women problem is one of the most disturbing for the father-to-be. There comes a point during the nine months when the wife, though technically able to continue to have sex, becomes so deeply absorbed in the coming event, so relentlessly pre-maternal, that she is no longer able to be the same kind of lover to her husband. It is not very appealing to make love to someone who is first and foremost a mother rather than a woman; undiluted maternity turns a man off. And so at about the seventh month the sex diminishes, and the man bravely resigns himself to semi- or total abstinence. The trouble is, having had little practice, most men aren't very good at abstinence. At this time, when they should be feeling most completely in communion with their wives, when their fidelity should be flawless, they find themselves more fiercely tempted than ever before. And for some reason, either mercy or perversity, single women seem readier to minister to that temptation.

In some simpler, older societies, I am told, this period presents no difficulty. It is quietly expected that the husband, deprived of the services of his wife, will seek satisfaction elsewhere. I myself can recall being shocked, when I was a teenager working summers as a manual laborer, at the what-the-hell attitude of my fellow workmen whose wives were expecting.

We middle-class types are less open about such things and more apt to repress. A friend told me that during his wife's first pregnancy he found himself wildly attracted to a girl in his office who had never looked like much to him before. "I never touched her," he said, "but that only seemed to make it worse. She'd pass by my office door and I'd find myself following her down the hall like a puppy. One evening when my wife had about two weeks to go I was sitting in the living room dreaming about the girl, and without meaning to I said out loud: 'Gee, that girl Ginny in the office really has the cutest little figure!' My wife, who was feeling as big as a house by then, said nothing. But then, after more reverie, I asked her: 'How long after the baby comes will it take for you to get back your figure?' That's when she burst into tears. She wouldn't speak to me for days."

I mentioned the aggravation of living with a pregnant woman. It's just the normal aggravation (usually heavily outweighed by manifold pleasures) but intensified a degree or two. Women, that is, become more so during pregnancy, especially, I think, in regard to preliminaries. As natural ritualists, women love preliminaries. A woman dressing and making herself up is savoring preliminaries. A woman in her lover's bed craves preliminaries. And having a baby is, for the expectant mother, a half year or more of sweet preliminaries. There is the buying or borrowing of the maternity clothes, the preparation of the nursery, the gathering of the layette, the swathing of the bassinet. There is the seemingly interminable discussion of the virtues of breast-feeding, followed by the debate over which kind of bottle is better. And of course there is the matter of choosing a name for the baby, a relatively simple task which women endlessly prolong, not so much out of indecision as out of a sense that preliminaries are not to be rushed.

Here again the baby routine is rigged against a man's nature—or at least the "nature" our culture has imbued him with. Men like to dress fast, love fast, decide fast. The little ritual preliminaries that a pregnant woman dotes on and with which she dawdles away her incubation are fun and touching for the husband too—at least at first. But when she wonders aloud for the nineteenth time whether to gamble on either pink or blue for the color of the baby's blanket or instead to compromise on yellow, her husband may grind his teeth.

It is commonly said that a husband is jealous of the attention his wife gets during pregnancy, jealous even of the wife's ability to create life—a sort of uterus envy on his part. Perhaps. I know that men often do have sympathetic pregnancy symptoms. When my wife had morning sickness, I didn't feel so hot either. An acquaintance tells me he several times thought he felt something kicking inside when his wife was feeling the same thing, though it may have been indigestion.

A less-noted affliction of the expectant father is Dagwood-phobia. No man with any spirit likes the idea of falling into a cliché, and the weariest of all the domestic clichés is the expectant father bit.

"Oh, my God," a man says to himself upon hearing of his oncoming paternity, "I'm going to have to pace up and down the waiting room like those guys in cartoons and then I'm going to have to buy flowers for my wife." It's like the embarrassment and faint rebelliousness a man feels when it occurs to him that getting married is going to involve a wedding, with the rented clothes and the insipid song about cutting the cake and the routine about the bride and groom dancing together alone on the dance floor while everybody else watches. "I'm not going to have to go through all that crap, am I?" he asks himself. And all the time he knows full well that, yes, he is going to have to go through all that crap, partly because he himself actually wants to, has in fact been looking forward to going through all that crap and would feel cheated, somehow, if one single absurdity of it were denied him.

When my first child was being born, I forced myself to stay in my chair in the waiting room. The other men were staying in their chairs too. After I'd been there three hours or so, one of the men uttered a great sigh, sprang from his chair and began to pace. Promptly, several other men began to pace, and soon we all were pacing, on and off. I, for one, felt better for it, possibly because the exercise helped relieve the tension but also because there was something inside me insisting that I was *supposed* to be pacing.

A friend of mine, a maverick of sorts, says he's always been a little sorry that he fought off the urge, when his son was born, to buy the traditional box of cigars to hand out to the boys at the office. What he is saying is that he has learned that clichés aren't necessarily wrong, they're just old. And this fact, itself the root cliché, is something women never seem to need to learn. As ritualists, women are not put off as easily by life's operational banalities. Upon encountering a cliché, a woman will try to give it her own touch, to make it work for her. She instinctively understands the usefulness of petty ritual in getting a person from the beginning of an experience to its end without undue trauma. A man, however, especially a young man, feels obliged to stamp and roar at clichés, which, as we have seen, is what the whole birth procedure seems to consist of.

A woman should know, therefore, and not be appalled, that as happy as her husband is about the baby, within him there may be a certain amount of stamping and roaring going on.

Of all the clichés that beset the father-to-be, I might add, the hoariest is the one that says all fathers naturally prefer to have a boy. The counter-cliché is when the father-to-be replies that, no, it doesn't matter to him, a boy or a girl, either one will be fine. I, happily, was beset by neither cliché, because I knew from the very beginning that, whether I liked it or not, I was going to have a son. I just knew it. What else, after all, could I have? I worried about other things—whether my son would be as rough on me as I sometimes had been on my own father, whether the doctor's knife might slip during the circumcision and with a single stroke carve years of paradise out of the little fellow's life. But as to the gender of the child, I never had a moment's doubt.

And so when at 7:00 A.M. on that notable morning, after my wife had spent all night in labor, Doctor Rugart came into the waiting room and said, "Well, Tom, you're the father of. . .," I was already thinking Son, and my chest was already swelling with pride. And when he continued with ". . . a fine baby girl," the hand I had raised to meet his involuntarily sank. I couldn't lift it. I wasn't just disappointed, I was thunderstruck. The doctor, who had been through it all before, reached down for my hand and dragged it up and shook it, too weary to disguise the fact that he thought me a familiar kind of fool.

(One evening five or six months later, I was gazing down into my daughter's crib, a pastime I'd acquired, and suddenly a question sprang into my mind: What if she'd been a boy? And then I had another of those involuntary reactions: I shuddered.)

The first glimpse of his child is another small ordeal for the father. It is not always love at first sight, as one encounters that miniature stranger. In fact, it can be frightening. Mothers never seem to have much trouble understanding that babies are bound to look odd for a while, having just been squeezed through a knothole, but fathers seem doomed to despair over the pinched and florid little faces. That may be because one of those anxieties that a husband experiences while his wife is being serenely pregnant is that some unfortunate hereditary trait, probably from her side of the family, will reappear in his child. Looking at a newborn, one can believe the worst.

One can also be frightened in other ways. A newborn baby typically looks as if it is angry with you—so angry that you feel guilty instantly, whereas you had thought it would be years before the child found you out. My first response, upon seeing my daughter, was to recall something a friend of my wife's had told me. She said that when she was little, her father had kissed her too warmly, too intimately, and that this had been pleasant but also upsetting and undoubtedly one of the things that had driven her to the psychoanalyst's couch. And so, ridiculously, when my daughter gave me that angry little scowl, something inside me said: "She knows—she knows I'm going to kiss her too warmly."

The point I am making is that for husbands, the birth of the first baby can be an unpredictable, unexpectedly trying time, a time when they may not be quite themselves. I, for one, find it a little embarrassing to think back upon. I remember, for example, my attitude toward the woman who shared the hospital room with my wife. She had just had her eighth child, and whenever a visitor would ask her about it, she would say, "Don't mention that baby! I'm here for a rest." Such a humorless, highstrung state was I in that I found her remark almost irreverent.

The silly behavior reached its climax a few days after the baby was born when the woman at the hospital desk showed me a picture of my child and said I could buy it for five dollars. The photo was extremely overlit, and the child was a ghastly white. Obviously the hospital had let some hack of a photographer go into the nursery, hold a flashgun in my baby's face and fire it off point-blank. I was enraged. I was sure the baby's retinas had been singed, if not her psyche—it must have been like Hiroshima for the child. I'm not the type who complains to strangers, but I yelled at the woman at the desk and actually threatened to bring suit against the hospital and contemplated trying to get a local newspaper to mount a crusade against the practice. Six floors up, in the maternity wing, my wife communed with her unharmed infant. When they showed her the photo, she loved it.

In due course, the mother and child come home from the hospital and true family life begins, and in the ordinary urgencies of that new life, the anxieties are quickly forgotten. Now there is an actual new human being for the husband to relate to, not just a lump under a maternity jumper, and there are practical new routines for him to occupy himself with, such as learning to hold his breath while changing diapers. And by and large his wife is her old self again. The hormones have eased off, and she is no longer playing Earth Mother, no longer maddeningly remote or ethereal.

Of course the husband may not readjust immediately. It may take him a while to realize that his wife is no longer Queen of the World and he her footman. It may be necessary, in fact, for him to be apprised of the new situation by his wife herself—as was a friend of mine an hour after his first child was born. The maternity-ward nurse had summoned him to his wife's chamber, where she was resting after the delivery. Her face was pale against the pillow and her eyes were closed, so he tiptoed into the room and stood silent by the bed. As he gazed down upon her almost worshipfully, her eyes popped open. "For God's sake, Peter," she said, reaching up and pulling him down for a hearty kiss, "I'm still your wife!"

WHO MAKES THE BABIES?

PAUL R. EHRLICH AND JOHN P. HOLDREN

Many middle- and upper-class Americans hold the convenient belief that the growth of the population of the United States is due mainly to excessive reproduction among the poor and ethnic minorities. In reality, fewer than one-third of the babies born in the U.S. each year belong to the poor, and fewer than 20 percent to the nonwhite. Evidently, then, the backbone of our population growth is supplied by the parents of "Middle America," many of whom assure themselves that having a third or fourth child is reasonable because they can "afford" it. Unfortunately, the heaviest costs of excess births do not show up in the family checkbook. Rather, they are measured in terms of stress on nonrenewable resources, on the life-support systems of the biosphere, and on the overburdened institutions of our society.

The seriousness of population growth among the affluent is magnified by their disproportionate pressure on resources and environment. This fact is most easily demonstrated quantitatively in an international context by comparing per capita consumption in rich and poor countries. For example, the average American consumes fifty times as much steel, 170 times as much synthetic rubber and newsprint, and 300 times as much plastic as the average citizen of India. The ratio of per capita energy consumption (perhaps the best single indicator of environmental impact) for the same two countries is 56 to 1.

Similar arguments, applied within the boundaries of the United States, indicate that a poor person in our own population has far less opportunity to loot and pollute than does the average American. Thus the slightly higher birth rate among U.S. poor is more than compensated for, in terms of stress on resources and environment, by their lower per capita impact (and the fact that they comprise a relatively small fraction of the population). The higher birth rate is of course a liability, but its consequences are most serious for the poor themselves. Statistically, not only are large families more likely to *be* poor, they are also more likely to *remain* poor. It is also worth noting that, although the poor have had relatively little to do with generating our environmental deterioration, they are often disproportionately its victims. The urban poor are confined to the cores of cities where air pollution is heaviest and urban decay and overcrowding are worst. Migrant farm workers may be spared the evils of modern urban life, but they suffer directly from agricultural pollution, especially misuse of pesticides.

It is particularly unfortunate that the Nixon administration has chosen to label the government's new policy of extending family planning services to the poor as "population control." This terminology has reinforced the erroneous beliefs of much of the public about the source of American population growth. More importantly, it has aroused considerable resentment among minorities, particularly black leaders, who often see such policies as a form of genocide aimed at blacks.

(Apparently, the public, including nonwhite minorities themselves, tends to equate "poor" with blacks, Chicanos, and American Indians, because higher proportions of these groups are in low-income categories. Nevertheless, the majority of the poor are white, and the majority of nonwhite people are not poor. For instance, only about 30 percent of black families were classified as poor in 1967.)

In any case, the fears of genocide and economically selective programs have been fed by the attitudes of some population control advocates who seem mainly interested in controlling the reproduction of someone else, and by occasional abuses in existing birth control programs for the poor. Those who have encouraged such abuses, and others preoccupied with variations in the birth rate among different components of our population, should take consolation that a straightforward and noncontroversial remedy is available. Specifically, among blacks and other minorities as well as whites, reproduction rates are closely correlated with income and educational levels. (Affluent black couples, for instance, have slightly fewer children on the average than do comparable white couples.) Thus, it would appear that minority and white birth rates will become indistinguishable as soon as minorities are provided the same economic, educational, and social opportunities as are now enjoyed by the rest of us.

In the meantime, of course, contraception and subsidized abortions should be available to all Americans, white, black, or brown, married or unmarried. No one should be subjected to compulsory pregnancy. Government support of these measures through national health and welfare services is necessary and long overdue. At the same time, it must be recognized that programs envisioned as purely voluntary and noncoercive by Congress and federal agencies may be coercively administered on the local level. To guard against this possibility, local administration should be in the hands of the recipients of the services and their peers.

Finally, the subsidized provision of contraceptives and abortions should not be misconstrued as population control. Rather, these measures are the logical continuation of family planning, which has been part of the American scene for more than two generations. Population control is the conscious manipulation of population size and growth rate on the societal rather than the family level. If the failure of family planning to stabilize the American population necessitates the escalation to population control measures of some sort, the new efforts should certainly be aimed first at the middle and upper classes, where the societal (as opposed to personal) consequences of growth are greatest.

GROUP SEX
(Book Review by Gordon Bermant)

Gilbert D. Bartell

You need to be careful talking about group sex—you can never tell what your friends are going to think. I once lost a friend because of a disagreement over the worth of Robert Rimmer's *The Harrad Experiment*. My friend thought this novel about group marriage among super-bright college students was deep and true while I found it shallow and false. She took my criticisms to be some kind of reverse ploy in a complicated sex game and hasn't spoken to me since. So now I'm a little gun-shy. Fortunately this new book by Gilbert Bartell states its case clearly enough that one can get to the facts about group sex without having to take up sides about *Group Sex* at the same time.

The book reports on the results of a new and needed research genre: participant observation in the social life of sexually deviant groups. The value of the approach is that when the results are well and honestly written the humanity of the business comes through with all its complexity to engage the reader's empathy and forestall premature generalizations. Bartell has achieved clarity without condescension and explicitness without prurience or clinical overtone. The approach and style are similar to Martin Hoffman's *The Gay World*.

For about three years Bartell and his wife Joan observed and partially participated in the world of "organized swingers" in and around Chicago. Most swingers are married couples who have sex with other married couples in pairs, trios . . . n-triples, depending upon taste and opportunity. Please keep in mind that this is primarily a scene for married couples; the acceptance of singles, particularly single men, is marginal. Also, remember that a couple seldom swings with another couple more than twice; swingers fear emotional involvement more than venereal disease.

There is the inevitable specialized vocabulary: "closed swinging" is when Mr. A goes off with Mrs. B while Mrs. A joins Mr. B in another bedroom. In "open swinging" the pairs don't bother to separate but rather explore the available combinations with an important exception to

Reprinted from *Psychology Today* Magazine, June 1971. Copyright © Communications/Research/Machines, Inc.

which I'll return. "Roman culture" is a party with more than two pairs swinging open, "French culture" is oral sex, "Greek culture" is anal sex, and "B and D" means binding and discipline or generally any sado-masochistic variant. "Swinging" is preferred to "swapping" for several reasons, including its ambiguity, which comes in handy when approaching a strange couple at a bar.

Major portions of the book describe how swingers get together, how they bridge the embarrassing gap between initial social contact and sexual overture, who does what to whom and how many times at a party, and so on. All this makes racy reading. But Bartell moves beyond taking the easy shots and tries to place his material in social context. He views organized swinging as a response to the dreary reality of middle-American existence. He characterizes swingers as individuals who have bought the commercial message that they are the Now Generation, the Beautiful People. Ninety-nine per cent of the men read *Playboy,* and by swinging they try to turn that brand of wet dream into reality.

A few points deserve particular emphasis. First is the degree of organization swingers bring to their enterprise. If the dedication to mailing, phoning, cataloging and traveling that swingers exhibit in making contacts could be harnessed, say, for a grass-roots political campaign, the results would be something to reckon with. As it turns out, the advantage would fall to the right of the political spectrum, for about 40 per cent of those Bartell talked to expressed appreciation of George Wallace. Most of the swingers in Bartell's sample were antiblack and antihippie, and virtually all expressed orthodox religious affiliations. These findings support the thesis that organized swinging is more a deviance specific to sex than the harbinger of a breakaway trend toward new lifestyles. If you know a couple whose station wagon has an American-flag decal on the window and an electric vibrator shaped like a phallus in the glove compartment, then you know a typical swinging couple of Bartell's variety.

There is an interesting asymmetry in the homosexual practices of organized swingers. During open swinging and parties, contact between and among women is often approved or encouraged—but woe unto the man who touches another. Parties can turn into fights following charges of male homosexual advance. This difference in ranges of permissible activity is one of the major cues to the dynamic of organized swinging. It follows the dominant pornographic themes: ordinary stag films and hard-core books often feature contact between women, but male homosexual pornography is always a specialty item. The pornographer knows that the image of two or more women having sex together turns men on but that the vice reversed is without commercial erotic appeal. Situational lesbianism poses little threat for swinging men because it is part of the tableau rehearsed in fantasy. Moreover it partially relieves their burden of satisfying what they secretly or unconsciously take to be the women's insatiable and now unbridled lust. (There is a high premium on performance among swingers; yet, perhaps not surprisingly given the nature of the autonomic nervous system, Bartell found that fewer than a quarter of the men could regularly achieve erection during the parties.) But these men have no concept of situational male homosexual activity and even the hint of an approach is a real threat. So, again, the orthodox nature of the swinger's sexual consciousness is revealed: typical masturbation fantasies are engineered into reality by dint of organizational effort before the event and liberal liquor intake during it. All in all, a dreary scene.

But what are the alternatives for the swingers? Many of them argue, and Bartell agrees in part, that "the family that swings together stays together." The falling away from a monogamous ideal that occurs in swinging is at least not compounded by the dishonesty of clandestine affairs or the exploitation of prostitutes. And Bartell points out that the general social context of the swinging scene provides satisfaction for people who might not otherwise achieve such popularity.

On the other hand it seems reasonably clear that swinging as described here is essentially a masculine invention and depends for its success on an initial wifely compliance that evolves eventually into more or less enthusiasm. I've tried to think through possible differences between husbands and wives in the satisfactions and utilities that they achieve through swinging. I suspect that women put swinging sex to different uses from those of men, but I can't get totally clear on this (and neither can Bartell—an inevitable masculine bias?). It may be that—much to everyone's surprise and disquiet—the women finish what the men have begun. But the safest bet is that many kinds of fish are being fried when swingers get together.

Regardless of the truth about swinging women, the most likely truth about swinging men was put quite precisely by one of Bartell's informants when he said, "People will tell you they do all sorts of things, but when it comes right down to it they're only interested in going off to another room and screwing your wife."

So there you have it: the more things change, the more they stay the same.

THE REPORT OF THE COMMISSION ON OBSCENITY AND PORNOGRAPHY

PART 1. OVERVIEW OF FINDINGS

The Effects of Explicit Sexual Materials[1]

The Effects Panel of the Commission undertook to develop a program of research designed to provide information on the kinds of effects which result from exposure to sexually explicit materials, and the conditions under which these effects occur. The research program embraced both inquiries into public and professional belief regarding the effects of such materials, and empirical research bearing on the actual occurrence and condition of the effects. The areas of potential effect to which the research was addressed included sexual arousal, emotions, attitudes, overt sexual behavior, moral character, and criminal and other antisocial behavior related to sex.

Research procedures included (1) surveys employing national probability samples of adults and young persons; (2) quasi-experimental studies of selected populations; (3) controlled experimental studies; and (4) studies of rates and incidence of sex offenses and illegitimacy at the national level. A major study, which is cited frequently in these pages, was a national survey of American adults and youth which involved face-to-face interviews with a random probability sample of 2,486 adults and 769 young persons between the ages of 15 and 20 in the continental United States.[2]

The strength and weaknesses of the various research methods utilized are discussed in Section A of the Report of the Effects Panel of the Commission.[3] That Report is based upon the many technical studies which generated the data from which the Panel's conclusions were derived.

A. Opinion concerning effects of sexual materials

There is no consensus among Americans regarding what they consider to be the effects of viewing or reading explicit sexual materials.

The excerpts which make up this article are from the Bantam Book publication of government materials prepared by the New York Times, October 1970.

A diverse and perhaps inconsistent set of beliefs concerning the effects of sexual materials is held by large and necessarily overlapping portions of American men and women. Between 40% and 60% believe that sexual materials provide information about sex, provide entertainment, lead to moral breakdown, improve sexual relationships of married couples, lead people to commit rape, produce boredom with sexual materials, encourage innovation in marital sexual technique and lead people to lose respect for women. Some of these presumed effects are obviously socially undesirable while others may be regarded as socially neutral or desirable. When questioned about effects, persons were more likely to report having personally experienced desirable than undesirable ones. Among those who believed undesirable effects had occurred, there was a greater likelihood of attributing their occurrences to others than to self. But mostly, the undesirable effects were just believed to have happened without reference to self or personal acquaintances.

Surveys of psychiatrists, psychologists, sex educators, social workers, counselors and similar professional workers reveal that large majorities of such groups believe that sexual materials do not have harmful effects on either adults or adolescents. On the other hand, a survey of police chiefs found that 58% believed that "obscene" books played a significant role in causing juvenile delinquency.

B. Empirical evidence concerning effects

A number of empirical studies conducted recently by psychiatrists, psychologists, and sociologists attempted to assess the effects of exposure to explicit sexual materials. This body of research includes several study designs, a wide range of subjects and respondents, and a variety of effect indicators. Some questions in this area are not answered by the existing research, some are answered more fully than others, and many questions have yet to be asked. Continued research efforts which embrace both replicative studies and inquiries into areas not yet investigated are needed to extend and clarify existing findings and to specify more concretely the conditions under which specific effects occur. The findings of available research are summarized below.

Experimental and survey studies show that exposure to erotic stimuli produces sexual arousal in substantial portions of both males and females. Arousal is dependent on both characteristics of the stimulus and characteristics of the viewer or user.

Recent research casts doubt on the common belief that women are vastly less aroused by erotic stimuli than are men. The supposed lack of female response may well be due to social and cultural inhibitions against reporting such arousal and to the fact that erotic material is generally oriented to a male audience. When viewing erotic stimuli, more women report the physiological sensations that are associated with sexual arousal than directly report being sexually aroused.

Research also shows that young persons are more likely to be aroused by erotica than are older persons. Persons who are college educated, religiously inactive, and sexually experienced are more likely to report arousal than persons who are less educated, religiously active and sexually inexperienced.

Several studies show that depictions of conventional sexual behavior are generally regarded as more stimulating than depictions of less conventional activity. Heterosexual themes elicit more frequent and stronger arousal responses than depictions of homosexual activity; petting and coitus themes elicit greater arousal than oral sexuality, which in turn elicits more than sadomasochistic themes.

Satiation

The only experimental study on the subject to date found that continued or repeated exposure to erotic stimuli over 15 days resulted in satiation (marked diminution) of sexual arousal and interest in such material. In this experiment, the introduction of novel sex stimuli partially rejuvenated satiated interest, but only briefly. There was also partial recovery of interest after two months of nonexposure.

Effects Upon Sexual Behavior

When people are exposed to erotic materials, some persons increase masturbatory or coital behavior, a smaller proportion decrease it, but the majority of persons report no change in these behaviors. Increases in either of these behaviors are short lived and generally disappear within 48 hours. When masturbation follows exposure, it tends to occur among individuals with established masturbatory patterns or among persons with established but unavailable sexual partners. When coital frequencies increase following exposure to sex stimuli, such activation generally occurs among sexually experienced persons with established and available sexual partners. In one study, middle-aged married couples reported increases in both the frequency and variety of coital performance during the 24 hours after the couples viewed erotic films.

In general, established patterns of sexual behavior were found to be very stable and not altered substantially by exposure to erotica. When sexual activity occurred following the viewing or reading of these materials, it constituted a temporary activation of individuals' preexisting patterns of sexual behavior.

Other common consequences of exposure to erotic stimuli are increased frequencies of erotic dreams, sexual fantasy, and conversation about sexual matters. These responses occur among both males and females. Sexual dreaming and fantasy occur as a result of exposure more often among unmarried than married persons, but conversation about sex occurs among both married and unmarried persons. Two studies found that a substantial number of married couples reported more agreeable and enhanced marital communication and an increased willingness to discuss sexual matters with each other after exposure to erotic stimuli.

Attitudinal Responses

Exposure to erotic stimuli appears to have little or no effect on already established attitudinal commitments regarding either sexuality or sexual morality. A series of four studies employing a large array of indicators found practically no significant differences in such attitudes before and after single or repeated exposures to erotica. One study did find that after exposure persons became more tolerant in reference to other persons' sexual activities although their own sexual standards did not change. One study reported that some persons' attitudes toward premarital intercourse became more liberal after exposure, while other persons' attitudes became more conservative, but another study found no changes in this regard. The overall picture is almost completely a tableau of no significant change.

Several surveys suggest that there is a correlation between experience with erotic materials and general attitudes about sex: Those who have more tolerant or liberal sexual attitudes tend also to have greater experience with sexual materials. Taken together, experimental and survey studies suggest that persons who are more sexually tolerant are also less rejecting of sexual material. Several studies show that after experience with erotic material, persons become less fearful of possible detrimental effects of exposure.

Emotional and Judgmental Responses

Several studies show that persons who are unfamiliar with erotic materials may experience strong and conflicting emotional reactions when first exposed to sexual stimuli. Multiple responses, such as attraction and repulsion to an unfamiliar object, are commonly observed in the research literature on psychosensory stimulation from a variety of nonsexual as well as sexual stimuli. These emotional responses are short-lived and, as with psychosexual stimulations, do not persist long after removal of the stimulus.

Extremely varied responses to erotic stimuli occur in the judgmental realm, as, for example, in the labeling of material as obscene or pornographic. Characteristics of both the viewer and the stimulus influence the response: For any given stimulus, some persons are more likely to judge it "obscene" than are others; and for persons of a given psychological or social type, some erotic themes are more likely to be judged "obscene" than are others. In general, persons who are older, less educated, religiously active, less experienced with erotic materials, or feel sexually guilty are most likely to judge a given erotic stimulus "obscene." There is some indication that stimuli may have to evoke both positive responses (interesting or stimulating), and negative responses (offensive or unpleasant) before they are judged obscene or pornographic.

Criminal and Delinquent Behavior

Delinquent and nondelinquent youth report generally similar experiences with explicit sexual materials. Exposure to sexual materials is widespread among both groups. The age of first exposure, the kinds of materials to which they are exposed, the amount of their exposure, the circumstances of exposure, and their reactions to erotic stimuli are essentially the same, particularly when family and neighborhood backgrounds are held constant. There is some evidence that peer group pressure accounts for both sexual experience and exposure to erotic materials among youth. A study of a heterogeneous group of young people found that exposure to erotica had no impact upon moral character over and above that of a generally deviant background.

Statistical studies of the relationship between availability of erotic materials and the rates of sex crimes in Denmark indicate that the increased availability of explicit sexual materials has been accompanied by a decrease in the incidence of sexual crime. Analysis of police records of the same types of sex crimes in Copenhagen during the past 12 years revealed that a dramatic decrease in reported sex crimes occurred during this period and that the decrease coincided with changes in Danish law which permitted wider availability of explicit sexual materials. Other research showed that the decrease in reported sexual offenses cannot be attributed to concurrent changes in the social and legal definitions of sex crimes or in public attitudes toward reporting such crimes to the police, or in police reporting procedures.

Statistical studies of the relationship between the availability of erotic material and the rates of sex crimes in the United States present a more complex picture. During the period in which there has been a marked increase in the availability of erotic materials, some specific rates of arrest for sex crimes have increased (e.g., forcible rape) and others have declined (e.g., overall juvenile rates). For juveniles, the overall rate of arrests for sex crimes decreased even though arrests for non-sexual crimes increased by more than 100%. For adults, arrests for sex offenses increased slightly more than did arrests for nonsex offenses. The conclusion is that, for America, the relationship between the availability of erotica and changes in sex crime rates neither proves nor disproves the possibility that availability of erotica leads to crime, but the massive overall increases in sex crimes that have been alleged do not seem to have occurred.

Available research indicates that sex offenders have had less adolescent experience with erotica than other adults. They do not differ significantly from other adults in relation to adult experience with erotica, in relation to reported arousal or in relation to the likelihood of engaging in sexual behavior during or following exposure. Available evidence suggests that sex offenders' early inexperience with erotic material is a reflection of their more generally deprived sexual environment. The relative absence of experience appears to constitute another indicator of atypical and inadequate sexual socialization.

In sum, empirical research designed to clarify the question has found no evidence to date that exposure to explicit sexual materials plays a significant role in the causation of delinquent or criminal behavior among youth or adults.[4] The Commission cannot conclude that exposure to erotic materials is a factor in the causation of sex crime or sex delinquency.

NOTES

1. The Report of the Effects Panel of the Commission provides a more thorough discussion and documentation of this overview.
2. The study was conducted by Response Analysis Corporation of Princeton, New Jersey, and the Institute of Survey Research of Temple University, Philadelphia, Pennsylvania.
3. See also the Preface of the Commission's Report.
4. Commissioners G. William Jones, Joseph T. Klapper, and Morris A. Lipton believe "that in the interest of precision a distinction should be made between two types of statements which occur in this Report. One type, to which we subscribe, is that research to date does not indicate that a causal relationship exists between exposure to erotica and the various social ills to which the research has been addressed. There are, however, also statements to the effect that 'no evidence' exists, and we believe these should more accurately read 'no reliable evidence.' Occasional aberrant findings, some of very doubtful validity, are noted and discussed in the Report of the Effects Panel. In our opinion, none of these, either individually or in sum, are of sufficient merit to constitute reliable evidence or to alter the summary conclusion that the research to date does not indicate a causal relationship."

Positive Approaches: Sex Education,
Industry Self-Regulation, and
Citizens Action Groups*

Regardless of the effects of exposure, there is still a considerable amount of uneasiness about explicit sexual materials and their pervasiveness in our society. In discussions about obscenity and pornography, the fact is often overlooked that legal control on the availability of explicit sexual materials is not the only, or necessarily the most effective, method of dealing with these materials.

Apart from legal controls, a great deal of support exists in our society for several other methods of dealing with obscenity and pornography. According to a national survey, nearly everyone approves, for example, of parents teaching children "what is good for them and what is not." A very large proportion, approximately three-quarters, of the adults in our survey also approve of dealing with sexual materials by providing instruction in school that teaches children "what is good for them," by industry regulating itself in terms of the kinds of materials it makes available, by librarians keeping "objectionable materials" off the shelves, and by groups of citizens organizing themselves to keep "objectionable things" out of the community.

The Commission has explored the effectiveness of sex education, industry self-regulation, and organized citizen action as methods of dealing with the availability of sexually explicit materials.

A. Sex education

A large majority of sex educators and counselors are of the opinion that most adolescents are interested in explicit sexual materials, and that this interest is a product of natural curiosity about sex. They also feel that if adolescents had access to adequate information regarding sex, through appropriate sex education, their interest in pornography would be reduced.

There is mounting evidence of dissatisfaction with existing sources of sex information. Although adults indicate that parents are the most preferred source of sex information for children and that other children are the least preferred source, these same adults indicate that child peers had been a principal actual source of *their* sex information. Other sources of information indicated by adults as preferred sources, such as church,

---

*The Report of the Positive Approaches Panel of the Commission provides a more thorough discussion and documentation of this overview.

school, and physician, were also minor actual sources for them. Studies of today's adolescents reveal that their peers are still the principal source of sex information and that parents, church, and physician are minor sources. Schools, however, are a more important source of sex information today than they were a generation ago.

This trend toward delegating some responsibility for sex education to the schools is approved by a substantial majority of adults in our country. The amount of support for sex education in the schools varies among different segments of our society, however: People who are older, who have less formal education, and who have conservative attitudes toward sex are less likely to support sex education.

Young people report dissatisfaction with the sex information they get both at home and at school. They report that at home parents are frequently embarrassed or uninformed and most do not talk openly and honestly about sex, while at school, the information they are given tends to be irrelevant, insufficient, or is made available too late. In the absence of satisfactory information from preferred sources, young people tend to turn to their friends, and to books and periodicals, although they recognize that these may not always be reliable sources. Young people would prefer to receive information from more appropriate and more reliable sources and in a more timely fashion, and think that more responsibility should be delegated to the schools.

More desired sources of sex information are not necessarily more reliable. Parents, a preferred source of sex information, are often neither well informed about sex nor expert in communicating with children. Formal courses in sex education are relatively new in universities and colleges and there are few teachers who are well prepared for imparting sexual information to young people. Studies indicate that physicians are often no better informed about some significant aspects of human sexuality than the generally educated citizen and may be no more at ease in discussing some sexual matters. This is also true for professional religious workers.

Training of professional workers in the area of sex education is beginning to receive some attention, but opportunities for formal training are still not widely available. Less than 15% of our colleges and universities offer any training in this area and such training is frequently only in summer workshops. Even so, the amount of professional training currently available represents a considerable increase in opportunity over what was available as recently as two years ago. The American Association of Sex Educators and Counselors devotes a great part of its annual national meeting to practical seminars and workshops in order to supplement the sparse existing training opportunities.

Medical schools are now beginning to include courses in normal human sexuality in their curricula. At the present time, about half of the medical schools in the United States devote any portion of their curricula specifically to human sexuality and for the most part the courses offered are elective. This represents a tremendous increase in training opportunity as compared with two years ago. Within theological schools discussion of sex education is only beginning.

Commercially prepared teaching materials for sex education courses at all levels are now becoming available; however, materials for use in the training of professionals are still severely limited. In fact, at least two medical schools and one religiously affiliated private training institute for professional workers have used what is generally termed "hardcore pornography" in their sex education courses because no other materials are available explicitly depicting the wide range of sexual behavior with which professionals in human sexuality must be familiar.

Training of professionals in sex education must overcome not only the absence of adequate information about sex, but also existing attitudes which inhibit the open discussion of sex without embarrassment or titillation. The experience of the two medical schools and the private training institute suggests that the use of pictorial depictions of explicit sexual activity with discussion provides not only information but also a reduction of inhibition and embarrassment in talking about sex. It should be noted that a similar finding was obtained in some of the experimental studies of the effects of explicit sexual materials.

Many schools have implemented sex education programs in the past few years and these represent a wide variety of approaches in terms of content and context. Some courses start in elementary school and continue through high school, while others are initiated only in junior high or even senior high school. Some sex education courses are integrated with other courses, and some are separate courses under a variety of different titles. The content of different courses varies from principal focus on comparative structure of reproductive systems, to focus on the social content of sexual activity, to emphasis on moral sanctions constraining sexual expression. Thus, there is little professional consensus regarding the appropriate scope of sex education.

The recency of the introduction of sex education into the curriculum and the pluralism that exists regarding the definition of goals, content and context, have resulted in the almost total absence of empirical research aimed at evaluating programs of sex education. The Commission has been able to discover only two formal studies. One is still in the process of data analysis and no results are as yet available. The other indicates that girls who had a particular sex education course were less likely to have illegitimate children than girls who had not taken the course and that boys who took the course were less likely to be divorced later, at the time the study was conducted, than were boys who had not had the course in sex education.

Sex education in the schools has been advocated because the existing alternatives for communicating about sex with young people are felt by so many people, both adults and young people themselves, to be inadequate or undesirable.

Although sex education has been endorsed by a variety of national organizations, such as the National Congress of Parents and Teachers, the National Council of Churches, the National Education Association, the American Medical Association, and the American Psychiatric Association, and although a majority of adults in our society favor sex education in the schools organized opposition to sex education has emerged in the past two years at both national and local levels. This opposition has resulted in a decelerating rate of introduction of new sex education programs in the schools. It has also engendered sensitivities which have made it very difficult to conduct empirical research to evaluate the consequences of sex education. Such opposition has also, however, forced the advocates of sex education in the schools to assess their programs more critically and to recognize the need for more empirical research data about the consequences of these programs as well as the need for education of parents and the general public.

It is increasingly apparent that parents, as well as children, are in need of adequate information about sexuality. Education of parents may help to bridge the communication gap between them and their children and thereby reduce some of the burden of sex education on other institutions.

Institutions other than the school are now recognizing the need for more adequate sex education and are beginning to assume responsibilities in this area. This is particularly true of religious institutions. A number of national religious organizations have begun to discuss sexuality seriously and several are active in producing and disseminating sex education materials.

At the present time, the amount, and frequently the quality, of sex education available to young people is limited. However, to the extent that interest in erotica on the part of young people is motivated by natural curiosity and the desire to know more about sex, sex education would appear to be potentially powerful in reducing this interest and thereby decreasing the possibility of exposure to misinformation or information outside of its proper context. Sex education programs also offer the opportunity for parents, school, and church to cooperate in helping to form within the individual a set of positive values and attitudes toward sexuality. . . .

PART 2. RECOMMENDATIONS OF THE COMMISSION

Non-Legislative Recommendations

The Commission believes that much of the "problem" regarding materials which depict explicit sexual activity stems from the inability or reluctance of people in our society to be open and direct in dealing with sexual matters. This most often manifests itself in the inhibition of talking openly and directly about sex. Professionals use highly technical language when they discuss sex; others of us escape by using euphemisms— or by not talking about sex at all. Direct and open conversation about sex between parent and child is too rare in our society.

Failure to talk openly and directly about sex has several consequences. It overemphasizes sex, gives it a magical, nonnatural quality, making it more attractive and fascinating. It diverts the expression of sexual interest out of more legitimate channels, into less legitimate channels. Such failure makes teaching children and adolescents to become fully and adequately functioning sexual adults a more difficult task. And it clogs legitimate channels for transmitting sexual information and forces people to use clandestine and unreliable sources.

The Commission believes that interest in sex is normal, healthy, good. Interest in sex begins very early in life and continues throughout the life cycle although the strength of this interest varies from stage to stage. With the onset of puberty, physiological and hormonal changes occur which both quicken interest and make the individual more responsive to sexual interest. The individual needs information about sex in order to understand himself, place his new experiences in a proper context, and cope with his new feelings.

The basic institutions of marriage and the family are built in our society primarily on sexual attraction, love, and sexual expression. These institutions can function successfully only to the extent that they have a healthy base. Thus the very foundation of our society rests upon healthy sexual attitudes grounded in appropriate and accurate sexual information.

Sexual information is so important and so necessary that if people cannot obtain it openly and directly from legitimate sources and through accurate and legitimate channels, they will seek it through whatever channels and sources are available. Clandestine sources may not only be inaccurate but may also be distorted and provide a warped context.

The Commission believes that accurate, appropriate sex information provided openly and directly through legitimate channels and from reliable sources in healthy contexts can compete successfully with potentially distorted, warped, inaccurate, and unreliable information from clandestine, illegitimate sources; and it believes that the attitudes and orientations toward sex produced by the open communication of appropriate sex information from reliable sources through legitimate channels will be normal and healthy, providing a solid foundation for the basic institutions of our society.

The Commission, therefore, presents the following positive approaches to deal with the problem of obscenity and pornography.

1. The Commission recommends that a massive sex education effort be launched. This sex education effort should be characterized by the following:

a. its purpose should be to contribute to healthy attitudes and orientations to sexual relationships so as to provide a sound foundation for our society's basic institutions of marriage and family;
b. it should be aimed at achieving an acceptance of sex as a normal and natural part of life and of oneself as a sexual being;
c. it should not aim for orthodoxy; rather it should be designed to allow for a pluralism of values;
d. it should be based on facts and encompass not only biological and physiological information but also social, psychological, and religious information;
e. it should be differentiated so that content can be shaped appropriately for the individual's age, sex, and circumstances;
f. it should be aimed, as appropriate, to all segments of our society, adults as well as children and adolescents;
g. it should be a joint function of several institutions of our society: family, school, church, etc.;
h. special attention should be given to the training of those who will have central places in the legitimate communication channels—parents, teachers, physicians, clergy, social service workers, etc.;
i. it will require cooperation of private and public organizations at local, regional, and national levels with appropriate funding;
j. it will be aided by the imaginative utilization of new educational technologies for example, educational television could be used to reach several members of a family in a family context.

The Commission feels that such a sex education program would provide a powerful positive approach to the problems of obscenity and pornography. By providing accurate and reliable sex information through legitimate sources, it would reduce interest in and dependence upon clandestine and less legitimate sources. By providing healthy attitudes and orientations toward sexual relationships, it would provide better protection for the individual against distorted or warped ideas he may encounter regarding sex. By providing greater ease in talking about sexual matters in appropriate contexts, the shock and offensiveness of encounters with sex would be reduced.

2. The Commission recommends continued open discussion, based on factual information, on the issues regarding obscenity and pornography.

Discussion has in the past been carried on with few facts available and the debate has necessarily reflected, to a large extent, prejudices and fears. Congress asked the Commission to secure more factual information before making recommendations. Some of the facts developed by the Commission are contrary to widely held assumptions. These findings provide new perspectives on the issues.

The information developed by the Commission should be given wide distribution, so that it may sharpen the issues and focus the discussion.

3. The Commission recommends that additional factual information be developed.

The Commission's effort to develop information has been limited by time, financial resources, and the paucity of previously existing research. Many of its findings are tentative and many questions remain to be answered. We trust that our modest pioneering work in empirical research into several problem areas will help to open the way for more extensive and long-term research based on more refined methods directed to answering more refined questions. We urge both private and public sources to provide the financial resources necessary for the continued development of factual information so that the continuing discussion may be further enriched.

The Federal Government has special responsibilities for continuing research in these areas and has existing structures which can facilitate further inquiry. Many of the questions raised about obscenity and pornography have direct relevance to already existing programs in the National Institute of Mental Health, the National Institute of Child Health and Human Development, and the United States Office of Education. The Commission urges these agencies to broaden their concerns to include a wider range of topics relating to human sexuality, specifically including encounters with explicit sexual materials.

4. The Commission recommends that citizens organize themselves at local, regional, and national levels to aid in the implementation of the foregoing recommendations.

The sex education effort recommended by the Commission can be achieved only with broad and active citizen participation. Widespread discussion of the issues regarding the availability of explicit sexual materials implies broad and active citizen participation. A continuing research program aimed at clarifying factual issues regarding the impact of explicit sexual materials on those who encounter them will occur only with the support and cooperation of citizens.

Organized citizen groups can be more constructive and effective if they truly represent a broad spectrum of the public's thinking and feeling. People tend to assume, in the absence of other information, that most peoples' opinions are similar to their own. However, we know that opinions in the sexual realm vary greatly—that there is no unanimity of values in this area. Therefore, every group should attempt to include as wide a variety of opinion as is possible.

The aim of citizen groups should be to provide a forum whereby all views may be presented for thoughtful consideration. We live in a free, pluralistic society which places its trust in the competition of ideas in a free market place. Persuasion is a preferred technique. Coercion, repression and censorship in order to promote a given set of views are not tolerable in our society.

Legislative Recommendations

On the basis of its findings, the Commission makes the following legislative recommendations. The disagreements of particular Commissioners with aspects of the Commission's legislative recommendations are noted below, where the recommendations are discussed in detail. Commissioners Link, Hill, and Keating have filed a joint dissenting statement. In addition, Commissioners Keating and Link have submitted separate remarks. Commissioners Larsen and Wolfgang have filed statements explaining their dissent from certain Commission recommendations. A number of other Commissioners have filed short separate statements.

In general outline, the Commission recommends that federal, state, and local legislation should not seek to interfere with the right of adults who wish to do so to read, obtain, or view explicit sexual materials. On the other hand, we recommend legislative regulations upon the sale of sexual materials to young persons who do not have the consent of their parents, and we also recommend legislation to protect persons from having sexual materials thrust upon them without their consent through the mails or through open public display. . . .

PART 4. SEPARATE STATEMENTS BY COMMISSION MEMBERS

Report of Commissioners Morton A. Hill, S. J. and Winfrey C. Link— Concurred in by Charles H. Keating, Jr.*

Overview

The Commission's majority report is a Magna Carta for the pornographer.

It is slanted and biased in favor of protecting the business of obscenity and pornography, which the Commission was mandated by the Congress to regulate.

The Commission leadership and majority recommend that most existing legal barriers between society and pornography be pulled down. In so doing, the Commission goes far beyond its mandate and assumes the role of counsel for the filth merchant—a role not assigned by the Congress of the United States.

The Commission leadership and majority recommend repeal of obscenity law for "consenting adults." It goes on, then, to recommend legislation for minors, public display and thrusting of pornography on persons through the mails.

The American people should be made aware of the fact that this is precisely the situation as it exists in Denmark today. The Commission, in short, is presumptuously recommending that the United States follow Denmark's lead in giving pornography free rein.

We feel impelled to issue this report in vigorous dissent.

The conclusions and recommendations in the majority report will be found deeply offensive to Congress and to tens of millions of Americans. And what the American people do not know is that the scanty and manipulated evidence contained within this report is wholly inadequate to support the conclusions and sustain the recommendations. Thus, both conclusions and recommendations are, in our view, fraudulent.

What the American people have here for the two million dollars voted by Congress, and paid by the taxpayer, is a shoddy piece of scholarship that will be quoted ad nauseam by cultural polluters and their attorneys within society.

The fundamental "finding" on which the entire report is based is: that "empirical research" has come up with "no reliable evidence to

*Mr. Keating while concurring in this report is preparing a separate dissent.

indicate that exposure to explicitly sexual materials plays a significant role in the causation of delinquent or criminal behavior among youth or adults."

The inference from this statement, i.e., pornography is harmless, is not only insupportable on the slanted evidence presented; it is preposterous. How isolate one factor and say it causes or does not cause criminal behavior? How determine that one book or one film caused one man to commit rape or murder? A man's entire life goes into one criminal act. No one factor can be said to have caused that act.

The Commission has deliberately and carefully avoided coming to grips with the basic underlying issue. The government interest in regulating pornography has always related primarily to the prevention of moral corruption and *not* to prevention of overt criminal acts and conduct, or the protection of persons from being shocked and/or offended.

The basic question is whether and to what extent society may establish and maintain certain moral standards. If it is conceded that society has a legitimate concern in maintaining moral standards, it follows logically that government has a legitimate interest in at least attempting to protect such standards against any source which threatens them.

The Commission report simply ignores this issue, and relegates government's interest to little more than a footnote—passing it off with the extremist cliche that it is "unwise" for government to attempt to legislate morality. Obscenity law in no way legislates individual morality, but provides protection for public morality. The Supreme Court itself has never denied society's interest in maintaining moral standards, but has instead ruled for the protection of the "social interest in order and morality."

The Commission report ignores another basic issue: the phrase "utterly without redeeming social value." This language has been propagandized by extremists and profit-seekers, and it is so propagandized in this report as being the law of the land. It is not the law of the land, since no Supreme Court ever voiced such an opinion, yet this erroneous concept has been built into the statutes of the states as a result of extremists asserting that it is a necessary "test" enunciated by the Supreme Court. This erroneous conception has led to a vast upsurge in the traffic in pornography in the past four years. The fact is, it is nothing more than an opinion of three judges, binding on no one, neither court nor legislature.

In sum, the conclusions and recommendations of the Commission majority represent the preconceived views of the Chairman and his appointed counsel that the Commission should arrive at those conclusions most compatible with the viewpoint of the American Civil Liberties Union. Both men singlemindedly steered the Commission to this objective.

In the interest of truth and understanding, it should be noted here that the policy of ACLU has been that obscenity is protected speech. Mr. Lockhart, the Chairman of the Commission, has long been a member of the American Civil Liberties Union. Mr. Bender, his general counsel, is an executive of the Philadelphia Civil Liberties Union.

The two million dollars voted by Congress have gone primarily to "scholars" who would return conclusions amenable to the extreme and minority views of Mr. Lockhart, Mr. Bender and the ACLU. . . .

Critique of commission behavioral research

1. Introduction

Dr. Victor B. Cline, University of Utah psychologist and specialist in social science research methodology and statistics, has called the Commission's Effects Panel Report—upon which the majority report and its recommendations are based—"seriously flawed, and omitting some critical data on negative effects."

Dr. Cline is the author of over 30 published research papers, principal investigator on a number of research projects funded by the Office of Naval Research, National Institutes of Mental Health, Offices of Education, etc. He teaches courses in clinical, experimental, and child psychology, and is a practising clinical psychologist.

Testifying before the Commission in Los Angeles on May 4, Dr. Cline called for, and has since repeatedly called for, the assemblage of an unbiased panel of scientists to (a) evaluate the original research sponsored by the Commission, and (b) assess what conclusions might legitimately be drawn from the assembled evidence. The Commission leadership and majority have ignored his request. In view of this, the signers of this dissenting report asked Dr. Cline to serve as an unpaid consultant. He agreed to do so, in the interest of scientific honesty and truth.

Following is Dr. Cline's evaluation of the Commission report, Effects Panel report, and "findings."

A careful review and study of the Commission majority report, their conclusions and recommendations, and the empirical research studies on which they were based, reveal a great number of serious flaws, omissions and grave shortcomings which make parts of the report suspect and to some extent lacking in credibility.

Readers of the majority report are at the "mercy" of the writers of that report, and must assume that evidence is being presented fairly and in good faith on both sides of the issue. This is also true for most Commission members themselves. It should be stated that members of the Commission Minority were allowed to look at most of the Commission-sponsored 85 research studies but only after repeated, dogged requests. And then a number were finally and most reluctantly released to them perilously close to the Commission-set deadline for this dissent.

A number of the research studies upon which the report is based suggest significant statistical relationships between pornography, sexual deviancy and promiscuity. Yet, some vital data suggesting this linkage are omitted or "concealed." Findings from seriously flawed research studies or findings which do not follow from the data are sometimes presented as fact without mentioning their very serious limitations. . . .

3. The Propper Study

The Commission in the summary of their Effects Panel Report conclude:

In sum, the empirical research has found no evidence to date that exposure to explicit sexual materials plays a significant role in the causation of delinquent or criminal behavior among youth or adults. The Commission cannot conclude that exposure to erotic materials is a factor in the causation of sex crime or sex delinquency.

Based on the above paragraph, cited again and again in various forms throughout the whole report, we have the basis for recommending the removal of all pornography controls for adults and all controls (except pictorial pornography) for children.[1]

Yet if we review the research of Propper, in his study of 476 reformatory inmates (see Table 1) we noted again and again a relationship between high exposure to pornography and "sexually promiscuous" and deviant behavior at very early ages, as well as affiliation with groups high in criminal activity and sex deviancy. This study was financed and contracted by the Commission, and while they refer to Propper's study often, no mention is made of any of these specific results in the Commission Report. This study was for many months in the hands of the professional committee that assembled and wrote the report as well as available for inspection of any of the Commission members who wished to read it (but no one else). As the reader can scarcely fail to note,

1. Control of unsolicited mail order pornography and open public displays are recommended.

there are striking statistical relationships between heavy use of pornography and various kinds of sexual "acting out," deviancy, and affiliation with high crime risk groups.

4. The Davis and Braucht Research

Davis and Braucht (1970) in a study of seven different populations of subjects comprising 365 people assessed the relationship between exposure to pornography and moral character, deviance in the home, neighborhood, sex behavior, etc. Samples of city jail inmates, Mexican-American college students, black college students, white fraternity men, conservative protestant students and Catholic seminarians were studied intensively. In addition each had one female friend fill out a character scale about their behavior.

TABLE 1

"Exposure to Sexually Oriented Materials
Among Young Male Prison Offenders" (1970)
(By Martin Propper)

Sample: 476 male reformatory inmates, ages 16-21

Activity Engaged In	Subjects Having Lo Exposure to Pornography	Subjects Having Hi Exposure to Pornography	Source
1. Age of first intercourse 11 or under	37%	53%	Table 31
2. Age of first intercourse 14 or under	65%	86%	Table 31
3. Having sex intercourse 3 or more times a week prior to incarceration	28%	45%	Table 29
4. Having intercourse with 7 or more partners	63%	96%	Table 28
5. Intercourse with *more* than 1 person at a time	35%	59%	Page 68
6. Engaged in *passive* mouth sex organ contact (sometimes or frequently)	27%	56%	Table 34
7. Engaged in *active* mouth sex organ contact (sometimes or frequently)	16%	49%	Table 33
8. *No* homosexual experience	53%	37%	Page 66

(*Continued*)

TABLE 1 (*Continued*)

"Exposure to Sexually Oriented Materials
Among Young Male Prison Offenders" (1970)
(By Martin Propper)

Sample: 476 male reformatory inmates, ages 16-21

Activity Engaged In	Subjects Having Lo Exposure to Pornography	Subjects Having Hi Exposure to Pornography	Source
9. Several times to frequently did anal intercourse	20%	40%	Table 35
10. Belongs to a high sex deviant peer group[1]	44%	78%	Table 36 Page 72
11. Belongs to high anti-social "crime" group[2]	55%	82%	Table 37 Page 73

	Seeing Textual Depictions of Homosexual Activity	
	Never	10 or more times
12. Participation in homosexual activity one or more times	12%	40%

13. Table 32 in the Propper study also reveals among the younger age boys
a very high relationship between (a) the *age* at which they saw a picture
of sexual intercourse, and (b) the *age* at which they first engaged personally in sexual intercourse. This means that if a boy saw pictures of
intercourse at a very early age, he engaged in intercourse at a very early
age. If he saw intercourse pictures later, he engaged in intercourse later.
While the data do not provide evidence of causal linkage it certainly raises
the possibility. It also reminds one of Bandura's work in "imitative learning" where children learn by imitating what they've seen.

1. The sex behaviors which constituted this measure included: (a) sex intercourse,
(b) "gang bangs," (c) going to a whore, (d) getting a girl pregnant, (e) participating in orgies.
2. The activities which constituted this measure included: (a) friends' suggestions
to violate the law, (b) friends in jail or reform school, (c) friends in trouble with
the law, (d) purchase of stolen goods by friends, and (e) friends who were members of gangs.

In their study, which was impressive in its rigorous methodology and
statistical treatment, they state, "*One finds exposure to pornography is
the strongest predictor of sexual deviance among the early age of exposure subjects* [p. 35]." Later, they again note, "*In general, then, exposure to pornography in the 'early age of exposure' subgroup was related
to a variety of precocious heterosexual and deviant sexual behaviors* [p.
36]." They note that since exposure in this subgroup is NOT related to
having deviant peers (bad associations and companions) and similar type

variables, it would be difficult to blame the sexual promiscuity and deviancy of these subjects on other influences such as being influenced by friends (rather than pornography) into these kinds of anti-social activities.

It should be noted that this research was contracted and financed by the Commission, was in the hands of the Commission staff for many months, is referred to many times in their report—but not a single mention is made of these negative finds. In fact, the September 3 issue of *The New York Daily News* and an earlier edition of the *Washington Post* carried stories on their research linking exposure to pornography with sex deviancy. This is a particularly important finding in that it suggests real dangers in exposing children and young adolescents to heavy quantities of pornography, the strong implication being that pornography can affect and stimulate precocious heterosexual activity and deviant sex behavior (homosexuality). Obviously more research must be done here, but like with the early studies linking smoking with lung cancer, it would seem most irresponsible not to report such findings and especially in the Commission's Effects Panel Report when so few people have access to the original research, and where publication in the scientific literature would be at least one or two years in the future.

5. The Berger Research

Alan Berger and associates in Illinois had contracts with the Commission to do two studies. In one they surveyed 473 adolescents primarily in the age range of 14-18 (from working class backgrounds) with an extensive questionnaire which asked questions about their exposure to pornography, their sexual behavior, etc. In the second study 1177 college students were interviewed about similar issues. In carefully reviewing these findings it is once again distressing to note that those data "not favorable" to the majority point of view are either played down or not mentioned.

The two most significant (highest) relationships (between independent variables) were between having been exposed to large amounts of pornography and engaging in high levels of sexual activity. This was true for both high school students (gamma .394 [males] page 48) and college age subjects (gamma .380, page 62). These relationships are lower (but still significant) for women. An example of this relationship can be seen in Table 2, p. 84.

There are also substantial relationships between exposure to pornography (high) and grades (low), especially in high school, but also college for males (gammas of —.256, page 30; and —.216, page 67). The

TABLE 2

	Amount of Pornography Exposed to Student	Percent College Males Engaging in Sex Intercourse, etc.
Hi	5-6	77%
	4	62%
	3	60%
	2	44%
Lo	1	4%

relationship between these two in college declines when one controls out the influence of high school grades, but still remains true for the top college men academically (who have low pornography exposure indices).

In their study of the 473 high school students they found a relationship between frequency of seeing movies depicting sexual intercourse and the adolescent engaging in intercourse (their Table 46, page 101, is duplicated in part below).

TABLE 3

	Frequency of adolescents seeing movies depicting sex intercourse			
	Not at all	1-4 times	5-10 times	11 or more times
Percent of Males engaging in premarital intercourse	53	62	73	88
Percent of Females engaging in premarital intercourse	10	29	44	

The above data are in the Commission financed reports, but are not discussed or presented, despite the fact that they have an important bearing on the "effects" question.

And while it is recognized that there are some people in our society with more libertarian views who would not be concerned if pornography did "cause" more young people to engage in premarital intercourse, there are still others, including many parents, who would be concerned and would wish to be so informed. The Commission Report fails in fully informing its readers about such associations or linkages as noted above.

6. The Mosher and Katz Study

In another Commission sponsored study by Mosher and Katz (1970) studying male aggression against women in a laboratory setting, they concluded (page 23) that, "The data clearly support the proposition that aggression against women increases when that aggression is instrumental to securing sexual stimulation (through seeing pornography)." This finding was particularly true for men with severe conscience systems as well as for those feeling guilt about being aggressive. This suggests that the need for sexual stimulation (via pornography) can overrule conscience and guilt in "permitting" aggressive behavior towards women. And while this is only a laboratory demonstration, with many limitations, it still constitutes another "negative effects" type of evidence in which virtually no attention is paid by the writers of the Commission report.

7. The Goldstein Study

In another Commission financed research project by Goldstein (1970) a study was made of the exposure to pornography and its relationship to sex activities of groups of sex offenders and others. In all, nine separate groups of male subjects were studied and compared. They found that the rapists were the group reporting the highest "excitation to masturbation" rates by pornography both in the adult (80%) as well as teen (90%) years. Considering the crime they were imprisoned for, this suggests that pornography (with accompanying masturbation) did not serve adequately as a catharsis, prevent a sex crime or "keep them off the streets." Fifty-five percent of the rapists report being "excited to sex relations by pornography." When reporting on "peak experiences" in exposure to pornography during their teens, 80% of the rapists report "wishing to try the act" that they had witnessed or seen demonstrated in the pornography exposed to them. This is far higher than with any other group. When asked if in fact *they did follow through* with such sexual activity immediately or shortly thereafter 30% of the rapists replied "yes." An even higher number of blacks (38% replied "yes") which is consistent with many studies showing very high rates of sexual activity early in life for this group. Even among the "normal" controls 28% replied "yes." If we can accept what they say at face value, this would suggest that pornography potentially does affect behavior and possibly adversely. This would also suggest serious concerns about exposing young people, especially to thematic material involving pornographic-violence. Since the writers of the Commission Report base most of their findings on data using "verbal self report" there is little reason not to at least consider as partially valid what these people say about pornography and its influence in their lives. When one asks them about their *adult* years and to what extent they "tried out behaviorally" what pornography had suggested to them, the figures drop somewhat (15% for rapists, 25% for child molesters, etc.) but still suggest an "effect."

8. *The Opinions of Professional Workers*
   About Pornography

In their summary section the Commission states, "Professional workers in the area of human conduct generally believe that sexual materials
do not have harmful effects." While this appears to be true these conclusions are based on a mail-back survey in which only a third of their
sample responded. They also neglect to state that in this study 254 psychiatrists and psychologists *had* cases where they reported they had
seen/found a direct causal linkage between involvement with pornography and a sex crime. While another 324 professionals reported seeing
cases where such a relationship was suspected, this totals in actual
numbers 578. While these therapists represent a minority group percent-
agewise, it would seem to this reviewer irresponsible to gloss over them
as if they didn't exist. What if 900 of 1000 physicians indicated that they
had observed no relationship between cancer of the cervix and use of
the coil contraceptive, but the other 100 physicians indicated that in
their practice they had come across cases where there was a suspected
or definite relationship. Do we discount the experience of the minority
because they are outvoted where a possible health hazard is involved?

Additionally they do not report (though they were aware of its
existence) of another survey conducted by a religious group, the Arch-
diocese of New Jersey, in 1967 of professionals seeing a relationship
between involvement with pornography and anti-social sex behavior. The
majority of therapists here reported noting such a relationship at some
time during their practice. This study is also flawed because of a low
return of "mail-backs" by the professionals. But such is also true of the
Lipkin and Carns study. Such omission of contrary evidence is difficult
to understand.

9. *Sex Offenders Report Pornography*
   Contributed to Their Crime

In another Commission sponsored study by Walker (1970) seven
groups of adult males (sex offenders, mental hospital patients, university
students, etc.) were tested and interviewed relative to exposure to pornography and a great deal of personal background data. In their analysis
of the data they found that the sex offenders significantly, more often
than their controls (non sex offenders who they were compared with),
increased their sexual activity after viewing pornography. A significant
minority (39%) of the sex offenders indicated that "pornography had
something to do with their committing the sex offense they were con-
victed of." The researchers also found that their offenders significantly

more often claimed that they had been influenced by pornography to commit a sexual crime.

The writers of the Commission Report note this evidence and rightly raise the possibility that these sex offenders may be "scapegoating" here (blaming something or somebody else for their problem). This possibility is certainly a reasonable one. The alternate possibility, that they might indeed be telling the truth, however, *is* another reasonable alternative. And until this issue is settled it would seem most injudicious and unwise to claim that pornography has "no effects" or that "no effects" can be demonstrated which would constitute the basis for major social change, repeal of laws, etc.

10. Three Examples of Improper Reporting of Research Data

    (a) The Berninghausen and Faunce Study
    (b) The Kutschinsky Study
    (c) The Walker Research

(a) The Berninghausen and Faunce Study

In Chapter V of the Effects Panel Report, the Commission states

A comparison study of thirty-nine delinquents and thirty-nine nondelinquent youth (Berninghausen & Faunce, 1964) found no significant differences between these groups in the number of "sensational" (obscene) books they had read. Non-delinquent youth were somewhat more likely (75%) than delinquent youth (56%) however, to report having read at least one "possibly erotic" book.

But what the Commission doesn't tell the reader is that:

(a) a significantly greater number of delinquent boys (than non-delinquent) had read two or more adult books (with erotic content); and a significantly greater number of delinquents had read three or more "erotic books" than the non-delinquents.

(b) the authors of the research concluded that "limitations of the study precluded having any great confidence in the stability of the conclusion" meaning the findings are unreliable and probably shouldn't be cited.

The writers of the Commission Report make three errors:

(a) They cite data to prove a point from a "worthless" study.
(b) They don't tell the reader that the study is flawed.
(c) They present only that evidence which favors their point of view. They again fail to cite contrary findings.

Since most readers will never read the original study they are "at the mercy" of the writers of this report to present complete and honest data. Once again we see an example of where this did not occur. . . .

12. Misuse of Questionnaire and Verbal Self Report Data

Nearly all of the studies presented in evidence relied heavily on "verbal self report" without outside verification. Caution must be exercised in interpreting these kind of data. A number of factors can make these data suspect: (a) The subjects may consciously falsify or distort (especially if the questions might "incriminate" or would require revealing damaging evidence against oneself—this might be particularly true for the prison sex offender inmates), (b) Questions in the sexual area in particular could lead to defensiveness, distortion, or "protective dishonesty" of response (such as having married couples, as in the Commission's Mann study (1970), check off in a daily diary (kept home) whether or not they had had an extramarital sexual experience the night before, and "Did you orally stimulate your partner's genitals to climax?" etc.), (c) The fact that it has been repeatedly demonstrated that slight changes in wording of a question can make major differences in the number of people who will respond "yes" or agree. This was demonstrated in this study in a most dramatic fashion when in the Commission sponsored national survey (by Abelson) only 23% of the males admitted that pornography sexually aroused them vs. 77% agreeing to this in the Kinsey studies. Similar differences were found for women (8% Abelson, 23% Kinsey). Who can you believe? Similar gross differences were found when asking people if they felt pornography should be controlled by legislation and laws. Not only is this true across several different studies, but also across several questions within a single study.

Example: Harris Poll (1969): 76% of U.S. wants pornographic literature outlawed.

Gallup Poll (1969): 85% of the U.S. favor stricter laws on pornography.

Abelson (1970): 2% of U.S. viewed pornography as a serious national problem. (A Commission Study)

However, when one looks at the question which Abelson in this Commission financed study asked U.S. citizens, it's not difficult to figure out why they got such a low percent: "Would you please tell me what you think are the two or three most serious problems facing the country today?" It is doubtful that even the most concerned citizen would list "pornography" as among the first two or three when the country is faced with the problems of war, racial conflict, youth rebellion, law and order disruption, drugs, pollution, etc. And as might be expected these head the list.

Thus when in recommending abolition of nearly all laws regulating pornography the Commission report justifies this by saying: "*A majority of the American people presently are of the view that adults should be legally able to read or see explicit sexual materials if they wish to do so.*" They are basing this only on *some* of the responses of U.S. citizens to *Abelson's* survey but not other data from the *same* survey (e.g., 88% would prohibit putting sex scenes in movies that were put there for entertainment)[1] and of course are rejecting out-of-the-hand results of the Harris and Gallup polls (see above) who have been in business for several decades. This kind of manipulation of statistics and reporting of data is indefensible especially when most Americans or even social scientists will never have an opportunity to view the original data on which these recommendations are based.

1. When the question is worded slightly differently we, as might be expected, get slightly different results: "If a sexual scene were essential to plot development" (not just for entertainment) only 69% would wish to prohibit it.

AREA 3

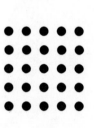

ENCOUNTER IN
MARITAL ROLES

DIVISION OF LABOR
IN TWO-INCOME FAMILIES

ROBERT O. BLOOD, JR.

By definition, the wife's employment takes her out of the home, normally for 40 hours a week plus commuting time. These are usually the hours during which the housewife (i.e., non-working wife) does the bulk of her housework. The traditional division of labor gives the husband sole responsibility for earning the family income and the wife general responsibility for the housework. Only those tasks which are too heavy or too technical for the wife are performed by the husband.

The traditional division of labor is challenged by the wife's exodus from the house. Husband and wife then share the responsibility for earning money on a roughly equal basis. The average American husband works a 40-hour week and most wives do the same. Some married couples even share the same ride to work, so their departure and returns are simultaneous. Insofar as husband and wife have equal time available, in the long run housework should theoretically be shared equally.

Modification of the division of labor in the direction of equality is accelerated by the inability of working wives to complete their housework unaided. To be sure, increased income makes it possible to purchase labor-saving devices and the notorious TV dinners, to hire part-time maid service and utilize commercial services such as laundries and restaurants. Moreover, many wives who managed to keep reasonably well occupied when they spent full-time at home discover that they can accomplish a surprising amount in shorter periods if they have to. Both the wife and the members of her family may lower their standards of housekeeping under the new circumstances. Yet, despite all these shortcuts and the added non-family personnel, the chances are that the working wife is unable to get the housework done without her husband's cooperation. Provided he has no legitimate excuse (i.e., no counter-

From Robert O. Blood, Jr., "The Effect of the Wife's Employment on the Husband-Wife Relationship," in Jerold Heiss, Ed., *Family Roles and Interaction: An Anthology*, © 1968 by Rand McNally & Company, Chicago, pages 259-64. References cited in the original have been deleted.

claims upon his time), he is likely to respond by increased participation in the domestic division of labor.*

Five research projects have tested the hypothesis that the wife's employment increases the husband's share in the division of labor. In all five cases, the hypothesis is confirmed. Blood and Hamblin find that the median husband's share of the housework is 15 per cent when the wife does not work and 25 per cent when the wife is employed. This is not just a relative difference but an absolute increase in the number of hours per week which the husband spends in housework.

Using the child's report of whether household tasks are done by the father only, the mother only, or both parents, Hoffman finds that the working wife does fewer tasks and her husband more in four different task areas: fathers', mothers', common, and child-care.

Nolan finds that employed wives shift the burden of housekeeping both onto their husbands and onto commercial services. The amount of time devoted to household operations is reduced by decreasing home canning, freezing, and sewing, and increasing use of prepared mixes in baking. Husbands of working wives help out more in virtually all areas of feminine activity, including foods (meal preparation, baking, dishwashing), clothing (washing and ironing), and cleaning (dusting, picking up, cleaning floors and baths, making beds). Such husbands also help more with the children, both at bedtime and with homework.

Analogous to Nolan's finding that housekeeping is shifted to commercial resources is Powell's discovery that Florida working wives depend heavily on paid housekeepers. The availability of Negro women as cheap labor in the Deep South reduces the impact of the wife's departure on the husband. Despite the employment of maids, husbands of working wives do more tasks in Powell's preschool and school-age samples, leaving only those in the adolescent stage of the family life cycle who fail to respond to the wife's need. The disappointment of their wives with this non-responsiveness is suggested in the poor marital adjustment of the adolescent group. In other words, husbands who fail to respond to the employed wife's need for household assistance can expect to suffer the consequences. The statistically normal and morally normative impact of the wife's employment on the division of labor is for the husband's share to increase.

The dramatic impact of the wife's employment on the division of labor in the home can be seen in Table 1. These data are from a repre-

---

*The author reports elsewhere that farmers have such a legitimate excuse in the accessibility of their farm chores evenings and weekends. This is presumably one of the reasons why farm wives are less apt to be employed.

TABLE 1

Wife's Share of Household Tasks By Husband's Income
and Wife's Employment Status

Wife's Share of Household Tasks	Husband's Income Under $5,000		Husband's Income $5,000 or More	
	Wife Not Working	Wife Working	Wife Not Working	Wife Working
	Per Cent			
Very low	7	27	7	23
Low	29	39	32	46
Moderate	34	20	33	19
High	18	6	23	8
Not ascertained	11	8	5	4
Total	99	100	100	100
Number of families	184	66	284	48

sentative sample of white married women in the Detroit Metropolitan Area.
The data represent a summary index of eight household tasks performed
by the husband always, usually, or half the time, or by the wife usually
or always. It will be noted that three times as many working wives fall
at the "very low" end of the continuum, and three times as many housewives at the "high" end.

Detailed analysis shows that the wife's employment results in substantial increases in the number of husbands who assume all the responsibility for mowing the lawn and shoveling the sidewalk. It also results
in substantial decreases in the number of wives who carry sole responsibilities for getting the husband's breakfast, doing the evening dishes, and
straightening up the living room when company is coming. Working
wives also tend to do less household repairing and do less grocery shopping by themselves (especially in the lower income group where the
main shift is to joint shopping). The only task which working wives
maintain as active an interest in is the economic one of "keeping track
of the money and bills." Here the wife's lessened time is offset by an
increased sense of involvement in the family finances—so no significant
change occurs.

The general result of the husband's increased responsibility for traditional masculine tasks and his increased sharing of the traditional feminine ones is an increase in the degree of conformity to the masculine
role and a decrease in conformity to the feminine role in working-wife

marriages. These complementary trends are expressed in Tables 2 and 3 where the masculine tasks include the sidewalk, lawn, and repairs, while the feminine tasks are breakfast, the dishes, the living room, and the groceries. This state of affairs (which also appears in Hoffman's data) means that the wife's employment introduces greater flexibility into the handling of the traditional feminine tasks but *less* flexibility into the

TABLE 2

Conformity to Masculine Role in the Division of Labor
By Husband's Income and Wife's Employment Status

	Husband's Income Under $5,000		Husband's Income $5,000 or More	
Conformity to Masculine Role	Wife Not Working	Wife Working	Wife Not Working	Wife Working
	Per Cent			
Low	12	5	15	6
Moderate	16	18	21	13
High	25	21	23	19
Very high	40	53	37	63
Not ascertained	7	3	4	—
Total	100	100	100	101
Number of families	184	66	284	48

TABLE 3

Conformity to Feminine Role in the Division of Labor
By Husband's Income and Wife's Employment Status

	Husband's Income Under $5,000		Husband's Income $5,000 or More	
Conformity to Feminine Role	Wife Not Working	Wife Working	Wife Not Working	Wife Working
	Per Cent			
Low	12	50	18	31
Moderate	33	26	31	27
High	24	12	27	25
Very high	26	8	21	13
Not ascertained	5	5	3	4
Total	100	101	100	100
Number of families	184	66	284	48

handling of masculine ones. Hence, it would be misleading to describe dual income families as involving more sharing of *all* household tasks. Only in the sense of a greater equalization of the *amount* of work done by husband and wife do such families experience more sharing in general.

To summarize, husbands of working wives usually do more housework, their wives less. The wife curtails her normal sharing in masculine tasks. On the other hand, the husband enters domains traditionally reserved to wives. Only household tasks so technical that the male partner cannot learn them or so closely linked to employment that the wife's entrance into the occupational world reinforces her participation in them resist the pressure to change created by the wife's exodus from the home.

That these shifts in the division of labor are not always accomplished smoothly is suggested by conflicts in working-wife families. Nye finds that dual-income couples quarrel more frequently than one-income couples. He also finds some tendency for the former group to argue about more topics, the chief difference significantly being in the area of "house and furniture."

Gianopulos and Mitchell do not compare working wives as a whole with non-working wives in their analysis of cases from the files of the Marriage Council of Philadelphia. Their "finding" that husbands who disapprove of their wives' working have more marital conflict involves circular reasoning. However, the authors make a useful analysis of areas in which conflict occurs. When conflict occurs in working-wife families, it does not spread randomly over all aspects of marriage. For instance, there is no increase in difficulties over in-laws, friendships, or sexual or religious matters. Almost all the significant differences are concentrated in the "domestic-economic" field. Most relevant to the division of labor are conflicts focussed on household management (where wives are especially touchy), on the husband's work and children (sore points for the husbands), and on the wife's working and financial matters (which both partners report as trouble spots).

The Detroit Area Study provides further support to these tendencies (with the added value of an income control). Working-wife conflicts over financial matters are concentrated at low-income levels. When the husband earns less than $5,000 a year, 23 per cent of the working wives but only 17 per cent of the non-working wives report that money has been their chief area of disagreement.* Conversely, disagreements over marital roles are concentrated in higher income brackets. Above $5,000, only

---

*Although not significantly different within the rigorous limits of the one chief area of disagreement, these data may reflect a significant tendency for low-income working couples to disagree *more often* about money.

2 per cent of the non-working wives but 10 per cent (five times as many) of the working wives report that marital roles have been their chief bone of contention.

These three studies suggest that when the wife goes to work, new conflicts arise between husband and wife. However, these conflicts do not pervade all aspects of the marriage but reflect the stresses created by the wife's absence from the home. Cause-and-effect relationships can be assumed in the difficulties two-income couples have over household management, over whether the wife should work, and over children.* These difficulties reflect the obstacle which the wife's work places in the way of getting housework done and caring for the children.

By contrast, the higher incidence of conflicts over money and the husband's work seem likely to be selective factors. Dual-income couples quarrel over money not because of the extra income but in spite of it. Indeed, it is because they have financial difficulties that the wife goes to work. Longitudinal research is needed to show how much financial conflicts are resolved by the extra income and how much they persist due to the working wife's greater involvement in financial decision-making. The husband's job, similarly, is likely to appear troublesome to working-wife couples primarily because it fails to provide an adequate income and thereby propels the wife into the labor market.

To conclude, the division of labor in the home is profoundly altered by the wife's daily departure from the home. Some couples make this transition smoothly but others experience difficulties along the way, difficulties which are concentrated around the reassignment of housekeeping and child-rearing tasks to fit changed family circumstances. The less the financial necessity for the wife to work, the less gracefully the husband takes on these added responsibilities at home. So, the need for the wife's employment significantly affects the stress resulting from changes in the division of labor in the home.

*Because working wives are often childless, greater difficulties regarding children are revealed only when the presence of children is controlled in the analysis. In the Detroit Area Study this variable is uncontrolled with the result that fewer working wives report children as their chief disagreement.

MOTHER WENT TO WORK . . .
AND FATHER STAYED HOME

Jorie Lueloff

A poster on the wall of the living room where Steve Everett is relaxing as he knits on a bulky ski sweater reads, "Love is the hardest lesson."

That lesson is one Steve and Marge Everett are determined to learn, so determined that they recently devoted a year to a brave experiment: Marge went to work and paid the bills while Steve stayed at home in Chicago's Oak Park suburb to take care of their two children and the domestic chores. The experience revolutionized their attitudes and their whole approach to life. It also quite possibly saved their marriage.

Knitting is a pastime Steve happened to pick up during his year of housekeeping (for some reason it's not particularly startling to see a tall, bearded man built like a lumberjack wielding needles—not when he does it with such businesslike, unfussy competence). And while Steve's knitting isn't an especially important aspect of the life-style the Everetts have evolved since that year, it does symbolize their recently acquired freedom from stereotyped male and female roles they found destructive. "We were at a point where the marriage was faltering—I wondered if we should go on together," Steve says. Then smile lines like sun rays crinkle around his blue eyes. "Now, if I had it to do over, I know I'd marry Marge again. We're closer than I ever dreamed we could be."

When Marge Everett talks about the year of role-reversal, her face—round Dutch-girl cheeks and a tilted nose give away her ancestry—is thoughtful and her words come slowly. "I *don't* know how we got through it. When we first mentioned it to friends, they would pick up that something was wrong with our marriage. And of course something was. But we had a commitment to each other that made us want to try to do something before we faced the prospect of divorce."

Nothing melodramatic or extraordinary either in their past lives or in the course of events that followed the Everetts' marriage in 1963 portended their marital crisis—or their capacity to literally turn their world upside down to try to deal with it. Marge was a typical bride in white lace and veil, and her background was just as conventional as her wedding gown. The daughter of two Chicago schoolteachers, she got her own teaching degree at a small Presbyterian college in Wisconsin. After graduation she taught primary school and lived at home until her marriage.

Like many brides, Marge loved the idea of being a wife and, eventually, a mother. "I guess I took a romantic view of it," she says now. "I really looked forward to being a housewife and doing all the things housewives do—like fixing up the house and making glamorous meals and all that. I wasn't by any stretch of imagination a likely prospect for the women's liberation movement."

Neither was the groom. Steve had grown up on a cattle ranch in Nebraska, where, when he finished his chores, he went hunting and trapping. After college, he did a hitch in the Navy and then taught school. He knew exactly what he wanted from a wife. "She would be a baby-maker and housecleaner," he recalls. His concept was based, in large part, on his own family. "I saw my mother go to bridge clubs and stuff like that. She kept the floors clean and washed my clothes—and I thought, 'That's what a woman's supposed to do.'"

In the early months of their marriage Marge willingly filled the traditional role of housekeeper with one exception—she continued to teach. Since she had more experience than Steve, she also made more money, and this bothered him. When Steve decided to go on to graduate school, Marge paid all the bills and took care of their tiny, two-room apartment. "I thought it was my duty as a woman to help him get ahead at a sacrifice to myself. Later I resented the fact that he got his Master's and there was no thought of my going for one."

It took about a year for the romance of housework to fade, but the real disenchantment set in in June 1965, when Marge quit work and then had Andy. She had looked forward to motherhood as a woman's crowning achievement all her life—and it was a letdown to find herself lonely and unhappy.

For one thing, she missed her job. "Shortly after Andy was born," she remembers, "the school called and asked me to come back. For a minute I was tempted, but then I heard Andy crying in the background and said, 'No, I don't think so.'" Anne was born two years later, and Marge was not exactly thrilled. "When Andy was small, he cried a lot and that made me very nervous and frustrated. And then to have another small child and start the whole thing all over again! Well, from then on, the frustration just grew!"

By the time the Everetts celebrated their sixth wedding anniversary, Marge was thoroughly dissatisfied with her life. "I had to take care of the kids all day and most of the night too. I had to clean the house just to see it get dirty again. I had to get all the meals." But worse than the physical work was the psychological isolation. "My world grew so small. For four years I lived through Steve's life." Steve's homecoming was the highlight of her day, and she often jumped him at the door for news of the "outside" world. It was a greeting Steve didn't relish.

"I hated it," he says. "I didn't always feel like rehashing every little thing I'd done during the day."

Then, too, when guests came to their house, usually teacher friends of Steve's, Marge resented missing out on conversations because he left all the hospitality functions to her. She wanted to talk with Steve about her growing despair and desperation, but "I couldn't because he was still in the typical male role. He got out in the world and met all these people that I assumed were more interesting than I, and I was afraid if I didn't at least keep the house up, I might lose him. Truthfully, I felt I loved him more than he loved me—because at that point he didn't show affection the way he does now."

The situation was brought into sharp focus on a camping trip they took that summer with some friends. Three times during the evening one of the Everett children cried, and each time it was Marge—not Steve—who left the party of adults to check on them. "I didn't say anything to Steve, but I was so angry that by the third time I hated his guts."

Finally, the other couples got after Steve for letting Marge do all the work. "Don't you take any responsibility within your own family?" they asked and began discussing it.

Marge was so relieved she started crying and walked away from the group. "That was such a feeling—that other people understood! I'd felt resentments so many times before and held them in. Now someone else was drawing his attention to the unfairness."

Steve's first reaction was puzzlement. "At the time I thought all the criticism was unjustified. Now, looking back, I think it was pretty mild." But it did strike a chord, and the Everetts regard the camping trip as a major turning point.

From that time on, Steve says, "I gradually woke up to the fact that Marjorie was my servant—that that's the role of women in general and I was doing my part to help keep women down." As a history teacher he felt especially guilty. "What does American history really mean," he asked, "if I go home to a wife who considers herself a slave?"

Meanwhile, Marge took a course on existentialism and began reading books and articles on psychology and woman's role and discussing them with Steve. He invited her to present a review of Ashley Montagu's *The*

Natural Superiority of Women to the sociology class he taught at summer school. Together they joined a sensitivity training group, which Marge says "helped me to know myself better and gave me the courage to bring up my complaints without feeling I would damage our marriage by being negative."

After a lot of talk and study, the Everetts came up with an idea that most men (including Steve a few years earlier) would automatically reject. It involved changing places with each other for a full school year. In a practical sense, the Everetts were in an ideal situation for a role switch. Since both were teachers, their earning power was roughly comparable. Steve was due for a year's sabbatical, so the timing was perfect. They did have some qualms about the psychological effects of a role reversal. They wondered what would happen to a male ego cut off from the competitive jungle and left at home to file recipes. Does a woman who becomes a provider also become an emasculator? And what about Andy and Anne, then at the impressionable ages of four and two? How would a little boy identify with a father who cooked breakfast while Mommy paid the bills? And who would be the female model for a little girl—a bread-baking father or a breadwinning mother? "At first we were afraid to take the risk, but then we decided we *had* to take it."

In the fall of 1969, Marge went back to work teaching first grade, and Steve stayed home with the children. The family routine remained the same, but now it was Steve who got up to start breakfast and dress the youngsters while Marge got in the family car and drove off to school at 7:45. After she left, Steve took out a cook book and planned the meals. "Lunch wasn't too difficult, but supper was a real sweat. At first, I started it at one o'clock in the afternoon. Later, when I settled down, I started it at three."

Marge left him the car once a week. On other days getting around was a problem. For shopping expeditions, Steve devised his own means of transportation, one that brought him a lot of stares. He put both children on his bike—Anne in front and Andy behind—tied a grocery cart on the back, then jumped on and pedaled to the neighborhood market.

When Marge got home from school at 4:30, she did the things most people do after a day of work. "Sometimes I'd read the paper or flop on the couch. Usually I played with the kids, too. It was so nice to see them! I wasn't bitchy and I didn't take things out on them the way I did when I was home all day." Still, it was a little while before she got over feeling guilty about leaving the children. "As a woman, I was brought up to believe it was my role to stay home and take care of the children. It's really pretty hard to shove off all that conditioning."

Furthermore—deep down—she didn't really believe that Steve could care for the children as well as she could. "I didn't think he knew all the things he had to know to take care of them—like how they look when they're tired and how to feed them properly. I also thought he considered me overprotective, and that he'd be completely permissive and let them run wild. I had the feeling that I was the only one who could take care of the children."

On the other hand, she had the secret suspicion that Steve was going to outdo her on her own turf, the kitchen. "I don't like cooking or the mess it creates. I just knew it was the kind of thing where he was going to show me up." She was right. Now Marge will admit that she was surprised and even annoyed by the ease with which Steve handled cooking tasks. Having conquered casseroles, he went on to baking bread and pies—things Marge had never been a success at. "That blew my mind. I felt guilty because he did a better job of cooking than I did. But finally I could accept that it just wasn't my thing."

Although Steve coped with the housework pretty well, it wasn't nearly so simple as he'd thought. "When we started," Marge recalls, "Steve announced he was going to organize his day. He was going to prove that all a wife must do is organize and there will be plenty of time for everything. He found out this just doesn't work with kids, phones and other interruptions. He found out you really can't plan your time."

Worse than the work itself, Steve discovered, was the tedium of jobs like doing the laundry, sweeping the floors, cleaning the bathroom, and ironing and folding clothes. What galled him most was "knowing that tomorrow you're going to have to do the same things all over again."

There were also some deep, serious concerns that kept cropping up. Steve's biggest fear was of losing his male identity. "I thought if I lost that, I would lose my authority and strength." He was also afraid that people would think he was homosexual. Several times he was tempted to back out of the deal. "There were periods when I'd think, 'This is too weird. We've got to stop.' I really would have liked to run out on it." But he stuck it out.

As the experiment progressed, Steve found himself looking forward to Marge's homecoming more and more each evening. "One night she was late getting home and I caught myself running back and forth and looking out the window for the car and worrying about dinner spoiling. And all of a sudden it just shook me—realizing that Marge had been doing the same thing and going through these same feelings. But when she'd gotten angry at me for coming home late, I thought there was something wrong with her."

Again and again, the Everetts found themselves having the same experiences and conversations they'd had before—with the roles and dialogue reversed. Before the switch, Marge had complained when Steve came home too tired for conversation. More than one argument started when he turned on the news and fell asleep in front of the television set. "One night," says Marge, "I came home from work and flopped down on the couch. And Steve said, 'Do you have to do that? I'd like some time to talk.' Well," Marge continues, "I could only laugh and cry at the same time, because the same thing he wanted, I had wanted so many times before."

On another day—when Steve was halfway through his housekeeping routine—he went to make the beds and found that Marge had done it before leaving for work. He remembers it as one of the most touching moments of the year. "It made me realize how important those little things are," he says. "I realized how a little help can free you for ten minutes to read a book or something."

Meanwhile, Marge was having a marvelous time. "Being home for four years had given me the feeling that I wasn't too worthwhile, that I had nothing to offer. What could I do besides fold diapers? Not that it's not important to fold diapers and do housework—it's just different when you're doing something outside. What I did for my students and people on the outside brought me alive. I was receiving praise for what I could do as a person. I wasn't being taken for granted. I began to feel like someone."

While Marge was gaining self-confidence, Steve was finding out what it's like to go without recognition—unless you count compliments on your meat loaf. The main compensation was getting to know his children better. And as he grew closer to them, he made some discoveries. "I could never understand before how Marge could get angry with the children—how anyone could be upset with two such beautiful children. But one day after I'd scrubbed the kitchen floor, they came running in and got it dirty. While I was yelling at them, I suddenly realized I'd never been around them long enough to get really mad or upset."

Another incident brought into focus the full extent of Steve's obligations as caretaker of the children. It happened on a day he planned to attend a funeral. "Just as I was ready to go, Anne threw up. I had a sick child on my hands and I couldn't go where I wanted. It made me see that if I was going to be responsible for the kids, I would just be pinned down by them."

The experiment is over now. Steve is teaching again and Marge is back at home. But things aren't the same as they were before. Both have become more sensitive to the other's feelings, and more able to express their own. From Marge's point of view, "It's like discovering a person that had been concealed. Steve was brought up like most men, being told 'Don't cry' and 'Don't show anything.' He's broken through that and finds he can explore his feelings. I'd been brought up not to show anger. If I did, I'd feel guilty, which was harder still. But with Steve able to accept our working through it, I've been able to get past the guilt."

Steve says, "The 'me' when I got married didn't have feelings. It didn't occur to me then to ask Marge 'What do you want from life?' 'What makes you happy or sad?' Now I have respect for what's happening to the other person. Sensitivity training helped open up the possibility to release feelings—it dawned on me that a 'me' existed I hadn't known about.

"The experiment was probably the most important thing that's happened to me in my life. But I was lucky—I knew it was coming to an end, and I had Marge's understanding of what life is like when you're confined to the house. I don't think a male can experience the hell a woman does."

Marge notices that she's less apt to have attacks of "my nasties"—sniping at Steve about personal gripes in the company of other people. And now that they're verbalizing and ventilating their feelings, the snide gestures have decreased, too. "Steve used to come into the house and look around kind of checking to see if I'd done my thing—once *I* even caught myself doing that when I came home from work."

Steve agrees. "There's no game-playing to get the other person to do what we think he or she should do. The roles have been broken and the sly little manipulations are gone. It used to be that if I wanted Marge to slim down I'd say, 'Why don't you put a mirror on the refrigerator?' That would be my ego talking, not my concern for her well-being and fulfillment. It's terrible that so much of life is into the game of images, competition, power, role-playing. What a waste to use your family for that, when it can be the source for exploring the reason that you live, the purposes of your life." As for that old devil housework, the Everetts now share the battle. In short, role-sharing has replaced role-reversal. "Steve washed the kitchen floor the other night because he wanted to," said his wife recently, giving him a grateful (and unguilty) look. "Before the role reversal, if he helped me out he got across the idea that he was doing me a big favor—that he was doing it *for* me, not with me. And he used to be grumpy about it, too."

Steve acknowledges the change. "I don't feel like a helper anymore, I feel like part of the unit. There's no set pattern. One week I bake cookies, the next week I don't. This morning I made breakfast, yesterday Marge did." Both of them cook meals, change sheets, make beds, scrub floors, dust and do laundry.

Now that she's been relieved of a lot of chores, Marge has more time to do what she wants. She reads more, takes a philosophy course at night school, and spends one morning a week doing office work at the Women's Liberation Union. One of her favorite projects is an informal women's consciousness-raising group. "The common bond is we're all housewives and we've all experienced that lonely, isolated feeling." It's entirely different from the clubs she tried a few years ago. "Those groups used to do a lot of good things—like collect clothes for the poor— but the people never really got to know each other. This group is different because we talk about our own lives. It's really digging deep to find out who you are."

Marge is convinced that her year of role reversal saved her from a second-rate existence. She's no longer living entirely through Steve and the children. She and Steve still argue about some of the same things, but the bouts are fewer and faster thanks to greater mutual understanding and clearer communications. "Fights that would have gone on for eight or nine hours before are now over in half an hour."

Although it might seem that a year of being housebound would prompt Steve to get out and stay away as much as possible, he comes home earlier and spends more time with the family than ever before. "I have more of a feeling now that I belong," he says.

Also Marge doesn't jump him the second he walks in the door these days. "Now I have my own life, too," she says. "There's more meaning to my life than just what Steve's doing." In turn, this relieves Steve of a burden.

"Marge isn't getting all her status from me any more. She's getting it from her own people, her own world."

The Everetts believe their children have benefited from the experiment. Although Anne and Andy were a little confused during the first few weeks—they kept calling Steve "Mommy"—adjustment was quick, and they had the great advantage of getting to know their father better than most youngsters do. They now turn to Steve as often as Marge—

much to her relief. "I love them," she says, "but it's so much better when somebody shares the responsibility."

Whereas skinned knees used to be solely Marge's province, Andy and Anne now run to the handiest parent. Steve often changes the children's clothes and tells them bedtime stories. "Before, Marge always put them to bed. Now I do it half the time—whenever expediency dictates. As a result, instead of 'Daddy' or 'Mommy' being just a role, they see us more as people."

But the Everetts believe the main change wrought by the experiment was in themselves. As Steve puts it, "The home is a functional situation and all the duties of the house can be shared by all the members of the family. This leaves time for them to enjoy each other, react to each other spontaneously and also frees them to grow in the way they want to grow."

In line with their new philosophy, the Everetts now work very hard to free each other for special projects that are personally important. For example, when Marge was working on her applications to graduate school a few months ago, Steve did all the cleaning up after supper. When Steve was caught up in volunteer work for a local political campaign, Marge did more of the housework and child-tending than usual.

The future promises an even bigger change. This fall—eight years after Marge put Steve through graduate school—he's going to do the same for her. But in a very real sense, both Everetts have already undertaken "advanced studies" in responding to the challenge on their poster: *Love is the hardest lesson.*

WHY WORKING MOTHERS HAVE HAPPIER CHILDREN

Dr. Bruno Bettelheim

"I'm a working mother," began one member of our discussion group. "I teach and I feel good about it. My children complain once in a while, but usually only when I come home very tired or preoccupied. Most of the time they really seem quite proud that their mother is a teacher. I know that getting out of the house and doing something I believe in is good for me, but I sometimes wonder if I'm fooling myself—if my working isn't bad for my children. I read the other day that two out of five mothers are now working. Among my own friends, all of whom could manage on the husband's income alone, the percentage is even higher. And it's funny, because we grew up with the idea that if a mother didn't devote all her time to her children, they'd be emotionally deprived."

No doubt many mothers must work to support themselves and their children. But so far as the child is concerned, what matters most is the mother's attitude toward working. If she hates it, the child will suffer. If she gets real satisfaction from it, the child will pick up her enthusiasm and will look at life optimistically, thus contributing to the well-being of both.

A non-working mother said she had looked forward to living just for her husband and children, but found the reality of it disappointing. She tried spare-time work at home, thinking it would satisfy her need for something interesting to do, but it didn't give her the stimulation of adult contact she craved. She couldn't bear the thought of a rigid, 40-hour work week that would take her away from her baby too long. So she stayed at home, just waiting for the day her youngest child would go to school and she could take a job.

In the meantime she suffered because her husband couldn't understand why she felt she had failed utterly if her bread didn't rise or why she felt guilty if she forgot to defrost the refrigerator.

I pointed out that if she were engaged in other meaningful activities, the importance of the trivia that now comprise her "doll-house" dream world would not mushroom out of proportion. This mother needs to feel that what she does is significant; therefore the things she does—washing dishes, making beds, etc.—become significant.

"I was one of those women who expected that I'd just love to stay home with my kid and enjoy every moment of it," remarked another mother. "But after he was born, I could hardly wait till he got to kindergarten so I could start working part-time. I became disappointed in myself that I didn't enjoy being at home with him, that I felt my life was empty and I wanted to get out. I guess my disappointment did something to him. Now we are much better off; when he and I come home, we have a good time together."

Part of her disappointment, I suggested, may have been the consequence of unreasonable expectations. It is true that some mothers love to stay home and take care of their children. But others, even those who dreamed how wonderful motherhood would be, often feel let down by the reality of it all. More and more young mothers find housework stultifying.

The reason is that in so many respects we are living in a time of transition—and this includes family life. Though most girls still want to have a husband and children, they want many other things, too. For 15 years or more, a girl is encouraged to compete with boys in class, to enlarge her mind, to develop her initiative. Until she marries, she studies the same subjects or works at the same jobs as her male friends. Then she must switch from studying or working to being a wife and mother. After years of apparent equality, it is made clear to her that males are really "more equal," and she may well resent this.

Our educational system, while preparing girls for an equal occupational life, advocates the values of a now antiquated form of marital life. What school reader ever shows a mother working outside the home? Yet millions do.

When work around the house is unfulfilling, a young mother's children become the natural target for her energies. Motherhood has been depicted to her as a tremendous experience, but unless she is fascinated by the minute stages in her baby's development, she seldom finds that any new enrichment has entered her life to replace the old. To fill the emptiness, she turns to watching over her children's psychological problems and educational life.

Sadly enough, the children would often be better off with less watching over and with more real support where they need it. But a nonworking mother is often in a poor position to give her child that support when, for example, he is doing badly in school or in the world.

Having overinvested emotionally in her child's achievement, she sees all this investment put in jeopardy when he fails at something. So, as likely as not, she bawls him out when understanding and compassion are needed. She may fail as a mother because her inner needs make her work at it too hard.

"Now that I've taken a job," one mother said, "I feel guilty about walking out on my family. Don't my children suffer from having a working mother?"

Throughout the history of mankind, most women have been working mothers. Yet many middle-class American women have the idea that working mothers are deserting their families. Before the age of modern technology, the human economy couldn't have succeeded without working mothers.

It is our change in attitude toward work that makes the working mother uneasy. For ages, the whole family worked together and work was viewed as the significant bond that held them together. Suddenly, within two generations, family cohesion no longer rests on economic necessity but on affection, which doesn't always work as the sole family bond. All the things intended to tie parents and children together emotionally too often end up as artificial stratagems. A mother may make desperate efforts to be a child with her children, or she may prematurely introduce them to adult views so that they can compensate for the adult companionship and stimulation she is missing by staying home. In either case, the affectionate relationship becomes a subtle enslavement. It is this psychological enslavement that the working mother tries to escape from into her job; if she does it successfully, she also helps her child escape it.

"You're right," said a mother. "My son is three. As long as he was a baby, things went fine, but now that he gets into everything, I seem to be after him all day long, nagging him and scolding him, and that makes me feel awful."

TODDLERS

Her boy was now a toddler, and that's the age when many a mother gets restless and irritated with her child. Even with the best of intentions it is not easy to arrange things in the modern home for a toddler, who needs constant supervision. Thus a mother may find herself constantly nagging her child. Worse, she feels she no longer has a moment to herself, that she is becoming a "non-person," as one mother put it.

She is depressed to find she is so often annoyed or bored with her child, although she wants to be a happy, loving mother.

This same period is terribly important in the development of the child's personality. He is learning and reaching out to the world, trying to master it. He is getting answers to his basic questions: "Am I welcome in this world? Do I gain by reaching out to it?"

At this critical moment the child is in the sole care of a person who often finds herself in a state of psychological exhaustion. A lot of love is needed to compensate for the endless do's and don'ts that modern living imposes. When the mother is the sole educator of a very young child, her tremendous importance as the giver of love is wasted in having to supervise every minute of the small child's active day. When her husband comes home, she's dead tired.

She can barely wait for the child's bedtime, when she can finally have a bit of life of her own. But she is often too tired to enjoy it.

This was not so in the past, nor is it so today in most of the world, where children are still brought up in the "extended family"—that is, by older siblings, cousins, aunts or grandparents. In such families, parents are reserved for the real decisions, for setting the overall pattern of their children's lives and education, but are not taken up with the minutiae of child-rearing.

It benefits neither child nor mother if all the no's and do's and don'ts come from her—the most important person in the child's world. When a child is criticized by a person who is terribly important to him and whose love he cannot afford to lose, even a small reprimand becomes an anxious experience. On the other hand, if he is taught the same things by someone less important, he may feel chastened but never frightened. Hence he resents the admonition less strongly, and this less important person gets less of a negative reaction.

"That's all very fine," said a mother. "But who's going to take this kind of care of our children when we're out working? We tried the grandparents, and they liked it so long as all they had to do was have a good time with the child for a few hours. But when we were gone for three days and they had all the responsibility, it was more than they could take."

I agreed that we cannot simply recreate the extended family in our modern situation. Certainly a baby-sitter, no matter how good, is not the answer. There is always the worry as to whether she will arrive in time and will be able to deal with emergencies. Moreover, even the best baby-sitter does not offer the companionship of age-mates, which the toddler needs so much. Our greatest living child psychologist, Piaget, has stressed how much a child needs to engage with other children in what he calls their "collective monologue"—chattering away in concert without anybody's taking it very seriously. By playing with each other, Piaget says, children learn the "rules of the game," and this learning is very important if, later in life, they are to be able to cooperate with others. The child who has always had his mother at his beck and call may never learn the give and take that makes life with others possible.

Some young mothers are now demanding that day-care centers be created, not just because they want to be free to work, but because they know the centers are good for their children. For this movement to succeed, we need to adopt an entirely new attitude about what is best for mothers and children. So long as the working mother feels that no matter how good working may be for her, it is still bad for her child, little good will come of it for either of them. It is time to re-examine the notion that only the mother who stays home with her child has true motherly feelings. We must realize that it is better for both mother and child if the do's and don'ts are imposed during part of the day by someone professionally trained for the task, someone who is not so intimately tied to the child that an emotional uproar results when the child rejects one of her demands. The professional child-care worker can be much more patient; she doesn't have to worry about undone household chores while she spends her time with the child. What's more, she is assured of relief when her hours with the children are over.

FOR MUTUAL PLEASURE

Once mothers accept this point of view, they will be able to hand their children over to the professional worker for part of the day without ambiguous feelings, knowing that this is best for the children and themselves. Having several hours a day for their own adult pursuits, these mothers will be more than ready to use time with their children for mutual pleasure and growth.

If we are serious about work being a normal part of woman's life, employers will have to make the necessary arrangements so that working mothers can be just that—mothers who also work. This will mean that mothers should not come home from work too tired to take care of their children. It will require a shorter working day for mothers and enough flexibility in working hours to permit them to leave when their children need them. Such arrangements are small indeed compared with what is needed first—a more rational attitude about what is best for the child and for the mother in our modern world.

FATHERHOOD AND THE EMERGING FAMILY

LEONARD BENSON

Any forecast concerning fatherhood must be based upon certain assumptions about trends in the family, but there are overwhelming difficulties in predicting family developments because the family is not a self-contained social system, nor is it subject to strategies of legislative and administrative control. Although lip service is repeatedly given to the family's irreplaceable value to society, laws passed each year rarely deal directly with the family. Legislators attend to other matters, obliquely affecting family life to be sure, but in unformulated or unanticipated ways. Nor are corporations any more concerned than the legislature; they view the family as a sales target. The courts are usually more solicitous of domestic needs, but are not in a strategic position to initiate new and important family legislation.

Changes in the family are ultimately responsive to the most fundamental, and least supervised, changes in society. Yonina Talmon (1964) has observed that almost the entire social channeling of our selection of mates occurs as an unintended, unforeseen, or even undesired consequence of institutional arrangements made for other purposes. Trends toward earlier marriage and a higher marriage rate, for example, reflect this unsponsored, in a sense accidental, drift, with obscure implications for father; but, as we shall see, the changes that are occurring do seem to be related to the underlying transformation of the breadwinner role.

Various scholars have attempted to appraise the future of the family by more reliable means than humanistic reflection or intuition. Reuben Hill (1964), for example, has sought to pinpoint family trends through the intergenerational study of the family; more specifically, through the study of three generations within particular families. On the basis of his research he predicts greater overall family effectiveness, enhanced professional competence among those who work with family problems, improved economic well-being for the family, better family-life planning, and greater communication among family members. His two most questionable predictions concern the family's overall effectiveness and progress in communications. They emerge as hopes, not objective projections. Even if we could be assured that both trends have actually emerged in the past fifty years, it is impossible to know what kind of effectiveness will be required in the world of the future; certainly the entire matrix of communications in modern society is in a state of transformation, bearing unknown implications for husband-wife interaction. Hill's profile of the future freezes the non-family world and projects recent family trends in an otherwise static society, but that is something forecasts almost always do.

Charles Hobart (1963) has also written about the kind of family that can be expected to flourish in a society that is increasingly affluent in consumption and bureaucratic in management. He is optimistic that greater stress will be placed on "being" rather than "doing" within the family, on expressive rather than instrumental bonds, and that there will be a warmer, richer family center to life. He contrasts his view with that of Barrington Moore (1960), who contends that the family of the future will have to become more bureaucratized, just as everything else in society has responded to the principles of efficiency and rational organization.

Moore's position is easily misinterpreted. He correctly recognizes that as society becomes increasingly bureaucratized, aspects of the family must also succumb, yet essential aspects of family life can remain unbureaucratized as they always have. Indeed, there are no known strategies for bureaucratizing family intimacies as yet, only for surrounding them with greater comfort and with more effective labor-saving devices.

No intention is made by either Hobart or Moore to belittle the role of the family. Although it has receded in scope in modern society, it still remains the most meaningful social unit for most of the world's people—more meaningful than the corporation, the neighborhood, the political party, the church, the city, or the nation. Its universality is derived from the immediate satisfactions it offers and from its effectiveness in coping with daily problems. Nothing has come along to replace it, although other social agencies do have an increasing appeal; the nation-state, for example, has become relatively more important, but it cannot carry a primary symbolic load for many, perhaps not even for most, people. Hobart sees the family of the future as the basic source of affection and meaning in life, but one whose material subsistence is to be provided for by countless bureaucratically ordered, nonfamily agencies.

Hobart's point of view seems to reflect the mainstream of current thinking among American students of family life. But there is something that we tend to ignore, perhaps because it is so pervasive in our lives: the family-budget ethic, which is linked in America to the rhetoric of capitalism and private enterprise. This ethic, modified here and there over time though retained in essence, fosters opposition to government assistance to the family as an economic unit and to any enlargement of the public sector of our economy, except as it may be designed to strengthen or assist the private sector. The concepts of freedom, justice, and personal integrity, which are written into this ideological package, define for the individual an important dimension of his self-concept. As this ethic applies to man the father, each adult male is responsible for the economic well-being of his family, and he therefore takes pride in his success as a family provider and suffers if he is inept.

The successful man is not eager to share the rewards of his good fortune with men who fail, and the greatest prerogative of success is to be able to dispense its bounty to one's family and heirs. Paternal largesse has therefore been established as a carefully graded privilege the world over. Compounding the misfortunes of the unsuccessful man is the fact that his failure is a family tragedy, not merely a personal one. The lower-class child inevitably has trouble; if his father should leave home, as he very well may, the child's basic problem remains because public assistance is absolutely minimal (McKeany, 1960), an inherent consequence of the family-budget ethic and one that seems natural enough to those who have been reared in its discipline.

THE WELFARE ETHIC

In a smaller way, however, Americans retain a humanitarian welfare ethic, one that is also deeply rooted in our national experience and that is currently propelled by powerful political and economic forces. The welfare ethic is diffusive and can encompass anything from small acts of kindness to "wars on poverty." In its most vital form it promotes social arrangements by which each person is given the means and the encouragement to realize his own potentialities. We now recognize that the key to "equal opportunity" is the elimination of arbitrary advantages accorded to some children and denied to others; the perseverance of patterned inequality is always rooted in a status system by which some parents can provide opportunities for their children not available to all.

The contemporary effort to equalize life chances has led to the development of governmental programs in health, education, and welfare, with little thought of challenging the morality implicit in the family-budget system. But clearly the *equal-opportunities ethic* and the *family-budget ethic* clash. Welfare programs are usually oriented to the needs of family units, and they are most often designed to help families in which the father is inadequate, setting standards for services and consumption independent of the family's "ability to pay."

An inevitable consequence is that efforts are made to promote only those welfare services that do not openly challenge the family budget system. The latter is deeply entrenched, and its requirements take precedence over those specified by the welfare ethic. Thus family health and welfare services in the United States are essentially ameliorative rather than reformative or preventive (Robinson, 1963). A coherent welfare program is retarded by retention of the "each-family-for-itself" orientation in the dominating private sector of our economy, a veritable handicap system in the competition for status. If it can be argued that the greatest obstacle to man's rapport with humanity is status seeking, the basis for this isolation is the tradition of the family budget and its almost universal appeal to familism, with father as the key to the family's status.

The tenacity of the "father-as-breadwinner" doctrine prevents the resolution of problems of both the working mother and the modern welfare state. It is the basis for the supplementary character of mother's earning power, and it serves as the moral explanation by which to justify the unhappy state of those in the lower classes. In accordance with the ethic of paternal enterprise, one can logically resolve most social problems by saying, "If men would just do an honest day's work for an honest day's pay, we should not have all this misfortune."

The disabled father is not held responsible for his inadequacy as a breadwinner, of course, but the burden falls on his wife's shoulders. The discrepancy between what is expected of him and his potential fulfillment is enormous, much greater than would be the case for the disabled mother. Disability reduces father to a position that is antithetical to the expectations of adult men held by both the man and his wife.

An inverse relationship seems to exist between the father's breadwinner function and the progress of the welfare state and also between the breadwinner function and the expressive, "primary-group" functions of the family. Curiously, however, emphasis on the breadwinner has been displaced but the breadwinner role has not; thus father is psychologically tied to a role whose ethical validity is not nearly as strong as it once was. Men worry excessively about their earning power, but the satisfactions to be gained from "making good" are often insufficient to relieve the anxieties associated with striving.

It is possible that a modification of the breadwinner ethic might help to free parents from their obsession with the success potential of their children. It could be argued, for example, that we have made parenthood too close, too exclusive, and too isolated a function. A leading student of both American and Russian family life, David Mace (1962) contends that the Russian child learns in crèche and nursery to adjust to the wider life of the community as well as to the more circumscribed life of the home. Is it possible, he asks, that American parents, even good parents, cannot prepare their children for community living because the home provides a setting so distant from and so unlike the community at large? Do parents give their children not only security, but an exaggerated sense of their own importance and a limiting life style as far as community welfare is concerned?

In contrasting American parents with those in the Israeli Kibbutzim, Howard Halpern (1962) has explored similar questions. He contends that Americans are less generous in their relationships with both their own children and the larger community. Kibbutzim parents, on the other hand, have been so absorbed by the Kibbutz itself that, although they have countless hours of warmth, laughter, and fun with their children, they do not share the potentially deeper bond based on inconvenience, frustration, and even misery of growing up together in a home. Both Halpern and Mace suggest that nations with different cultural experiences have much to learn from one another as we search for new ways of expanding the sense of identity among children to include a larger share of the human race.

A worry of long standing in the United States is that community or public assistance to parents (not counting occasional charitable gestures from people of good will) undermines their desire to work and their sense of parental responsibility as well, despite solid evidence to the contrary. The Canadian family-allowances system, for example, has in no way diminished parental efforts in behalf of children, nor has it diminished the efforts of voluntary agencies to cope with family problems (Madison, 1964). The system has not been accompanied by any of the disastrous effects prophesied by its opponents, nor has it resulted in the proliferation of large families among the chronically dependent sections of the population or among Catholics.

In an economy capable of affluence even in wartime, a modification of the family-budget ethic, geared to the wages of father, is no longer hypothetical. A feasible modification might be likened to that which has already affected paternal authority. Fathers still have power over their children, but arbitrariness in its use is cushioned by a variety of specialized authorities now able to influence the life of the family. Even the socialization role of the family, and that of its father, has been declining; father's role in child rearing and his role as breadwinner may in fact decline together. Although father's difficulties in the lower classes and among nonwhites may be ameliorated by economic and social reform, the prime obstacle to decisive improvement is the breadwinner emphasis itself. A great many of our social problems can be alleviated only by altering the extremes of the breadwinner system so that a problem father will not necessarily produce a problem family, and a self-perpetuating one at that.

Three feasible changes exemplify the possibilities. First is the establishment of a truly public school system, one in which no assumptions need be made concerning supplementary home finances, facilities, or experiences. All books and supplies, all study accommodations, including travel, might well be furnished at public expense. Every effort could be made to guarantee that whatever is available in the best schools would be available in all and that schools in favored residential areas would not have superior facilities and teachers, as is currently the case. Even the quality of students in schools must be similar if they are to offer equal opportunities; in fact, the quality of the student body may be more important than any other factor in determining the effectiveness of a school (Coleman, et al., 1966).

Moreover, the age for entering school might very well be lowered. Growing knowledge of the plasticity of the human nervous system and of critical periods in development indicates that it is idle to talk about a society of equal opportunity as long as children are abandoned solely to their families during their most impressionable years. There is overwhelming evidence that this venerable custom is primarily responsible for the relative fixity of the social-class structure. And, as Robert Morison (1967) has pointed out, it seems increasingly unlikely that a complex, demanding society can rely exclusively on the haphazard educational procedures provided by home environments during the most teachable years of life, the first six.

The principal fear of those who would keep agencies of society out of the toddler's life seems to be that community controls over growth and development will reduce the freedom of the individual and, in the long run, produce a colorless, conformist society. But we all know that the most educated people are the ones who are least conformist and most innovative; the greatest conformist in all history has been the unlettered peasant. The real point of bringing education to the child at the earliest possible age is not to induce conformity but to cultivate the plasticity and adaptability of the human nervous system (Morison, 1967). Perhaps it is even possible in a single generation to rear healthy and alert children whose social and psychological orientation to life is entirely different from that of their parents, as suggested by the Kibbutzim experiences in Israel (Neubauer, 1965).

Another possibility is the establishment of a *first-class* network of public-health clinics for children, first-class in the sense that parents capable of paying extra could find no better facilities anywhere. Such an arrangement is well within the resource capacity of the United States in peacetime, although we still assume that people who are willing to pay extra should receive better health care, even for their children.

A third reform worthy of renewed consideration is the elimination of the inheritance of great wealth accumulated during the father's lifetime. The first two changes would resolve most of the social dilemmas now posed by the family-budget ethic, but several inequities would persist unless this third step was taken. One, for example, is the advantage wealthy young men now have in waging expensive political campaigns, without which election to the most important political offices has become increasingly difficult. Independently wealthy men have proved to be very useful public servants throughout American history, but their status has been based on unequal opportunity. As Emile Durkheim (1892) observed, the transmission of wealth by will is the last and most durable form of hereditary transmission.

Of course none of these changes will be made in the near future, although the trends are generally favorable. After all, people are not overwhelmingly committed to true equality of opportunity; many defer to the privileged classes, some revere them. The possibilities are mentioned here to call attention to the nature and implications of the family-budget system as it exists today. Even if these three modifications were made, life chances would still not be perfectly equal, but inequality would no longer be flagrantly perpetuated. Moreover, workers would still be paid unequal wages, so the family-budget system could be preserved in a restricted way. Some families would have more to spend than others, and those with similar incomes could plan their expenditures in dissimilar ways.

Certainly the distinction between the entrepreneurial family and the bureaucratic family, discussed in Chapter XII, has become more and more meaningless. We have learned that the bureaucratic family is every bit as budget conscious, and status conscious, as the entrepreneurial family, and we cannot conceive of a bureaucracy that does not rank its incumbents by function, grading their pay by rank. One will find no suggestion of a budgetless family here.

It is a mistake to think that the father's chief role must inevitably be that of breadwinner. It is also a mistake to think that the demise of his historical function as provider renders him obsolete. Even if he were relieved of his obligation to supply his children with the basic material resources for survival and the power to determine their social status, his work would be cut out for him. Helen Hacker (1957), for example, contends that the man's need to be free of doubts, uncertainties, or insecurities—his need to be "strong"—is the greatest burden of masculinity. Strength, of course, connotes many things, and the breadwinner emphasis is simply one interpretation, or distortion, of its many meanings. But the urge to be a *man* is felt in all cultures; if the wage-earner role is not glorified, other proofs of manhood will surely be established, and men will continue to serve as models for boys.

John Mogey (1957) was probably on the right track when he recognized that a reintegration of father in the family is occurring, after disasters in the early stages of the industrial revolution, in response to the trend toward an affluent, suburban life, and in association with the upgrading of work in general. As economic security reaches a larger part of the population, the father becomes more active in the family and is psychologically closer to both his wife and his children. We may very well be witnessing the establishment of an altogether new kind of family and a new basis for family stability.

In a sense, the family has become more important to father, even as he has become relatively less important to the family. Once father was the prime agent of family strength; now he is often reliant upon it, especially for emotional sustenance (Mogey and Morris, 1960). A system seems to be emerging in which an important function of the family is to guarantee the highly skilled male a sense of interpersonal security. The family becomes the key to father's endurance as a skilled organism in the bureaucratic world. Impersonal forms of bureaucratic organization replace the kinship network as the strategic principle for work and social effort, and the small family becomes the man's emotional "home base" in the process. Indeed, the rise of romantic love as a family affair has accompanied the rise of modern bureaucratic organization.

Thus, father is ideally an integrated member of the family and, as such, an agent of family and social stability, but he is also a source of value, of productivity, to society. As such, he stands in need of all the support that his family and the community at large can provide.

AREA 4

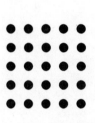

ENCOUNTER
IN PARENTHOOD

WHY ARE CHILDREN SO UNREASONABLE?

BETTY CANARY

NEA Staff Writer

Children are unreasonable. You teach them things like, Do Unto Others . . . and Respect Your Elders, and recite truisms long handed down from parent to child and what do they do? They start thinking, that's what they do. And they ask questions and expect YOU to do some explaining.

My son, for example, came home from school and asked, "Did you know Sept. 22 is Yom Kippur? That it's a Jewish holiday?"

"Yes, I know," I said.

"Then why don't we get out for vacation like they do on our church holidays?"

"Well, it's difficult to explain," I said.

Then, after watching a news broadcast of Irish Catholics and Irish Protestants fighting, he asked, "Why don't they stop that?"

"Well," I said.

"Don't they know it doesn't make any difference what church a person goes to . . .?"

"Oh," I hedged. "I'm sure they KNOW it's wrong to fight."

"Then why," he asked in his maddening way, "don't they STOP?"

"Well, . . ." I explained.

"Didn't you say we were part Irish?"

"Yes," I said proudly. "And your father's family is Dutch and German."

"Then we're half-breeds, right?"

"How ridiculous!" I said.

"But this book says a man who is part Indian and part Canadian is a half-breed, so what's the difference . . .?"

"Well, . . ." I explained.

"Did you see those Irish police throw rocks?" he asked.

"Remember," I recited, "our policeman is our friend!"

"What about the one who stopped Rick and yelled at him?" he asked. "You didn't think HE was very friendly."

"Your brother was only walking to the store," I said hotly, "and some policemen are rude just as some citizens are rude. The man had no right to . . ."

Reprinted by permission of Newspaper Enterprise Association, Inc.

"Boy, I'm glad Rick wasn't black!"

"What has that to do with it?"

"My friend, Jimmy, you know? HIS brother was just coming home from ball practice and the police took him to the station!"

"I'm sure it was a misunderstanding." I said. "It makes NO difference if you're black or white."

"Then why can't Jimmy join the swimming club?"

"You KNOW I told you that was wrong."

"So why can't he join?"

"Let's have a snack," I said, hoping to stop the questions.

"Are those children in Biafra still starving?" he asked through his tuna sandwich. "Why do we just let them starve? I can't understand . . ."

CAN I PRACTICE WHAT I PREACH?

Helen Jean Burn

Tonight I learned something, and I am going to write it all down word for word, just as it happened—now, while it is still fresh in my mind—because I don't want to forget it, ever.

The seven of us—my husband and I and our five children—were having dinner when Jamie (who is nine) accidentally told us about his sister's friend.

Our daughter, Angela, is fourteen. She is a very serious girl, reading books as fast as she can get them out of the library, getting excellent grades and showing a keen concern about the world and its problems. We think she is pretty. She's tall for her age, and slim. She has blue eyes and very long blonde hair. She doesn't date yet, which suits us just fine; she has lots of time. She doesn't feel that way, of course. She says most of the girls in her class are already going out with boys, to movies and bowling. I suppose her father and I would allow her to do these things, too. It's just that nobody has asked her yet.

She has told me her problem is shyness. All through junior high school, she's had a tendency to freeze up whenever she is around boys, and she can't think of anything to say to them. "They must think I'm stuck up," she told me, "but I can't act right around them, no matter how hard I try."

Naturally, I have reassured her that this is typical for her age and always goes away with the passage of time. And at last this seemed to be proving true for Angie. During the current school year—her ninth grade—she has been talking a great deal about a boy. I'll call him Russell Douglas. He is in most of her classes and the editor-in-chief of the school paper. (Angie is feature editor.) He gets outstanding grades and has been elected class president.

Angie seems to enjoy talking to him about the books they are reading, their favorite records and even very serious questions, like religion and social problems. He calls her up occasionally, too, and they go over their homework on the telephone.

After school, they frequently stay late to work on the paper, and have lots of fun clowning around. Often at dinnertime Angie tells us all the funny things Russell said and did that day. My husband and I smile at each other over our coffee cups; it's good to see Angie so happy.

Then tonight Jamie dropped that bombshell. He said, "Boy, that Russ sure is a neat dresser. He wears a jacket and tie every day. Most of the Negroes don't dress that well."

Angie said dryly, "Most of the white kids don't dress that well, either, and for you even to mention it is prejudiced."

No more was said, but I knew my husband was as shaken as I was. We had moved from a house in the suburbs into the city in order to be closer to his work and the night school he attends. While the population of our suburb was almost all white, in the city it is about half Negro. At the combination elementary and junior high school not far from our new home, the enrollment reflects this proportion.

I talked extensively with our children about what I expected of them when they made the change to an integrated school. They understood the importance of seeing every person as an individual and not as a member of a particular religion or nationality or race.

I needn't have been concerned. They loved the new school. They said some of the children there were very "rich" (the daughter of a well-known local television personality went there, and one or two of the pupils came in extremely expensive cars) and some of them were very "poor" (a classmate of Angie's managed to stay in school by working nights as a charwoman in an office building). Angie explained that this made the students less critical of one another, less inclined to be catty about looks and clothes and marks. At the old school, everyone lived in the same sort of development-type house and had nearly the same amount of money, so they all tried to dress and think and act alike, too. Although Angie didn't use these words, her feeling seemed to be that there had been enormous pressure on everyone to be as much like everyone else as possible.

Jamie noticed a big difference in the city, too. He said, "At the old school, we'd all been in the same class together since first grade. When a new kid came, we looked him over for about two weeks before we decided to say hello." But apparently in the city people move around and change schools more often, so that newcomers are more readily accepted. After his first day here, Jamie came home jubilant. The boys in his class had fought over which ones could sit next to him at lunch.

So the move from a strictly middle-class suburb into the big city's varied and mobile elements seemed to be a happy change for our children.

Learning now, however, that the only boy our daughter had ever felt comfortable with was a Negro—well it was a shock. In the silence that fell over our dinner table, I knew my husband and I had the same thought. We were remembering the old argument of the segregationists —that integration would inevitably lead to intermarriage. How would we feel if Angie wanted to date this boy? For that matter, how would his parents feel?

Repeatedly I reminded myself of all the good things I had heard about Russell—his outstanding grades, his leadership ability, his popularity with his classmates—and I told myself I should be glad Angie had such a friend. But I really wasn't. I couldn't stop seeing a mental picture of this boy and our daughter walking along a street hand in hand, stared at by passersby, perhaps even insulted or threatened. And I was frightened.

When the children left the table, my husband said, "If I were you, I'd let the whole thing drop. She's a sensible kid. Let's let her handle this herself." I didn't disagree with him, at least not aloud; but I lacked his confidence. He didn't know how much it meant to Angie to have a boy phoning her.

All the time I was washing the dinner dishes, I fretted silently, taking first one side of the argument and then the other. Was my fear, I wondered, entirely unselfish? Was my upbringing, in a generation when things were so different, a crippling handicap, which made it impossible for me to be objective about this situation? Was there left in me a deeply hidden core of prejudice that none of my fine preaching to the children about human dignity and fairness had managed to dissolve? Could it be that I was not emotionally ready for the progress I knew— intellectually—was right? Worse, was I going to be one of those hypocrites who say, "Integration is fine, but not on my block"?

Angie, like most youngsters, is swift to detect insincerity, or—as she would call it—a phony. If I failed to adhere to all those convictions I had been voicing for years, now that it had come down to our own personal experience, she would probably never trust me again. And who could blame her? Still, if I tried to be consistent in order to avoid hypocrisy, would I be even more selfish, pushing my child into a situation she couldn't possibly have enough experience to cope with?

By the time the dishes were done, I couldn't bear the anxiety any longer; I had to talk to Angie. I found her in her room doing homework.

How did I begin? I believe I mumbled something to the effect that maybe we had better talk about Russell. When I said his name, she stiffened—slightly, but quite visibly. And she turned to me a look that seemed to say, "All right, now we'll see just how sincere you really are." Or maybe I imagined it.

I suppose fine preaching and pretty speeches become a habit, because the next thing I said was, "I just wanted you to know that any friend you have will always be welcome in our home." Remembering now, several hours later, I am ashamed. I didn't mean that one little bit when I said it. All I was actually thinking was, How in the world are we going to get out of this predicament?

But Angie believed me and immediately looked relieved. She said, "Thanks, Mom. After what Jamie said, I was afraid you were upset."

Me, upset? I babbled away for a while, trying to explain that it was just rather unexpected. She had talked so much about Russell, but had never mentioned his race, and we just had a different mental picture of him.

At that point, I remember, she clenched her fists eagerly, her eyes alive with idealistic enthusiasm. She said, "But that's just it, don't you see? It never should be mentioned. It's absolutely unimportant. If people would only ignore it—"

I tried to explain to her that you can't ignore race; it isn't realistic. It is, unfortunately, a factor in our society at present. I think I even went so far as to say it wasn't even kind to pretend there is no problem.

She slumped in her chair a little, as though all the wind were suddenly gone from her sails. "I know," she said. "But I think you have to keep saying the truth about it, anyway. You always told us—"

Of course, I knew what I had always told her and the other children. At that moment I wished I could forget it.

Still, I was proud of her, and I said so. I told her I was so glad she was mature enough to choose her friends for their qualities as people, and I hoped that someday everybody would be able to do that, just as she and Russell were doing. But I would be failing her if I didn't try to help her see that trying to live an ideal in a very unideal world is terribly difficult. "You can't do it," I said, "by closing your eyes to the unpleasant things. You really have to be extremely clear-sighted about them."

Even as I spoke, I was asking myself questions. How clear-sighted had we adults been? Everybody I know is wholeheartedly in favor of integration. Yet have we really faced the inevitable result, that people who work and study together are going to get to understand and like each other? Are we then going to draw back and say that wasn't what we had in mind; all we wanted was to improve the quality of education?

Angie was doodling around the edges of her math homework. After a while, she said, "I may be wrong, but I think I am being what you say

I should be—clear sighted—about Russell and me. I'm not sure I can explain, but I think that's why what we have together is more than— more than whatever it is teen-agers usually feel."

My heart sank, but I managed to ask calmly what she meant.

She struggled to find words. She said that in her age group it is almost impossible for a boy and girl to be friends, because everyone is thinking about dating. A girl is afraid that if she kids around with a boy, he'll think she's flirting with him, and a boy is afraid to pay too much attention to a girl, for fear she'll expect him to ask her out. Angie had come to the conclusion that it was her fear of appearing to be angling for a date that had made her so tongue-tied around boys. But with Russell, she never felt that way.

"We never talk about it," she said, "but we both know that the way things are in this country, we couldn't possibly date each other. No matter how we might feel personally, we would be so uncomfortable that going out together wouldn't be any fun."

I began to understand at last. I had forgotten how painfully self-conscious teen-agers are. They must conform to what the rest of the crowd is wearing and doing; they are too insecure to be innovators.

I expected to feel relieved, but I wasn't. For some reason, I found myself wanting to shake my fist at the world I had, just a moment ago, been trying to get Angie to accept. Thinking back on it now, I wonder how I kept from taking her in my arms; perhaps I was too ashamed.

Anyway, I remember that her voice seemed to become more pained as she went along. "It hurt me at first—Russell's attitude, I mean. The minute we step out of school, he isn't my friend any more. He won't ride on the bus with me. When the class goes to a museum or a concert, he doesn't walk with me or sit beside me. But at least when we are inside the school, we can have fun together. The fact that we can't even consider dating each other makes it possible for us to be relaxed together, you know what I mean? It leaves us free to be friends."

She looked so vulnerable, so sad. My own throat was aching, but I was able to sound normal enough to say, "Russell sounds like a very fine, sensitive person. His friendship has been a great help to you, hasn't it?"

She nodded. On her math scratch paper she was drawing little boxes; they looked like cages, or maybe traps.

But for the moment I was more concerned about Russell. I said, "And what is your friendship doing for him?"

She said she thought it was helping him. When they first got to know each other, Russell had a "sort of shell" around him, as though he were proud and hurt at the same time. "Or maybe," she corrected, "it was afraid of being hurt, of trusting anyone who was white." Once, Angie told me, she said something to Russell about the fact that a lot of progress was being made in civil rights, because now most public places have to serve Negroes. Russell gave her an odd look, as if to say, "Are you kidding?" Then he asked her if she could imagine how it feels to go into a restaurant with your father and mother and have the hostess lead you past a couple of dozen empty tables and seat you far in the back behind a pillar, so the people passing the restaurant can't look in and see them serving you. "And, Mom," she said, "I can imagine it, and I don't think it's any better than not being served at all, do you?"

No, I had to agree it wasn't any better. Still, I must have felt a need to continue defending my generation, because I said, "You can make laws that change people's actions, but you can't make laws that change the way people feel. That takes education, and education takes time."

Of course, that cliché was no comfort: it seemed to upset her even more. She said, "But, Mom, it just isn't right! Those feelings shouldn't exist at all to need to be educated away. That's what hurts people like Russell. What has he done to deserve those feelings?" She said there are kids in her school—not many, but the ones there are "stick out like sore thumbs"—who just plain hate Negroes, period. They push in front of them in line, knock their books off the desks accidentally-on-purpose, trip them when they go down the aisle—do all sorts of spiteful little tricks.

I asked her what she did when that happened.

"I feel like smashing them right in the face, but then I'd be as bad as they are. So I just try to look at Russ or whichever of the Negroes it happens to, and I smile with all my heart, so he knows I know and that I care. I guess I'm trying to say, 'We're not all alike, any more than you are all alike.'"

I did put my arms around her then. I said, "I'm so glad you are there to smile and show you care, and I'm sure your friendship is helping him—I'm sure it's helping him a lot." I turned to leave, having got so much more than I had ever intended to give.

As I reached the door, Angie said, "Mom—thanks. I mean, for being the way you are. It's because of you that I'm not like the kids who knock Russell's books off the desk. It's because of what you taught me."

Now, late at night, in my quiet house, I am still wondering. What I taught her! Knowing how near I came to letting her down this evening, I find it hard to remember just what I did teach her. Oh, the words I can recall—the platitudes, the fine speeches I really did not mean.

Perhaps it was what I did not teach her. My own fears, the shrinking from change—these I kept to myself. Indeed, until tonight I had forgotten they were there. And that is right. Whatever is left over from the past, deep down in me, is my problem to overcome, not hers. It must never be transmitted to the next generation, to plague them the way we all—black and white—are being plagued. It deserves to die; it must die. And in my family, it is going to die with me.

HELPING CHILDREN GROW UP SEXUALLY—
HOW? WHEN? BY WHOM?

ELEANORE BRAUN LUCKEY

Today many parents who themselves were reared by mothers and fathers afraid to educate their children in sexual matters are now afraid *not* to educate their own children regarding sex. Social pressures on young people different from the kind they experienced when young, prevalent attitudes toward sex that reflect a changing value system in society as a whole, and behavior among many young people that they do not understand have left today's parents perplexed and anxious. As a result they are eagerly seeking help for themselves and for their children, whom they want to achieve "normal sexual maturity."

Community agencies, youth organizations, churches, and schools are all scurrying to initiate programs of sex education—sometimes called family life education, boy-girl relationships, or interpersonal development. Inservice training programs, workshops, and institutes are being organized for nurses, social workers, clergymen, teachers, counselors, health educators, community youth leaders, and parents. After a long period of being treated with silence or half-truths, blushes and snickers, the subject of sex can openly be talked about in "respectable" society. Young people's attitudes and behavior toward the opposite sex—and the consequences—are the subject of serious concern not just to adolescents and their parents but also to persons in the teaching and helping professions.

Nevertheless, the goals of sex education are not altogether clear. Nor is it clear just whose responsibility it is to give sex information to children and adolescents and to try to shape the attitudes that determine their moral values and sexual behavior. Dealing with the sexual problems of young people is especially difficult for adults brought up in a society confused about sex, one that has been filled with sexual stimuli and at the same time with harsh taboos against sexual expression. Social scientists are not surprised that the combination of stimulation and repression has resulted in a demand for a "better way" of dealing with sex.

In response to the demand, persons who work professionally with children, adolescents, and parents are seeking *the* way (if there is *one*)

From *Children*, vol. 14, no. 4, July-August 1967, pp. 130-135. Reprinted by permission of the publisher and the author. (Eleanore Luckey is head of the Department of Child Development and Family Relation, University of Connecticut.)

or *a* way (if there are *many*) to help children grow toward "sexual maturity." This goal in itself is difficult to define, and to chart a course leading to its achievement is even more challenging.

Sexual behavior among men and women and sexuality as it is manifested in masculinity and femininity vary from culture to culture. Anthropologists tell us that there is no sexual practice that has been universally sanctioned or prohibited; even incest, the sexual behavior that comes nearest to being universally tabooed, has been approved in some societies in some periods of history.

In any culture, what is "normal" depends upon the practices of the majority. Many behavior patterns that are quite objectionable in our society are sanctioned in others; for example, homosexual practices, sexual relationships between children, premarital sexual promiscuity, and wife swapping and borrowing are approved forms of behavior in some societies. It is not possible to speak of what is or is not "normal" unless we specify the society to which we refer.

NORMALITY? MATURITY?

Even in this country alone the wide range of sexual behavior and values existing today make "the norm" impossible to define. At one extreme are those people who advocate complete sexual freedom amounting to anarchy; at the other extreme are those who condone the use of sex only for reproduction. Between these extremes lies immense variation in attitude and practice. For example, chastity before marriage is held to be a supreme value; it is considered "a good thing"; it is thought not to be very important; it is valued not at all; it is considered a poor thing. Masturbation is valued as a means of releasing sexual tension; it is considered an acceptable adolescent pastime; it is thought to be a shameful practice or a sin. Marital practices vary: there is no consensus on how frequently coitus should take place, nor on the appropriate position, nor on the amount or kind of foreplay that is acceptable. Most social scientists agree that it would be difficult if not impossible to define the norm of sexual behavior in contemporary American society. Even if such a norm could be defined, the definition would be meaningless, for sexual expression is a highly individual matter, an integral part of the total personality.

Sexual maturity rather than sexual normality may be a better goal for sex education. Even so, we must make assumptions that cannot be validated about the nature of man and the patterns of his maturing. By careful measurement and observation we have learned a great deal about the physical growth and development of boys and girls; we know about many of the factors that contribute to or detract from soundness and roundness of body; we have been able to trace general developmental patterns from the prenatal period to maturity and then to decadence. Intellectual growth has been more difficult to discover and predict in a sequential pattern, but in general we know a good deal about such aspects of growth as language development, concept development, learning, and creativity.

What we know of emotional growth is still largely theory or educated guesses; and social patterns that propel a child on to becoming a socially mature adult are known to vary from generation to generation. Even so, through keen observation, crude but persistent evaluation, and creative speculation, we can draw at least some tentative conclusions about the emotional and social development of the human being.

When we realize that sexual growth includes factors that are physical, intellectual, emotional, and social, it becomes clear that with the incompleteness of our knowledge it is impossible to trace a sequential pattern of sexual development and to predict maturity with any degree of precision. This is a task to be explored by scientific research. We cannot wait for the results, however, to define our social goals in broad terms and to plan the practical steps toward their achievement.

THE GOALS

As with other social goals, the consideration of educational goals requires two foci: the individual and the group in which he lives. Managing these two compatibly is a constant challenge for a democratic society. It is a greater challenge today than ever before, for in our rapidly changing society young people are demanding greater freedom in individual behavior than in any previous generation.

Our society has not yet provided an adequate way of caring for children born out of wedlock; it is therefore desirable today to discourage out-of-wedlock births. This is one social goal on which we can secure a great deal of agreement. Another is the elimination of venereal disease. So far, we have found no medically satisfactory way of preventing venereal infection. Both of these goals are served when premarital, promiscuous intercourse is avoided. Thus, at this point in our social development, it is reasonable to want to restrict premarital coitus.

However, with the increased effectiveness and availability of contraceptives and with the possible future development of immunizations against venereal diseases, the social consequences of promiscuous premarital sexual relationships will change. Insofar as morality is based on social consequences, when the consequences change the moral values change. What is immoral in today's society may be moral in tomorrow's. And what is right for today's generation of young people may be wrong for a generation to come.

One way to avoid getting hopelessly involved in dilemmas is to go beyond what is presently called "sexual morality" to a broader concept of morality, one based on the use of self and one's personal freedom for the benefit of others.

Broader definitions of goals are appropriate, too, in considering the individual's personal growth and satisfaction. Here the goal is not only a sexually fulfilled person but also one who accepts and values his total self—a person who understands himself, his behavior, and his value system and who has the integrity to defend his principles. The ultimate goal is a person who can communicate with others without fear, who can reveal himself, and who can listen to and be concerned about the welfare of others.

Sexuality can never be separated from personality, nor can sexual morality be separated from social morality. For this reason the term "sex education" tends to be misleading. By emphasizing sex it pulls the subject out of a total context. Unfortunately, our culture has for a long time treated a sexual relationship as a special and separate part of personal and social relationships rather than a normal, natural use of self in relating meaningfully to a person of the opposite sex.

Now, because of the need to provide information, to correct misconceptions, and to break the spell of silence, it will be hard for any program of sex education to avoid further isolating and emphasizing the sexual components of personality and interpersonal relationships. Nevertheless, the real goal of any program must be to help in the total development of young people so that they will become the kind of secure persons described above. If we can achieve this goal, we will not have to worry about sexual behavior.

HOW AND WHEN?

The questions of *how* and *when* are better dealt with together, because, except for always giving children frank, honest answers and explanations, the most important point about sex education is to provide the information in a normal context. Sexual matters need to be dealt with as the natural part of a total picture, whatever that picture may be. When children are curious about their own bodies—hands, feet, elbows, and "tummies"—they are also interested in their genitals and need to know proper terms for them. When children are interested in what happens to food in the human body and in why and how we breathe, they are also interested in the excretory functions and need proper explanations about them.

Most of a child's early questions about sex are occasioned by exposure to a situation that is new to him. He sees an adult body and notes that it is different from his own; he wants to know more about it. He sees a child of the other sex and notes that the genitals are different; he wants an explanation. He sees a pregnant woman and wants to know why her stomach is swollen, and he also may want to know how this came about. The child usually brings these questions to his mother because they occur to him before he reaches school age.

The way in which these early questions are answered largely determines what other questions the child will ask, how he will feel about asking them, and how he will feel about the answers. A parent reveals his own feelings about sex through common, everyday events in many ways. His attitudes will be regarded by his child as those of all adults, so that what questions the child asks or does not ask the teacher at school depend a great deal on the kind of reception they would get if asked at home.

In the school the teacher has continuous opportunities to answer questions bearing on sex that come up in the ordinary events of the day and in the content of every subject. From kindergarten through 12th grade, the child can be encouraged to develop a normal progression of interest in and an increasing body of information about family relationships and sex differences and functions and, in doing so, to form values and make decisions about behavior. In the elementary grades imparting information about animal and human reproduction is becoming a routine part of instruction. However, helping children understand their own developing masculinity or femininity is more difficult for the teacher because it involves a personal concept that can be discussed more naturally in the home than in the schoolroom; nonetheless, much thought about the meaning to oneself of one's sex can be stimulated at school through units in self-understanding and personality growth.

Many persons believe that the school has a better opportunity than the home to present the child with *information* regarding sex. This is partly true, at least, because teachers tend to be more knowledgeable than many parents about physiology, anatomy, health, psychology, and social problems. It is true, also, because as the child progresses through the grades the teaching becomes concentrated into subject areas, many of which relate specifically to sex and reproduction, to social-sexual-psychological development, and to social problems and health. Thus information about sex is not only a normal part of the subject matter in junior and senior high schools but is also an integral part that has to be conspicuously avoided if it is *not* to be included.

Every school subject, even one not directly concerned with sex information, has its contribution to make in helping children and young people understand interpersonal relationships, familial roles, and the relation of one's sex to these. Literature, music, art, history, and the social sciences especially offer such opportunities.

The home and the school are not alone in having opportunities to help the child develop a mature understanding of sex. Groups such as the Boy Scouts, Boys Clubs, Girl Scouts, Girls Clubs, Camp Fire Girls, Young Men's Christian Associations, Young Women's Christian Associations, and 4-H Clubs are dedicated to helping young people develop healthy bodies and well-rounded personalities. Most of these organizations work informally with adolescents or preadolescents in small groups over a span of a few years. They offer the young person an excellent opportunity to develop a self-confident personality, including an acceptance of his sexual identity; they also offer him practice in forming intimate, meaningful relationships with others, both of his own and the opposite sex. The sexual aspects of interpersonal relationships become especially important during adolescence when cultural expectation pushes young people toward dating, and their own heightened sex drive urges them toward exploration.

It is not possible to give information without at the same time conveying attitudes, and the attitudes of adults determine the values of the young, which in turn determine their behavior. The values that young people hold are those that have been demonstrated by the persons they respect.

The churches, of course, are specifically concerned with the values in our society and more than any other institution except the home are expected to take responsibility for the development of attitudes in keeping with their religious and moral precepts. However, such value positions are only meaningful to young people if they are clearly enunciated and are demonstrated as useful in today's society.

Perhaps the most consistent informers about adult attitudes and builders of young people's ideals today are not the traditional institutions that purposefully outline and pursue programs or policies of education but rather the mass media of communication: the television that the child watches from the time he is too small to respond to much

more than the movement and the sound to the time he is able to sit
for several hours absorbed in its entertainment programs and its ad-
vertisements that use sexual appeal to sell products; the magazine illustrations, the comic strips, the paperback book covers, the films that
make the sparsely clad body a common sight and the seductive female
or male an appealing personality. The child exists so constantly in the
midst of these stimuli that as his own understanding grows they become increasingly meaningful to him. This is sex education in the context of commercialism, of entertainment, and the message it conveys, while
often indirect, is powerful.

All these agencies of society—the home, the school, the community
agency, the church, the mass media—bring their messages to the child
in one way or another almost from infancy. Some of the messages are
direct, some are subtle; they are seen, heard, felt. Some of them are
quiet, some loud; some are conspicuous chiefly because of their absence.
Some are true; some, half-true; some, false. Altogether they are very inconsistent. As a result our children come to adolescence confused, curious, and often determined to find out on their own.

If the adults who touch the lives of children could determine what
their own values are, if they could know beyond question why they hold
these values, and if they could demonstrate them in their daily living,
children would get their message. If adults themselves could put sexual
matters into the normal context of living, young people would be better
able to do the same. The ultimate problem for adults is not so much
how to educate children and adolescents as how to work out their own
problems and how to convey their attitudes to the young people whose
lives they influence. That adults who are significant for them do not
readily have all the solutions will not distress the children nearly so
much as people seem to think. Children will not feel confused about seeking many of their own answers to the problems of interpersonal, inter-
sexual relations if they realize that adults too are honestly seeking solutions.

BY WHOM?

Who it is that is responsible for sex education becomes clearer when
we recognize that sex education is a segment of an individual's total
preparation for living in a complex world of interrelatedness, and that
information and attitudes specifically regarding sex are normal parts of
knowledge and of a social value structure. Every adult who deals with

children or adolescents in any way is likely at some time or another, in some way, to influence significantly the attitudes that help determine how a child will use himself—sexually as well as in other ways— in relation to other people.

Because most adults today have not had the advantage of growing up in a society in which the kind of sex education advocated here was available, many adults find it difficult to deal with their own attitudes and to communicate them in an open way to children and adolescents. Some adults, however, are able to do this better than others, and those who *can*, must! The opportunity that adults have to do so will largely be determined by their role in relation to the young. The parent has the longest and most intense relationship with the child and so the greatest opportunity; the teacher, the school nurse, the school counselor, and the principal each has significant opportunities from time to time, as does the youth leader, the clergyman, and the religious educator. So, too, does the advertising man, the sales manager, the editor, the journalist, the filmmaker, the television or radio director.

WHERE TO BEGIN?

In a wilderness that seems so vast, adults who are concerned with helping children and adolescents grow up sexually are likely to feel that it is all but a hopeless task. This, it is not. In addition to setting his own house in order and examining his own values and behavior and being open about them, the person who works professionally with young people can take a number of steps toward furthering a program of education that will make for mature sexual behavior in our society:

1. He can help other professional workers define their values and learn how to convey them to others. One of the most helpful tools for this kind of learning is the sensitivity group, sometimes called the T-group. Composed usually of about 10 persons with a professionally trained leader, the group is designed to encourage its members to explore their feelings and to interact in such a way that insight and self-understanding develop.[1]

2. He can take part in inservice training sessions, workshops, and institutes that provide the participants not only with information but also with an opportunity to clarify their own attitudes for themselves.

1. L. P. Bradford, J. R. Gibb, K. D. Benne, eds., *T-Group Theory and Laboratory Method* (New York: John Wiley & Sons, 1964).

Because acquiring information is usually accomplished much more quickly than acquiring insight into one's own feelings, the emphasis in the most effective groups is on the exploration of the participants' attitudes.

Many universities and colleges are now offering such courses, and many more would set them up if requested.

3. He can focus much of his educational efforts on parents, especially parents of infants and very young children. Because the parental influence is so constant and so intense, what parents believe, what they convey, and what they know are crucial influences in the development of the child's sexual attitudes.

Parents, however, often have uncertainties and fears about their own sexuality that inhibit their ability to help their children—for example, a mother who does not value her femininity will find it hard to help her daughter grow up to accept and value herself as a woman.

Parents also often need some of the skill that persons in the helping professions have in giving direct answers to questions about sex, and often they also need the information itself. Some parents, for example, have misconceptions about the effects of masturbation on the developing child; some do not understand the physiology of menstruation; and some have fears and apprehensions about their own sexual functions, the use of contraceptives, the effects of menopause, or their marital compatibility.

Thus many parents might benefit from the same kind of sensitivity group suggested for professional persons. The opportunity for parents to discuss such problems in a safe, accepting group of other adults could help them clarify their own feelings and thinking and learn how to deal with intimate matters openly and frankly. Such groups might be formed through a neighborhood house, an elementary-school guidance program, a parent-teacher association, a church, or any other local organization. A trained professional leader, however, is a *must*.

4. He can make known to the molders of the mass media his convictions regarding the use—and misuse—of sexual stimuli, particularly in advertising and in entertainment. If he finds that young people are being given a false or unclear picture about the meaning of sexual maturity through any form of mass communication, he can protest.

More important than all these steps, however, is the professional person's way of dealing directly with young people. Can he be open and willing to share his time, thoughts, and knowledge with the questing young? Anything less is not enough. The young have the right to honest answers—even when the adult's answer must be that he does not know or is himself confused.

AND SO—

Helping children grow into sexual maturity is not easy for a generation of adults who have grown up in a society frightened of sex. It can only be done by breaking through the silence and half-truths that have obscured their own knowledge and feeling and by establishing a broader objective than mere "sex education." This means striving for the development of the whole personality, for producing a man or woman able to feel genuine concern for the welfare of others, eager and able to establish intimate relationships with others, desirous of parenthood, and capable of assuming the responsibility of his own freedom.

Professional workers concerned about young people need to clarify their own attitudes and values and to develop ways of communicating them to others. When they do, they can be of special help to parents and to other professional workers—teachers, nurses, school counselors, principals, social workers, youth leaders, clergymen. They can influence the mass media's interpretation of sex and interpersonal relationships. They can help young people with the problems troubling them, always keeping sexual information in the context of the whole person, being honest and frank, and admitting that along with the young people, they, too, are *seeking*.

SPARE THE ROD, USE BEHAVIOR MOD

ROGER W. MCINTIRE

They had a bedtime problem in the Thompson household. Douglas Thompson, a strapping 18-year-old, couldn't get to sleep. Twenty-five or 30 times a night he would go to his mother's bedroom to tell her about his worries. Each visit took one or two minutes, and night would slip into morning as the worries went on.

Douglas' worries were small ones—had the downstairs' lights been turned off? Was the TV antenna properly oriented? Mrs. Thompson (the names are pseudonyms) usually reassured Douglas—yes, the lights are off; yes, the antenna is set right. Sometimes she spoke sharply. When Douglas did not talk to his mother it took a long time for him to get to sleep.

This had been going on for two years. Douglas had consulted a psychiatrist, taken sleeping pills and tranquilizers, and consulted a psychologist once a week for six months. Still he had the sleeping problem.

Change. I found all of this, on the whole, unsurprising. It seemed clear that Douglas' behavior persisted for three reasons: (1) the mother's attention and sympathy served as a reward, (2) this rewarding attention was given for the poor behavior, and (3) the behavior itself was easy.

To change the behavior, it was necessary to give the reward at a more appropriate time and for a better behavior, and to make the poor behavior more difficult to perform.

Mrs. Thompson was told not to listen to Douglas' worries after bedtime. Instead she was to set a special time early each evening to talk to Douglas in the living room for 30 minutes. If Douglas visited her bedroom after the discussion, then she was to cancel the next evening's talk in the living room. For his part Douglas was to keep a record, noting each night the time he entered his bedroom and, next morning, the approximate time he fell asleep. Also he was to log every worry as it came to him.

We were embarked on behavior-modification therapy. In the first week Douglas visited his mother's bedroom twice. During the second week he made one visit and after that the bedtime visits ceased altogether.

Reprinted from *Psychology Today* Magazine, December 1970. Copyright © Communications/Research/Machines, Inc. Adapted from *For Love of Children: Behavioral Psychology for Parents* by Roger McIntire, CRM Books, 1970.

By the third week the living-room sessions were lasting only 15 minutes, and before the seventh week, Douglas discontinued them.

Douglas' worries also dropped off dramatically. Within three weeks the number of items recorded in his bedroom worry diary dropped to almost none.

Cause. Douglas' behavior had been changed, but what about the underlying psychological cause of the problem? The behavioral approach eliminates long and possibly fruitless searches for underlying psychological causes that may or may not be susceptible to change and therefore may or may not be relevant in therapy.

A person's behavior is consistent with his experiences—his past successes and failures. We learn from practice, from trying certain behaviors and benefiting from the trials. It is a fundamental law of learning that *one learns what one does.* The things we practice are the things we learn best.

An accurate description of behaviors also points the way to alter those behaviors. For Douglas, the crucial procedure was to stop the bestowal of a subtle reward—his mother's concern and attention—for a bad behavior. Douglas had to test the new rules. When the consequences were as consistent as he was told they would be, his behavior changed.

This can be dangerous because one's behavior may become emotional when the usual routine doesn't get the usual results. I call this the vending-machine response. If a Coke machine fails to give you a Coke for your dime, do you thoughtfully and carefully change your behavior? No. You bang on its little buttons, kick it and insult it. So it takes courage and patience to withhold an expected reward as Douglas' mother did.

Praise. An easier and more positive behavioral approach is to look for something to reward. It may be necessary to settle for something less than perfect. For example, when one is teaching table manners to a two-year-old it may be necessary at first to praise any use of the spoon that gets food anywhere near the face. Later, praise may be saved for behavior nearer the target. What seems to elude most of us impatient adults is that we have to start *somewhere* and that the somewhere may have to be very far down indeed when we are dealing with children.

The most common error most of us make is to demand too much for too small a reward when we begin to teach something new to a child. The first little steps need big rewards. "But this is bribery," some protest. "Shouldn't a child do most of these things without reward, just for the joy of learning? Some children are good and do what is expected without any reward, don't they?"

First we must realize that good children get many and large social rewards and they snowball. For example, when a child starts off well, he is well-rewarded with praise; when he is well-rewarded, he keeps going; when he keeps going, he is further rewarded, and so on.

Snowballing can work the other way too. Some children are not rewarded for being good or learning. They expect no rewards because they have received none in the past. If a child starts slowly or poorly on something, he gets little encouragement; instead, he is badgered. The lack of reward slows him even more as he gets older. Performance that would have been rewarded is not, because "he should have been doing that years ago, anyway."

Candy. For example, in one study, 12 first- and second-grade children were diagnosed as "predicted reading failures" because they had failed a reading-readiness test. We divided the children into three groups. During the first week we determined their average error in word identification. Each group had an average error of about 40 per cent.

Then one group of children received concrete reinforcement—a raisin or a peanut or candy-coated chocolate—for each correct response. They also began with a very simple task that guaranteed success. We showed each child a picture-word combination and asked him to match it to a duplicate word card and say the word aloud. This technique helped the children fade into a learning task before going on to more difficult tasks. The remaining two groups received neither reinforcement nor the fading procedure.

The average error of the group that experienced reinforcement and fading dropped to five per cent. The other groups continued at a 40 per cent error rate. When we stopped the reinforcement and the fading for members of the first group, their error rate soared to 50 per cent.

We tried the candy reinforcement without the fading technique on one of the groups. The error rate declined, but only by four per cent.

The use of the fading technique alone was more effective than reinforcement alone. Average error dropped from about 40 to eight per cent.

When we used both reinforcement and fading on all three groups, the error rate dropped to less than five per cent. In general we had great success helping children who had been regarded as potential reading failures.

Colors. In another experiment, we demonstrated that we could bring tests and homework under behavioral control. We worked with a class of fifth-graders and a class of sixth-graders. Twice a week, for half an hour at a time, we had the students in a special-project room where there were models, educational games, teaching machines and materials for baking and cooking and ceramics.

We divided the activities into three levels, red, yellow and white. The red level included all activities. There were two ways for a child to get into the red groups: by getting 90 per cent or more in his spelling and math work or by improving his last score by 10 percentage points. Children in this group almost always chose to bake and cook.

The yellow level included games, work on ceramic candy dishes, or work on teaching machines. To be in the yellow level, a child had to remain within 10 percentage points of his previous score, in either direction. The white level was restricted to work with the teaching machines. A child fell into the white level when his score dropped more than 10 percentage points, but he could gain the highest reward and move into the most attractive group by improving his score by 10 percentage points.

Then we told the fifth-graders that their spelling work would no longer count for privileges in the special-project room. At the same time we told the sixth-graders that math would no longer count. Performance dropped immediately in the work that did not count.

Next we reversed the contingencies. We told the fifth-graders that math would no longer count but spelling would, and we told the sixth-graders that spelling would no longer count but math would. Once again performance scores dropped dramatically for the unrewarded work.

The results show that performance in school can be controlled with suitable rewards, and that abrupt withdrawal of rewards can affect performance, at least negatively.

Strike. We all are interested in some return for effort. I recall a father who rejected a reinforcement plan for correcting his son's behavior because he thought the boy should be grown-up enough to do the right thing without a payoff. When the counselor thanked the father for taking time off from work to talk about his son's problem, the father replied, "Oh, that's all right. We're on strike for a raise." Apparently, when his payoff was involved, it was different.

Attention, praise and general encouragement are effective rewards in the home. Of these, attention often has the greatest influence on a child's behavior. Because attention is so influential, a parent must be on guard not to support bad behavior by paying attention to it, as did one mother who turned from a talk with a neighbor to deal with her daughter who was screaming, "Mommy! Mommy! Mommy!" She yelled back, "What is it?" The daughter yelled "Hi!" and ran away.

The mother unintentionally gave an example of yelling by yelling herself and she reinforced the behavior by paying attention to her daughter when she yelled. Selecting behaviors to be rewarded or ignored is the main business of being a parent.

Nag. Some parents ride their children—*blow your nose, tuck in your shirt, don't touch.* They give the child a great deal of attention but little support and encouragement. Other parents seem to follow a rule: *when in doubt, reward; hardly ever punish.* A complete lack of limits provides no information about right and wrong behaviors. Both children and adults continually explore limits. If there are none, behaviors may get out of hand.

Ideally, as a child grows, the limits on his behaviors are lessened gradually; he should experience expanding responsibility and independence. Unfortunately for many children the pattern is a long period of limitations and then an abrupt change into independence.

The typical American teen-ager is thrown out of the nest at about 17, when he goes off to college or to work. He has to achieve instant adulthood and the process can be painful, especially when what he does has severe social consequences. Because the teen-ager must adjust to everything at once, he may find it too much; he may rebel, rejecting the behaviors so valued by the adult world.

Perhaps the commonest cause of this revolt is the failure of parents to let children make some of their own decisions when they are younger and learn to live with the consequences. Teen-agers who are allowed to make decisions and reap consequences experience the success and failure of their decisions. After successes, ideally, parents are encouraging; after failures, parents support youngsters by pointing out and helping with the search for alternate behaviors. A long period of trial and error is possible for a child whose parents are willing to permit it. When the young adult leaves home without this practice, there is no time for discussion, exploration or selection (or for rejection). He is rushing into adulthood and time has run out.

WHY PARENTS SHOULD TAKE A FIRM STAND

Dr. Bruno Bettelheim

From time immemorial children have tried to buffalo their parents. But, fortunately for most generations, parents didn't permit themselves to be buffaloed. Nowadays, however, parents seem strangely insecure. They often feel unsure about whether they should make decisions for their children, especially when the children protest, "You're trying to run my life!" Actually, as I will point out, parents show good judgment when they enforce guidelines for their children's behavior. For instance, this situation arose in one of the discussion groups I conduct with mothers at the Orthogenic School:

"For three years our son complained because he didn't want to go to college," said one mother. "He said, 'I have no choice. I *have* to go to college, otherwise I'll be drafted.' He flunked out of one school and dropped out of two others. Then he failed his draft physical and was classified 4F. Now there was no longer any need for him to go to college, but within two weeks he decided he wanted to go after all. Since then he's done magnificently; he enjoys his classes and gets excellent grades. Even more important, he used to feel that everything was wrong with the world, but now he's happy."

This young man finally found himself because he was able to make an important choice—and it turned out to be the right one for him. Nothing helps us to feel good about ourselves and the world more than to know we have made a right choice. People think that making right choices is a consequence of having a strong, well-integrated personality. Actually, it's the other way around: it is making choices—right ones—that builds a strong personality. On the other hand, consistently making wrong choices leads to a sick personality: the neurotic and the psychotic are people who habitually make wrong choices.

The young man who was unable to make a go of college as long as he was there just to avoid being drafted probably had a fairly well-established personality. But being unable to make the choice about college so weakened him that for the time being he could not cope with life. As soon as meaningful choices were again available to him, his old personal strength returned.

Not all students take this situation so hard. For some, having to go into the service is not the end of the world, while others are sufficiently motivated by their studies to feel that in going to college they have made a significant choice, and hence they do not feel debilitated. But, unfortunately, a sizable group of students are in the same boat as this young man. Having to stay in college because of the draft gives them a sense of inability to make meaningful choices, and because of this, they feel so weak as persons that they cannot cope with life. Many drop out, some by way of drugs.

In our affluent society, the college population in particular has grown up with the assumption that making a living is something they can take for granted. Whatever they do, they'll be able to survive, they won't starve, they won't be without a place to live, they won't lack medical care, etc. Their parents still worry about all that, because they grew up during or soon after the Depression. But to the new generation, these worries don't make sense. What parents want young people to do—worry about preparing for a job at which they will work hard to make a living—doesn't seem realistic. That's why people over 30 don't make sense to people under 30. If making a living is taken for granted, then the income worked for means little, and working for it seems empty. They still have to work for it, of course, but working for something that means so little gives them no strength.

One mother in our discussion group denied that children have no chance to make meaningful choices. On the contrary, she felt the trouble nowadays was that too much is put in the hands of children too early. This makes them think they can run the show. Of course they can't, and it all ends in a big mess. For example, a teacher asked her 12-year-old daughter what she thought of another teacher. Naturally, the child was flattered to be asked, but she also was aware that she knew too little to make a decision. The teacher insisted, however, and so the girl gave an answer she knew was not based on true understanding. Later she felt awful that she had condemned the other teacher.

One mother's 12-year-old son had an even worse experience. His young teacher, since he was the only male teacher in the school, strongly influenced the boys. This teacher told them about all the legal and illegal ways of getting out of the draft, and also that some drugs are all right and some are bad. Those are the problems they're going to grow up with, he said, and therefore they should decide which drugs to use and which not. With this kind of an attitude, he was practically giving them the go-ahead sign. And it isn't just one teacher or two who push children into serious choices. It's a trend. By the time they're 15, they're saying, "The hell with all adults. We can take over; we can make our own choices."

How this works is illustrated by the story of a 13-year-old, middle-class girl who had a big fight with her parents about her demands for independence. If she could not run her own life, she said, she'd run away. The parents said nothing. So she left the house, but made sure to slam the door so loudly that everyone would know she had left. There was only one way to leave her suburban home—by bus. She walked slowly to the bus stop the family always used, hoping her parents would come after her. There she waited for an hour and 15 minutes, letting seven buses go by, but nobody came for her. By then she concluded that she was not wanted, that she had been given the freedom to arrange her life as she pleased only because her parents did not care.

All children have fantasies of running away, but the question behind them is: Do my parents love me, or do they want to get rid of me? This girl could not possibly manage her own life at 13, and she ended up in desperate straits. But the parents viewed themselves as enlightened people who did not interfere with their child's independence.

"Things are very different when you know your own mind," said a mother. Her 14-year-old daughter was very active in a community center, attending meetings several evenings a week, starting at 6:30. This meant she was forever leaving the house before dinner. When the mother said that this practice had to stop, the girl disagreed. But the mother insisted. "In this family we eat together," she said. And with that, the girl, on her own, managed to change the starting time of the meetings to 7:15.

Here is an important lesson about choices. The girl was confronted with a clear but limited problem: how to arrange things so that she could attend the meetings and still have dinner with her family. Changing the time of the meetings was quite within her abilities, and so she was able to solve the problem very well and gain personal strength from doing so. Running her own life was far beyond the ability of the 13-year-old who ran away. She failed, and as a result she lost all trust in her ability to make things come out right; she turned to drugs and worse, just to forget how incompetent a person she felt she was. In fact, she was not altogether incompetent; she was only incompetent when confronted with what to her was an unsolvable problem: how to make a go on her own in this world at her age.

"How far does this go?" wondered a mother. The difficulty is that the conditions of big-city living make it very hard to give children neither too many, nor too few, nor too difficult choices. In smaller communities a child can more or less run free, because the parents or neighbors know where he is. Because there are fewer things to do, it is easier for them to select among the few choices without making wrong ones. Children need the right mixture of making their own choices (and learning from them) and being protected against making the wrong choices. It's easy to keep tabs all the time or not at all. It's much more difficult to keep the right balance, though that's what our children need. The parent must know exactly where she can trust and where she cannot.

"It's not just a matter of our trust," objected a mother. "We must help them realize what is a potentially dangerous situation. One day my son missed his school bus; it was the first time he had to take public transportation to school—it's quite a distance. About half an hour later I called the school to see if he had gotten there. This had nothing to do with trust, it had to do with my anxiety. When he came home that night he said, 'Gee, Mom, I'm twelve years old. Did you have to call?' I said, 'Sure, I had to call. How did I know that you got there safely?' I don't think he was angry at all."

She was lucky, I said, because some 12-year-olds might be angry, but what she did was the right thing to do. Because the children object, many parents believe that checking up, or whatever term you use, is the wrong thing to do. So they don't do it, and the child comes to think they don't care, or that he should be able to act all by himself. But if he can't act by himself, then his trust in himself is undermined. It's a strange thing; here we are worrying so when children object, instead of taking it for granted, as we do with a three-year-old who loudly objects if we tie his shoes, saying he can do it all by himself. We know his insistence that he can do it himself greatly enhances his self-respect, while he loves having us do it for him. In this way he can have the best of both worlds—proclaiming his independence and still enjoying the dependent satisfactions he craves. But when the 12-year-old objects for the same reasons, we fail to recognize that he too wants the best of both worlds—to be able to show himself and his friends how independent he is and still feel well protected.

The problem for parents is deciding which choices the child can safely make and learn from, and which we should not let him make because we foresee that, given his immaturity, he will make wrong choices and come to grief. This was the error in asking the 12-year-old if her teacher was good or not: at this age children are more concerned with good times than with good teaching. It's one thing to let a child make decisions that will not harm him; it's something else to project him into anxiety by asking him to make decisions that no 12-year-old should be asked to make, such as deciding if a teacher is good.

The same goes for any age, even for college people and the draft: Are these choices they can really safely make? What's eating the kids up isn't really the draft. Most countries have had obligatory military service for 150 years. Nobody likes it, but nowhere is it a tremendous problem. In this country, however, it has become a tremendous problem for kids who are told: "Make up your own mind whether you want to serve; it's up to you." To serve in the armed forces is always onerous at best and exceedingly dangerous at worst. For an 18-year-old to make such a decision is incredibly difficult. On the one hand, who wants to serve? But on the other, who wants to shirk his duty to his country? I think it is ridiculous to project young people into this kind of conflict. Now, I'm not for the draft. I hope we'll be able to do away with it. But to make youngsters start worrying about making such decisions when they're 15 or 16—this, I feel, places an impossible burden upon them.

If such a burden is destructive, making choices that prove to be without consequence may be even more so. Let me illustrate: many kids are picked up by the police—for smoking pot or petty theft or whatever. If police arrest had the consequences it used to have, the child would learn a great deal from having made the wrong choice, but our 13- or 15-year-old can't learn anything from a bad choice because the parents run interference for him. He gets a nice ride in the squad car with the siren going and a lollipop! And all he learned is that making the wrong choice has no bad consequences.

This goes even for the college boy. He thinks that college doesn't make sense, that the world doesn't make sense; but his parents still pay his college bills, and so his attitude has no consequence. If my son were to say that college makes no sense, I'd say, "Fine, don't go—find yourself a job." As likely as not, he would soon discover that without a college education he can't find a job he likes. So he learns that he made the wrong choice. Since he can still correct it, the mistake will make college all the more meaningful to him. On the other hand, if he finds a job he likes and does well in it, then he has made the right choice and will be stronger for it.

Whether or not to go to college is a choice our youngsters should be able to make freely. If they decide not to go and instead take a job, even if they later realize they made the wrong choice, they can learn from it and correct their mistake by going to college. And if their decision to go to college was the wrong choice, they can learn from it by leaving college and getting a job. But fear of being drafted robs them of such freedom of choice. Being drafted is irrevocable since they cannot freely leave the service when they find out it is the wrong place for them to be. Even at 18, they are too young to make irrevocable choices, so I believe it would be better if such choices were not offered to them. If it is absolutely necessary for them to serve, then the government should make the decision for them. At least then, the responsibility for serving or not serving, which is simply too great, would not be thrust upon them. When the consequences of a choice are far-reaching, or irreversible, the individual who must make the choice needs an appropriate maturity and knowledge of the world.

For example, we cannot let a 12-year-old child decide whether or not he wants to go to school. Making the wrong choice would have such destructive consequences that we cannot afford to let the child make his own choice, and so we have to make it for him.

We should permit our children to make choices only when, if they choose wrong, the consequences will not be utterly destructive. But when we decide to let them make a choice, then we must not prevent the choice from having consequences, so that they may learn from it for the future.

AREA 5

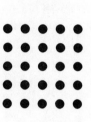

ENCOUNTER IN
THE NEW MARRIAGE

A VALENTINE'S GUIDE
TO THE 'NEW' WOMAN

Sandra Shevey

St. Valentine has seen many changes in how his day is celebrated. Two generations ago it was all the rage to send "ugly" cards pointing out the recipient's defects. One generation ago romance made a comeback, and all was hearts and flowers.

Today, however, what with so many young women wanting to be "liberated" from their customary sex roles, the average young man isn't quite sure how to treat this new breed of female. Here, then, is a handy guide to the kind of approach called for when one is courting the Liberated Woman who is "turned off" by old-fashioned male gallantry:

Watch Your Language. There's a whole new feminist vocabulary. Don't ask a liberated woman for a date. There are friendships, and they evolve. Guard yourself against such remarks as "you're a good-looking broad." This isn't man talk. It's just insulting to a woman. Don't call this woman lady, girl, doll, honey, or baby: belittling terms which define her as an object, a thing. Use her name.

To the liberated woman, "feminine" connotes a pretense, something unnatural—like batting one's eyelashes. If you dig her, say she's female, not feminine.

If she's an ardent feminist, be careful. Never insinuate she's a man hater—anti-men—just because she's pro-women. She'll never forgive you. Anyway, ridicule is a ploy used by a man to keep a woman in her place.

Who Calls Whom. After you've made each other's acquaintance and you decide you'd like to see one another again, who calls whom? It should be left casual, informal. She can call you, or you can call her. It will give you a chance to see what it's like on the other side—to accept or refuse a date as well as being accepted or not.

Calling for Her. This is largely circumstantial. If she has a car, let her pick you up. If you do, then vice-versa. If you both drive, flip a coin. If neither of you does, arrange to meet at a central place. Don't act as if you're responsible for her. A liberated woman detests paternalism.

Where to Go. The liberated gal may be as interested in a Women's Lib meeting as she is in spending the evening with you. Why not go along, take an interest in her activities.

The liberated woman is a great talker. Why not suggest dinner. Don't choose the place. Two decisions and you're a chauvinist. Better yet, be unconventional. Why not cook supper and let her bring the wine.

This gal's involved in politics, the community, so know what rallies and lectures are around.

Choosing the Wine. If you've agreed to have dinner out, play it by ear. Decisions can be shared which formerly were assumed by the man. If she frequents the restaurant in which you are dining, let her ask the headwaiter for a good table. What about the wine? She might be able to suggest a good Chablis if you're eating fish. You may let her deal with the wine steward.

Paying the Bill. Split the check, no if's, and's, or but's. The liberated woman doesn't want a man paying for her "services." You're spending the evening together because you like her, not because you're buying her time.

The Conversation. What to talk about with a liberated woman: the more heated the discussion the better. The liberated woman loves to argue, use her wits. Her being cute, sweet, pretty may be enough for you, but it's not for her. She will resent discussing trivia, also intellectual condescension. "Man is intellect, woman intuition" became obsolete the day the first woman entered a classroom. Encourage her to take pride in her accomplishments.

Know, too, that with this woman you're not in competition. You don't have to prove you're an authority. But believe in what you say. She can spot a phony.

Status Symbol. (An extra hint) Don't invite this woman out to impress friends, coworkers. She'll sense it and dislike you. She's not a possession, a decoration. This kind of invitation is out: "Would you enjoy meeting me for dinner? I've just finished a business conference, and some of the fellows have asked me to join them."

Compliments. Save them. They're usually patronizing: "Honey, I like that dress (better than the other one)"; or, "Your hair looks great that way (rather than hanging limp)." Seldom a man can flatter without sounding like he's instructing a woman. Sometimes compliments are exploitative: "Your skin is so soft"; "Your hair is so lovely." This kind of adoration makes the liberated woman feel as if she is being turned into an object.

Manners. Don't hold doors, help her on with her coat, carry packages, open cars, light her cigarette. They're taboo—ploys which keep woman in a subordinate, dependent role.

Boning Up on the Lib. Know something about woman's history: who were Elizabeth Cady Stanton, Emma Goldman, Elizabeth Blackwell? Read Kate Millet's "Sexual Politics" and Betty Friedan's "The Feminine Mystique." Become familiar with the ideas of Simone de Beauvoir, Ti-Grace Atkinson, and Robin Morgan.

Care about the Equal-Rights Amendment (on and off) in Congress and Women's Lib activities in your town: job discrimination, child-care centers, disparaging images of women on television as well as in films.

Criticism. Don't correct her manners. Keep quiet if she uses the wrong fork during dinner or mispronounces the name of a house specialty.

Oneupmanship is usually distasteful. Ask yourself, "Would I ever want her to correct me?"

Saying Good Night. The liberated woman has discarded the taboos and inhibitions handed down by Mother. So don't be surprised if she's affectionate. And don't be astonished if she's not. Women's Liberation means an option to choose.

Forget the Myths. "Machismo" might work for John Wayne, but the present-day woman doesn't like the drill sergeant, the conquering hero. She knows a tender, thoughtful man is much more satisfying. And forget what Dad told you about a woman wanting to be subdued. It frustrates her—all the time having to pretend she's weak and spineless. And what a bore!

So turn to that woman sitting next to you and strike up a conversation. Relax. Enjoy it. You might find out your initial fears were unwarranted and that you really enjoy being with her.

TODAY'S MARRIAGE OR THE NEW MARRIAGE— WHICH WAY FOR YOU?

Herbert A. Otto

Much of what happens (or what doesn't happen) in a contemporary marriage is determined by the implicit assumptions underlying the union. Some of these change during a marriage, others do not. To a considerable extent, *these underlying assumptions define the course of the marriage and provide a framework which shapes the nature of the relationship.* Some of these assumptions are verbalized at some time during the marriage while others are rarely, if ever, put into words. Among these assumptions are:

1. Marriage furnishes a means for the giving and taking of love, understanding, and for sexual fulfillment.
2. Sexual relations should take place only (or largely) between the two partners.
3. Marriage offers a measure of security, comfort, and stability, so that both partners soon learn to know what they can expect. Boundaries are set by husband and wife and it is their expectation that these will be respected.
4. Marriage involves a set of responsibilities and duties. It also involves certain roles—"what a husband is and should be" and "what a wife is and should be."
5. Marriage is for the raising and rearing of children and "having a family."
6. Marriage is a means of "weathering life's storms and ups-and-downs."
7. Marriage means companionship, someone to talk to.
8. Marriage is an insurance against a lonely old age.

In a similar manner, the implicit and explicit assumptions underlying the New Marriage will determine its course. For this reason, a New Marriage must begin with an exploration of these assumptions by both marital partners. As husband and wife enter into this process, openness and self-disclosure lead to increased personal authenticity and the emergence of a deeper understanding and vital togetherness. The concept of the New Marriage can offer new opportunities, open new doors, and add new creativity, excitement, and joy to married living.

If we conceive of the New Marriage as an exciting union which has as its main purpose the involvement of both partners in the adventure of actualizing each other's potential, then this purpose becomes a dynamic bond which fosters closeness while at the same time it meets the privacy needs of the partners. Implicit in the concept of the New Marriage is a deep respect for each other as a unique person with many individual capacities, talents, powers, and abilities which can be developed and brought to full flowering.

Also implicit is the concept that two parents who, in love and understanding, are dedicated to help each other actualize individual potential, are thereby doing more for the family than the heads of a child-centered marriage, where the efforts of the parents are subordinated to the needs of the children. The family devoted to the actualizing of the personal potential of its members provides necessary structure, as well as the freedom of group experiences, for growth as a family and individual growth experiences away from the family. These experiences are consciously designed and worked out by the family as a group, with primary emphasis on the needs and the wishes of the individuals involved. The actualization of a member's potential is first and foremost his own concern, but it is also the concern of the other family members who encourage, help, and assist. The primary emphasis, however, is on the individual's efforts to help himself. From this emphasis emerges a new freedom within the structure, and this marks the emergence of *The New Family*.

PRACTICING MARRIAGE WITHOUT A LICENSE

BETTY LIDDICK
Times Staff Writer

PART 1. SOME CASES

She was a young waitress in a seafood restaurant on the beach. He was a struggling songwriter. He wrote her a note: "Would you like to travel the world with me?" And they laughed and talked together and not much later, in a modern version of let-me-take-you-away-from-all this, he said, "Would you like to come to L.A. with me? It would be groovy."

It happens like that sometimes. Love—or lust—in an instant. A decade ago, it was a staple of movie scenarios, ending with a fairy tale wedding and they lived happily ever after.

But this is real life and today. The couple who met at the restaurant are still together and they are still happy. But they never married and see no reason to. And as for the forever part—forget it. That's just too impossible to contemplate.

Like uncounted thousands of others, the couple live together. Cohabitate, the law books call it (it's no crime in California unless one or both is a minor or already married). Shack up or live in sin, their mothers' generation called it.

Uncertain Effect

Whatever its label, living together is openly increasing. To listen to youth and Hollywood gossip columnists, you'd think it was epidemic, but it is only one of a number of experiments in living and its effect and implications are still uncertain.

Even the experts disagree. Dr. James Rue, general director of the American Institute of Family Relations and director of the Sir Thomas More Clinics of Southern California, laments the trend "because so many young people are being seriously damaged by what they feel is their best interests."

He believes, "In reality they leave a trail of havoc, depression, anxiety and insecurity the likes of which have not been seen in our culture."

Dr. Louis J. West, chairman of the UCLA school of psychiatric medicine and director of the Neuropsychiatric Institute, holds a completely divergent view. He maintains many young people "are repelled by today's smorgasbord of sexual opportunities" and living together is one of the healthier manifestations of the social revolution.

Sex Without Guilt

"If they want to enjoy sex without guilt, that doesn't mean they want to cheapen it," Dr. West says. "Many young people are searching for more meaningful relationships."

Meaningful . . . that word that's worn out its welcome. But it is this very personal and sometimes painful search for meaning, for self, that stamps today's living together uniquely new. It's not forced by circumstances like senior citizens who live together to keep full Social Security benefits or couples who can't marry because one partner cannot get a divorce.

And it's not a copout on marriage, the couples are quick to say, but a conviction that there is something better. The reasons range from the romantic ("It's more daring, adventuresome") to the coldly realistic ("It's economically, emotionally and sexually advantageous. Plus, if you like each other, it helps a lot").

What are the other attractions and the problems? Do the couples feel guilty? What do their families think? And who answers the telephone?

To find out, I talked to five couples, four unmarried and one who had just married after a year of living together. Some wouldn't stop talking if a train were bearing down on them. Others were quietly uncomfortable.

Dark Secrets

And at one awful visit, my questions brought dark secrets spilling out like an encounter gone awry. There were sure to be tears and recriminations after I left.

Despite their diversity, I found the couples all had in common:

—The philosophy that life is now, today. "Nothing is permanent."
—A belief that marriage is not only not viable, it's unnecessary. And hypocritical because of easy and rampant divorce. (One out of two California marriages break up.) All right, some couples concede, "Marriage is fine for people who want to be married. We don't."
—A fierce respect for the individual, his right to happiness on the job as well as in personal relationships.

—A reflection of current changing values, sometimes cloudy: "Since we care so much for each other, it would be more immoral to go out on a date, sleep together and separate afterward."

—A serious, almost touchingly naive "I have a friend" approach to their relationship. Sex is no big deal to this generation. "It's a quiet thing," says a 25-year-old woman about her affair. "It's not like Ezio Pinza coming out of the bushes singing 'Some Enchanted Evening.' "

—A predilection for choice. "You know the reason you stay is because you want to, not because there's a legal document saying you must."

—A love of freedom. "In life there are infinite numbers of possibilities. We want to leave as many open as we possibly can." "I didn't want to sign up with Jack LaLanne for two years of exercise, much less a marriage contract."

—A demand for anonymity. None wanted their names used despite their alleged openness about living together and their celebration of it as a way of life. "It would make my parents uptight . . ." "I'm starting this new business . . ." "It's just simply we don't want any nuts calling us . . ."

What does that anonymity say about their relationships and acceptance by society? That despite hotpants and X-rated movies and Warren Beatty and Julie Christie hugging it up in *Look,* the majority opts for the old morality?

Equivalent of Dogma

—A dislike for the state's role in their lives. Many feel the formality of a wedding is the equivalent of dogma, of falling in line behind the Establishment.

"Why do I need a minister to say it's cool for us to live together?" asks 22-year-old Kathy. "Love has married us."

She and Howard—the couple who met in the restaurant—are talking in their apartment on a Sunday afternoon. They haven't made that trip around the world yet, but they've been to 48 states and they are back at the beach now, enjoying a life they think is idyllic.

To get to their apartment, I walk along the bay, past expensive moored sailboats and comfortable, shiny houses with groomed lawns, only feet from the water. It's all very resort-like and restfully calm in the sort of way money provides.

A climb up the stairs to their apartment brings an even better view of the bay. There's an open porch with plants and inside it's a melange of pillows and books and records and candles and—you can almost feel it—options, their feeling of freedom, of doing what they want.

Howard has blue eyes and dozens of freckles and a rounding stomach. At 25, with one career in science behind him, he is a full-time college student on the edge of success in song writing.

He talks, talks, talks and he's totally engaging. He chain-smokes Marlboros and bites his nails and drinks coffee nonstop. He is the son of the fictitious Mrs. Portnoy and he is driven.

Kathy is lean and her dark hair falls to her waist. She appears more relaxed than Howard, but don't believe it. With her hair pulled back and with those determined dark eyes, she could head the ways and means committee of the Junior League and make a bundle. She is a good hostess ("Just plain soda?") and a good housekeeper and yes, by God, Howard will put the toothpaste cap on and empty the ashtray when it's full.

They are both so eager to talk they talk at once and the effect is like sitting in the middle of two stereos. They have been living together for two and one half years and it would seem, except for the ceremony, they are married. But that's the difference.

"I can't see any reason for getting married," Howard says. "What would it change besides saving tax money?"

They explain they have been taking a course in positive thinking and they try to see the world in positive terms, you are the master of your own fate philosophy with some Ayn Rand thrown in. And they see no positive reason to marry.

Howard, who had a restrictive upbringing, says, "I grew up with lots of have-tos in my life. I grew out of it . . . Marriage is another have-to on your head, a life-long contract.

'Nothing Is Forever'

"I'm living with all want-tos. I'd be committing a paradox to say till death do us part. What if you grow past the person you promised to be with forever? Nothing is forever. . . . It would be so hypocritical to sign a marriage contract. You wouldn't sign a contract to work at the same place all your life, would you?"

Although Howard would never marry as the institution is set up, now, he does favor contract marriage renewable every three years—but then only for the tax advantage. "It's profitable." A positive angle.

For Kathy, who had an unsuccessful marriage, at 17, marrying again would be "silly." A psychiatrist might say she is afraid of marriage, but she explains, "I wanted to live together at 17, but getting married made my parents so happy." Her parents, who live nearby, now approve. His parents, back in New York, don't, but they are cordial.

Not for Her

Kathy sees marriage simply as a celebration of two people meeting. But it's not for her.

"I've got to be independent . . . I'm not half Howard and half me," she says. "We remain individuals, knowing we can just leave. Because I know he can leave if he wants to, I work harder at pleasing him."

Insecurity?

"Sure, it's a good insecurity."

Theirs is no heavy-breathing, heart-clutching romance. From the start they agreed: "If something better comes along, we'll take it."

"If she feels she could find more happiness with someone else," Howard says, "she has to make that scene. She has the option to talk with others, to go out, to go to bed."

Yet they remain sexually faithful. "We want to be," says Howard. "If I wanted another girl, this relationship would be in bad shape anyway."

Their relationship is conventionally domestic. There's an occasional hassle about housekeeping. ("She's compulsive about it," Howard says. "She used to bug me about the toothpaste cap. That was a have-to so I didn't do it till she explained it made a stain.")

A Women's Lib dilemma about whether to work. "I felt strange taking his money," Kathy says, so she started her own small business.

A Wide Berth

Howard pays the bills; they share decision making. They give each other a wide berth. That afternoon Howard had bought two tickets for a concert. Kathy didn't want to go, so he took her father along. No fuss. No, "but I did it for you."

The only source of disagreement is children. Kathy could see their living together "being a bummer for future children." Howard thinks not.

The reaction of others to their relationship doesn't bother them. "The only opinion that matters is Kathy's and mine," Howard says. "If anybody does care, I don't care about them."

So why not use their names in this story?

"We know where we're at—others don't," he explains. And Kathy doesn't want to jeopardize her franchise sales business. In Howard's semi-show-biz work, it wouldn't matter.

He goes over to the piano and bangs out his newest song. Next year his income may hit six figures. He left his super secure job in government research to live an uncertain but creative life as a composer and it paid off. "When I left, my co-workers said, 'Gosh, you're lucky,' but they didn't realize they had the choice, too. No one makes you do things.

"I do what's good for me. I want to be here. I love Kathy (even if they split, they'd be good friends). That's happening now. When that's not happening, the relationship is over."

Kathy and Howard are still searching, but they are working on their relationship; they give, they care, they're open.

Not Anita and Paul. Couple No. 2, sign in please.

Their apartment is in the corner of a courtyard in North Hollywood. A couple of days of newspapers litter the porch. Inside, it's as empty as an $8 double, as if the occupants have given little of themselves to the place.

A low, backless sofa sags against the wall, the TV rages and a fluffy cat they found a few days ago leaps around loudly. It's clean, but it would definitely not make a color spread in Town and Country.

To make matters worse, I have the uneasy feeling there's an unsettled argument in the air. There is. Something about defrosting the dinner for supper . . . which they dismiss with a laugh.

Anita and Paul are appealing because they are so disarmingly straightforward. No hedging, no game playing. They are together because it's convenient and cheap. Isn't "one rent cheaper" than two? Won't he have "someone to bail him out" if he should ever go to jail?

"I have a friend," says Paul. "Security is the No. 1 reason for living together. It's kind of nasty coming home to an empty house. Now I have a steady date and naturally, the clincher, sex is always available. You don't have to think about it during the day."

These two are so honest—or tough—it's got to hurt. How else would she feel when he says right in front of her she's not the girl for him.

No denying Paul is handsome in a tousled sort of way. Tall, brown hair and eyes. President of his fraternity, glib with too eager smiles and too many jokes like he's up for reelection.

There's something vaguely corrupt about him. What is he hiding behind that barrage of nervous laughter?

Then you know: He has heartbreaker written all over him. Too many women will weep over him.

Twenty-nine-year-old Anita has the gamine charm of Shirley Mac-Laine. She is given to saying "hiya kid" and "sorry about that." A shade on the thin side, she moves with the grace of the model she once was ($100 a day). She has long straight red hair, pale freckles dotting almost translucent skin and sad green eyes that look as if they could cry on cue.

With a turbulent childhood and ugly divorce behind her, it's no surprise the psychic scars show. Her eight-year marriage had enough difficulties to sustain a soap opera: financial hardship, unfaithful husband, identity crisis, pregnancy just at the time she was considering divorce.

"I really don't want to talk about it," she says as we sit around the dining room table. But she does anyway. "My dad died when I was 6. I bet we must have moved 50 times.

"All my life I've been moving . . . My mother joined eight or nine churches. I stopped following her and started working when I was 13. Then I foolishly got married at 17. I just felt I was 50 years old all the while I was married."

She says after the divorce, she finally started living. "I went to art school and it changed my whole life." She left her office job and is freelancing as a writer-artist. "It's what I want to do." And it's also why she doesn't want her name used—you know, those sensitive accounts.

Paul, who's two years younger, works part-time as a messenger while he goes to college full-time. Their schedules leave little time for togetherness.

"It used to be a closer relationship," Paul says. "We were constantly seeing each other. Now our schedules are conflicting. She keeps long hours and I don't expect her to keep me company.

"There's a sort of new arrangement now, you see. The romantic love has sort of worn off now and she's going to work on her career and I respect her for that. We just don't see much of each other any more . . ."

Do they feel they're headed for a breakup?

"Sure," says Paul.

"Well, one of these days," says Anita. "Of course, we've been saying that for three years. Nobody can say what's going to happen in the future. You live for today. You try to do your best for the future. If he left tomorrow, we'd still be friends."

"Who knows," says Paul, "I might even marry her."

Like Anita, Paul grew up with a religious background. To his mother's delight, he was an altar boy for a half dozen years. He once thought about becoming a priest. But that was before his girlfriend became pregnant and he left for the Air Force ("It wouldn't have worked out to marry her").

After a succession of jobs as private detective, loan company employee and travel around the country and Europe, he has decided to become a teacher or counselor.

He met Anita when he was a model for her photographer-husband. After Anita's divorce, Paul was at her house so much, she asked one day, "Why are you paying for that extra room?" So he moved in to share expenses. Simple as that, 50-50. Strictly dollars and cents.

"We never planned on marriage," says Anita. "Some couples enter the relationship like a trial marriage or say they plan to get married, but we were just very fond of each other. There was never any pretense we would marry each other sometime to make everything right because we didn't think it was wrong to begin with."

Nor was living together an alternative to marriage. "I think it's better," says Anita, "as long as you're not going to have children. You don't take each other for granted or abuse each other.

"I don't ever want to get married because I had such a bad deal. If Paul wants to get married someday, it's better he finds someone who wants to."

And Paul most definitely wants to marry, perhaps in 10 years. "I just want to find the right girl."

Is Anita the right girl?

"Not for me," he says. "She's the right girl for someone else."

I look to Anita for a reaction. "There's no big thing there," she shrugs.

Mother Approves

"It's sort of different between us," Anita explains. "We're really good friends. In order to love anybody, you have to be good friends."

"We're 50% friends, 50% lovers," Paul says.

Acceptance of their status has been easy. "Living together is no big thing in California," Paul says. "Nobody cares in a big city."

"My friends like me for me," Anita says. "I felt guilty when I was married because I knew I didn't belong with that guy."

Her mother approves. And Paul's family? "When they start sending checks, I'll listen to them."

One disadvantage is that Anita feels compromised. When men find out about her status, she says, they proposition her. "If they know you sleep with somebody, they think you'll sleep with everybody."

Other disadvantages are the same as those in marriage, lack of privacy, for example. They have a quiet life and go out only a couple of times a month. On weekends, Anita sees her daughter.

How do they handle their common ground—money? Do they have a joint checking account?

"No, but we have a joint savings account," Paul says. "I put her name down, too, just in case something happens to me."

"I didn't know that!" Anita interrupts as Paul recites the account number. "My goodness, that's sweet . . ."

Do they share any promise of fidelity?

"Well, kinda. There isn't anything said definitely," says Anita. "But I'm a one-guy girl."

"We respect each other's rights, let's put it like that," Paul says. "I'm discreet."

No use stopping now. Is he faithful?

"That's a hell of a question to ask in front of her," he says, pointing to Anita.

"No, he's not," Anita says in a flat voice. "I don't mind. He's been good to me."

Final Answer

"No, I'm not very faithful," Paul answers finally. "Sometimes I am. It doesn't matter. I still love her." He shifts around on the chair. "See, I don't know if she's faithful or not. I don't think she'd ever tell me."

But in this uncomfortable setting, under the dining room light lit up like a precinct room, she does tell him embarrassingly, that yes she is faithful and he is quiet for a long while before speaking. "I didn't know that . . ."

For the first time tonight, or who knows how long, Anita and Paul are talking to each other. Maybe in some strange way, their way, they are closer.

"With me," Anita says, "making love is mental. With guys it's physical."

'They Don't Like Me'

"I know girls who go to bed with me one or two times and they don't really like me, I know," says Paul.

"It would be hard for me to do that," Anita tells him.

"It's hard for me," Paul says. "I don't really like that."

Leaving Anita and Paul is a reprieve from wrenching emotions. Next visit—Julie and Tim.

There they are—almost to order—two bright college kids carrying their books, so responsible and serious and customarily dewy-eyed and "terribly" in love that it's a joy just to look at them. Do young people like this still exist? Unweird, unfreaked, unhungup?

"You could say and you'd be right and it doesn't matter to me, I guess we're playing house," says Tim with a grin. He is huggable-handsome behind gold wire rim glasses.

We are talking one sunny spring morning in an office on the UCLA campus where he and Julie, both 20, are juniors. After wide dating experience, they have been going together for 2½ years and living together since October. For them, it's the most natural thing in the world, "even odd it should be any other way."

Just One Fear

There's just one unrelenting fear, one that makes Julie gulp whenever she hears footsteps at 2 in the morning: Their parents might find out.

Somehow, with an artfully obliging roommate to answer the phone at Julie's old apartment and their frantic races to hide her things in the closet when his parents come to visit, they've managed to keep their status a secret.

Hypocritical? They know it. And they feel the agonizing squeeze of guilt.

"In a way, we've set a trap for ourselves," says Tim. "If we told our parents now, they'd be hurt we didn't tell them earlier. It's really amazing they don't know. We've made some monumental slips, like saying our instead of mine."

As only children whose parents struggled to give them the things they didn't have, Tim and Julie feel special responsibilities not to disappoint their parents.

"They've banked everything on us," Julie says in her low solemn voice. She has forthright brown eyes, a fresh unmadeup face and long brown hair falling from a center part.

She says it all boils down to the fact their parents just wouldn't understand, even though they "communicate really well."

"I love my parents," Julie says. "I respect their morality. I don't want to hurt them unnecessarily."

Besides, part of the subterfuge is unknowingly financed by her parents. They pay the rent on her old apartment.

"I know I've had most of the things I wanted," Julie admits. "I guess everyone who grew up in this culture was relatively spoiled. My parents are putting me through college."

But she is no slacker. She worked two summers to help her career. She met Tim on their part-time jobs near the campus.

Their dating shocked friends because she was "a very straight social chick from Westwood" and he then was the "house freak" with long wild hair. Now they're easily accepted because, Tim says, "The people we're concerned about liking us are like us."

Introductions to strangers pose no problems. Tim simply says, "This is Julie.

"It would be pretty sappy to say this is my girlfriend."

Their decision to live together just sort of evolved. "We wanted to be with each other all the time. It wasn't a let's-try-it-out-before-marriage deal," Julie says.

Tim remembers she used to stay at his place two or three days at a time and it got to be a hassle living out of a suitcase. "One day I got annoyed and said, 'Next weekend go over and get all your stuff.' A couple of days later we were sitting around and realized, hey, we're living together."

Even now, he says, it really hasn't sunk in. "American culture pretty well drills into you that you can't have a meaningful relationship, one that isn't dirty, unless you're married.

"We were brought up to believe that this (living together) is a cardinal sin, mostly because it involves premarital sex . . . I guess we share a pretty conventional morality about sex: It does involve commitment."

Though they never intended their living together to be a trial marriage, in six months they will be wed in a "creative ceremony" of their own. "I've been to too many weddings where the only thing that's different is the names on the matches," says Julie. "I don't want to wait till the end of school for a June wedding," says Tim, putting a slur on June like a silent ick.

Julie believes their marriage will have more meaning and substance because they've lived together. "I can't imagine getting married and not having known the person. I know my mother's excuse is there won't be anything left to do. That's really absurd."

There have been adjustments, like learning to live with another person. Tim never even had a roommate. And there are the mundane things like housekeeping to contend with. But Julie and Tim say the novelty hasn't worn off.

Yes, they admit, they are "pretty insulated from economic realities." Because of their work-school schedules, they eat out most of the time. They both have cars. Tim pays the bills except food which they share.

They have discussed the remote possibility of children now and agree if Julie became pregnant, she would get an abortion. They aren't ready for the responsibility of a child.

Whatever their future together, it will be a mutual thing. After all, they're "best friends."

Tim sums it up: "The most important thing is we realize each other as individuals, with desires of our own. I have a consciousness of Julie as a person as well as someone I love. I'm not going to appropriate her ego because I love her. It took living together to realize that.

"I have changed. I'm more outward, more at ease. I wouldn't recommend it to everyone. There are some really sick relationships. But generally, it's better than a long period of engagement where you go over to her house with flowers and maybe her parents leave you alone for the night because you're engaged. That's more sordid than living together."

PART 2. FINANCIAL, LEGAL, MORAL
AND PSYCHOLOGICAL IMPLICATIONS
OF NON-MARRIAGE RELATIONSHIPS

High school kids used to ask counselors about kissing on the first date or going steady. Now they ask, "Why get married?"

In a rootless, uncertain time, when institutions are being challenged, marriage is a favorite target. Threatened perhaps, but continuing to grow. In Los Angeles County there were 62,457 marriages recorded in 1969 and 63,975 in 1970.

It's clear that living together will not replace marriage any time soon, but it is a significant part of our culture today and it brings special implications, rethinking and sometimes agonizing to a variety of areas.

Financial: A spokesman for the Internal Revenue Service points out unmarried couples living together cannot file a joint return and thus perhaps save money on their income tax. (The IRS follows individual states' views on common-law marriages; California doesn't recognize them.)

Couples can have joint savings and checking accounts and make loans together. In fact, one couple were delighted with their crisply official letter of welcome as depositors from a bank president.

The couples' handling of money, of course, is entirely personal and based on their circumstances.

The social impact made by those living together without benefit of a marriage certificate is just now being felt. The moral, legal, financial and psychological implications are considered in the second of a two-part series.

One couple, each with important careers, shared payment of the rent while they lived together for a year. They're married now and still pay that way.

Legal: Judge William P. Hogoboom, supervising judge of the County Family Law Department, who believes living together is part of the social revolution in our attitude toward moral standards, points out that the woman has no legal protection, no community property or rights to earnings. Children would be illegitimate, though the couple could subsequently marry and legitimatize the child.

Professional: It all depends upon the sensitivity of the employer and the values of the community.

"In my sphere of friends, marriage is not a requirement for respectability," says a young movie soundman who's studying for his master's in theater arts.

On the other hand, a schoolteacher might face some fingerwagging. Probably not from his school board ("We don't inquire into the private lives of our teachers," says Jerry Curtis, speaking for L.A. City Schools), but from parents who require "good examples" for their children.

Rarely are there written standards. They would and have been challenged. But as Ted Schmidt of Pacific Telephone says, "We want our employees to conduct themselves in a manner to give credit to themselves and our business."

A 26-year-old professional woman with a master's degree says all the while she worked for a large conservative company, she felt a "lingering fear that her boss would find out."

Sociological: It's a rare parent who accepts his child's cohabitation with understanding and approval. "My mother keeps saying, 'Why don't you ask Warren to marry you? You aren't getting any younger, dear,'" says a 25-year-old woman. "I feel badly hurting my parents. They are embarrassed."

Some parents struggle to understand, like the father who wrote to his son, "I'm certain many similar arrangements exist and I'm equally certain that today's standards are vastly different than those in which I was reared . . . I know it is unwise to adhere strictly to a set of values of an unchanging nature and that one must try to keep up with progressing standards."

But try as he might to approve, the father believes the arrangement is wrong. "You demean yourself by being convenient . . . You limit your opportunities for growth . . . If she is the person you ought to consider for a lifetime mate, it seems you both prejudice the absolute ecstasy and delight that planned dedication to one another assures . . . I hope you can find a gracious way to locate yourself again as an independent person . . . All this being said, we still love and respect your right to make your own decisions."

Moral: "I don't presume to judge," says the Rev. John McNassar of UCLA's Newman Center. "The consensus would be that it is an illicit relationship . . . but I can't say Frank and Susie are living in sin. I don't know what's on their minds."

Mr. McNassar feels as do others who work closely with young people that the healthiness of the relationship may be based on the reason for it.

"It's very difficult and not at all helpful to generalize," he says. "Some couples take it seriously. Others live together for convenience. Some consider it a real obligation; others don't.

"One of the problems is losing sight of what it means to be dedicated to one person on a permanent basis. It can take the edge off in an unfortunate way."

Little Contact

However, at the same time, Mr. McNassar sees good. "Some people are probably experiencing for the first time what it is to live day in and day out confronted with another person. This should have happened with the family, but many times a person has little contact with his family."

Father McNassar is not alarmed, he says, but "concerned in wondering what's going to happen when life gets into middle age."

One woman, just a few years out of college, has already thought of it. "I feel rather insecure in that it's nice to be doing this now, but I don't know if I'd like to be 40 years old and living with a guy and not knowing what's going to happen tomorrow.

Psychological: Take your pick of theories from two respected authorities. One sees living together as a sign of moral decay; another views it as a rebellion against moral decay.

Dr. James Rue, general director of the American Institute of Family Relations, is a friendly, graying father of eight who believes young people's experimenting with a morality that is new to them is a tragedy. "Living together is not giving. It's taking. Love is the giving of oneself for the well-being of others."

"I admire that young people don't want to accept the inadequate ways of doing things that their parents did. They see hypocrisy in many marriages and I join in with them, but in pursuit of a better way, I think they made a wrong turn."

Dr. Rue cites the lack of commitment in living together. "Commitment means I love you with all my heart and soul and love you so much I want you to feel secure with me forever—not as long as you please me sexually or pay my bills or don't get ill or find a better person. That's not commitment, that's convenience."

Certain types of persons are attracted to this way of living, Dr. Rue says. Like the young girl who may lack confidence. "She is willing to exchange herself for some form of security. A young woman who has emotional maturity and self worth won't settle for this."

Or the insecure man. "One who is unable to face responsibility, who doesn't want to be tied down. If the going gets tough, he cops out. It's like waiting for the other shoe to fall."

He says, too, that a couple's future relationships will have less chance for stability.

Opposes Trend

But even though he opposes the trend, he says, "I don't want to demean or castigate young people. They don't have to take this wrong turn. Why don't they say, we don't like the results of married life. We demand better preparation for marriage (state law does allow courts to require premarital counseling for those under 18).

"Professional men are supposed to pick up the debris (postmarital discord) and it frustrates the hell out of me," Dr. Rue says. "Why isn't there a stream of young people in here preparing for marriage? If you find the right reason to marry and are properly prepared, you stand the best chance for being magnificently happy."

Of the 1,000 hours of counseling weekly at the institute, 1% or less deals with premarital counseling.

"It's a pretty foreign idea," Dr. Rue admits, but education is the solution. "John should really know Mary before he marries her. Now it's little more than a blood test and good luck."

Dr. Rue would like to see preparation for marriage offered by parents, schools beginning with kindergarten, religion programs and the professional community.

"If we don't react through logic, patience and understanding, this could be a warning of the society that Toynbee warned of—'destruction from within.' "

On an individual basis, he believes because of the double standard, it's generally the girl who's the loser." (1) When she compromises herself, she develops a reputation among men. (2) There's the obvious worry about pregnancy—no contraceptive is 100% sure. (3) There's a gradual buildup of fear—he could leave tomorrow—and insecurity which turns to anxiety or depression."

'Much Healthier'

Dr. Louis J. West, chairman of the UCLA school of psychiatric medicine and director of the Neuropsychiatric Institute, says living together is "much healthier psychologically than those not willing to make the commitment."

Commitment?

"In many instances," Dr. West says, "living together represents the desire for more meaningful commitment than they see in many legal marriages because their bond is a human one."

Dr. West, youthful father of three, says there are no universal statements or formulas that apply to all those who choose to live together. "You have to look at each separately . . . Not all are engaging in an idealistic trial marriage by any means. Motivations range from old-fashioned love affairs to convenient living arrangements to other extremes.

"Nevertheless, I'm impressed by many of those young people who take a didactic relationship very seriously . . . Many are actually elevating the meaning of marriage. When they sign that contract they want it to mean more than what it means to those who make vows they don't really intend to keep."

Dr. West believes living together is a reaction to the secular and commercial view of marriage. "Young people today don't want their marriages to be a small business. They're searching for a transcendent meaning of their own. They're very serious in their hearts and have invested a spiritual quality to this 'disgraceful' living together.

"Lots of these youngsters," Dr. West continues, "are trying to find a way of living in which material values are diminished and human values are elevated. They want love relationships to be strictly human. They don't want to be involved with government of institutional church."

There are risks, sure. "As long as there are risks, there is still romance," Dr. West says. "That's something that's just about disappeared from the American scene."

The risks derive mostly from the attitudes of others, Dr. West says—government agencies, employers. "It's a strain upon any couple that could serve as a binding force to show the naysayers they were wrong. That's not good either."

Dr. West says most risks are to the woman, for reasons Dr. Rue outlined as well as emotional risks for both. "If they are really unable to make a deep, emotional commitment, trial marriage may not fulfill its potential. The couple may hold back. But that may be just as likely to happen in a legal marriage."

Would a couple be likely to have one relationship after another? Perhaps, Dr. West says, but then they might go from marriage to marriage, too.

Dr. West finds irony in that parents often avert their gaze from their children's promiscuity as long as they avoid scandal, but when they take up housekeeping, "the parents face criticism and come down on the kids like a ton of bricks.

"Couples who live together often show more confidence and maturity than those who flit from person to person, using sex as part of a superficial way of contact, but avoiding much more interpersonal relationships."

THE INTIMATE NETWORK OF FAMILIES AS A NEW STRUCTURE

FREDERICK H. STOLLER

As indicated, my concern is less with improving that abstract concept, society, than in enhancing the possibilities of rich, creative, fulfilling, and satisfying family experiences for the family members. The bulk of the argument, up to this point, has suggested that the family in isolation from others finds such rich experiences more difficult to attain. The alternative structure which is being proposed is the development of particular kinds of relationships and arrangements *between families,* i.e., intimate networks.

Under the circumstances previously described, the isolated family functions as a team when coming into contact with anyone outside the family circle. As described by Motz,[11] the family behaves much as if they had read Goffman's description of "front stage" and "back stage" performances carried out by teams that must deal with an audience or public.[12] All members of the family collaborate to maintain a particular appearance before others which is substantially different from that which they permit themselves when not in the presence of strangers. Any substantial experience with families in the presence of other families reveals how early the children learn to collaborate in this particular charade. A reordering of this type of family custom would be necessary for any enduring relationship between families to develop.

In view of the increasing mobility of the American family and the relatively low likelihood that the extended family could be revived as a significant part of the family experience, the compelling alternative involves the development of intimacy *between* several families. This arrangement has been called an *intimate network,* and specifies certain characteristics if the family experience is going to be affected in signifi-

11. Annabelle B. Motz, "The Family as a Company of Players," *Trans-action,* vol. 2, no. 3 (1965), pp. 27-30.
12. E. Goffman, *The Presentation of Self in Everyday Life* (Garden City, N.Y., Doubleday, 1959).

cant ways. Briefly defined, an intimate network of families could be described as a circle of three or four families who meet together regularly and frequently, share in reciprocal fashion any of their intimate secrets, offer one another a variety of services and do not hesitate to influence one another in terms of values and attitudes. Behind this definition is a picture of a brawling, noisy, often chaotic convocation which develops its own set of customs for the purpose of coming together in terms of rich experiences rather than merely being "correct" and, in the process, achieves movement in terms of its own views of its arrangements and ways of operating. Such an intimate family network would be neither stagnant nor polite but would involve an extension of the boundaries of the intimate family. In order to specify how this might come about, a closer look at the specifications of the intimate network is in order:

1. *A circle of families.* Once a set of parents have joined themselves to a group of families, they have acknowledged certain limitations of the isolated family. There is only a minimal vision of the potentialities of family life available to them because their experience with families outside their own childhood is nonexistent. Their own expertise as child-rearers (particularly with their own children) is no longer pushed as a supreme illusion; the difficulty of the task is accepted and the need for continuous help, insight, and an occasional shakeup from outside their immediate family circle is accepted. They face the possibility that the needs of various family members, including themselves, cannot be met without services being extended from outside the small circle of the immediate family. They realize that these services, when coming from community agencies rather than intimates, lack the meaning and warmth that could be a necessary part of the richer family experience.

The number of families to be accommodated within an intimate network should be sufficient to provide a variety of viewpoints and services, and a richness of close contact without blocking the sharing which would be a necessary feature of this arrangement. Two families would not be adequate to deal with many of the problems that would inevitably arise and would not provide enough variety. Depending upon the size of the families, judgment would similarly suggest that a group much beyond four would be difficult to manage. However, there is nothing inherent in such a number and experience could well alter this judgment.

2. *Regular and frequent meetings.* In order for intimacy and sharing to be attained and maintained, frequency of contact is required. Intimacy is a fragile quality and requires both frequency and regularity, particularly in the formative phases. When coming together is an infrequent occurrence, families will either be on their best behavior, or will reserve

such consultations solely for major crises. It is one of the goals of the intimate network to explore not only the large, obvious issues of family living, but also, the mundane, day-to-day features which probably color family life more meaningfully than those aspects parents are likely to believe "important." Families that come together for the purpose of being honest with one another will obviously meet painful situations, the avoidance of which will be inevitable if there are clear escape routes through irregularity of contact. Knowledge of the other families, and the courage to be honest with one another, are expected to result from frequent and regular meetings.

3. *Reciprocal sharing.* While there are always limitations to what is shared, families in the intimate network would have to develop the freedom to permit the other families to peer behind the scenes. If help is to be sought and given, there must be an openness about what is needed. Under such an arrangement, secrecy becomes as much a self-delusion as an attempt to confuse others about the reality that exists within the family. Therefore, such families must voluntarily be able to be open as to what is occurring, and as to the feelings and relationships that exist between all members, revealing to the others the details of how they live together. The retention of family secrets requires unwritten contracts within the family to be mutually protective at the cost of honesty; in order to maintain such collusion, a variety of subterranean agreements are required which can only be maintained at considerable cost.

Within the intimate network, the emphasis would, of necessity, have to be upon reciprocity. The burden is not upon a particular family to show themselves while the others withhold important aspects of their lives, nor upon one group of people to reveal themselves before a group of voyeurs, but rather, upon the circle itself to develop a freedom for all members to show themselves in a variety of ways and, as time goes on, with less and less reluctance. Should role patterns between families develop in an exclusively hierarchical order, a truly intimate network could not be established.

4. *Exchange of services.* A classic fairy story concerns a person offered three magic wishes, the clues these choices give to his values and the consequences they have for his life. In much the same fashion, a family faced with a possible exchange of services with other families is faced with an array of possibilities; the requests that are made will be a function of their version of the possibilities inherent in family living. Therefore, the types of requests made between the families within the intimate network will be important expressions of their versions of family life, and should change as these families engage in their mutual

exploration of such potentialities. Actual help for crises would be one expected exchange of services. But on a less dramatic level one can envision the development of an interfamily consultation service in which various members of each family are called upon to aid in negotiations which are constantly required within families from time to time. It is entirely conceivable that the requests for services will move into more unexpected areas as the families become more creative about their arrangements for family living.

Implicit in the kinds of services that are created within the family network are versions of what is possible and what is available if creativity is applied toward family living. Accepting what is possible within the isolated family demonstrates a poverty of conceptualization about the conduct of one's life and an acceptance of what is given. What can be accomplished within an isolated family arrangement is extremely limited and the resources of any given family diminish the kinds of satisfactions that can be extended to the various members of the family. Therefore, the system of services that are developed within a network will be an important aspect of the creativity which is being applied to the circumstances of family living.

5. *The extension of values.* As the network becomes more intimate, that is, as members become increasingly more free to deal with one another in a spontaneous manner, there would be less and less reluctance to express whatever comes to mind toward members of other families. Ultimately, such a development would involve the attempt to influence the other families in terms of the values and attitudes they hold close. To the degree that there are differences between the families, such an interchange would not necessarily mean the adoption of one or another of these value systems, but rather, a tug of war between the varying world views. Out of this type of struggle it is conceivable that *an intimate network could develop new systems of attitudes and values that did not exist before in any of the member families.* Such a development would be dependent upon the method that the family networks developed to resolve deadlocks that arise between the members. The possibilities of values and attitudes based upon broader explorations than is generally the case gives rise to the possibility that richer and more realistic systems can be developed than is possible under the prevailing system of isolated families.

COLD MOUNTAIN FARM

JOYCE GARDENER

Given: 450 acres of land, twelve usable for farming or pasture, the remainder being old, neglected apple orchards (also pear, plum, and cherry trees) and young woods, in a mountainous upstate New York dairy-farming area. A beautiful piece of land, with three running streams in the springtime, but only one good spring for water in the summer, close to the five-bedroomed house. The farm is one mile off the main road, at the end of a rugged dirt road, a mile from the closest neighbor. There is no rent, no electricity, no telephone—and to acquire any of these would be extremely costly.

The Group: Anarchists. Mostly in their twenties, with children under six. A fluctuating population, up to thirty. About four couples and one or two single people consider this home. Mostly former residents of NYC, but some from other parts of the East Coast. Interrelationships have existed for as long as five years.

History: Goes back two and a half years, to NYC, where a communal loft once existed, with shared dinners and other occasions. Or back three years, when at least two families shared an apartment together for a few months. Or to last spring and summer, when a group of NYC anarchists used half an acre of a friend's land to farm on weekends.

More concretely, June 1966, to a "Community Conference" at the School of Living in Heathcote, Md., out of which emerged a new community—"Sunrise Hill"—at Conway, Mass. At least one person, loosely connected with the NYC anarchists, went to live there.

The rest of us continued to farm our friend's land on weekends during the summer, meeting at least once a month at different places in the country during the winter—living together for a few days, getting to know one another better, and making plans to start our own farm the following spring. Some people from Sunrise Hill also attended these meetings.

We finally located this place through a friend. About that time, Sunrise Hill was suffering its final collapse—due to internal conflicts— and four people from there eventually would join us.

From "The Cold Mountain Farm," *Modern Utopian*, August 1967. Appearing also as "Cold Mountain Farm" in *Communes U.S.A.*, by Richard Fairfield (Penguin Books Inc., Baltimore, 1972). Reprinted by permission.

ONTO THE LAND

Starting a community farm is an incredibly difficult thing. We didn't fully realize this when we began. Setting up a new farm—or rather, rehabilitating an old and neglected one—was at least a season's work. Not to mention compensating for the work which should have been done the previous autumn.

It was still cold, there was occasional snow, the house was difficult to heat, and no one was prepared to move in. The dirt road was all but impassable, we walked the mile through snow and later mud—carrying babies, supplies, bedding, etc.

Meanwhile we had to find a tractor immediately to haul manure for compost heaps. They should have been started the year before as they require three months' time to rot properly and we wanted to farm organically. We'd have to prune the neglected fruit trees within a month, since pruning too late in the season would shock them.

On the many rainy days we had to make the house liveable: build shelves, worktable, bookshelves, a tool shed, a mail box; install a sink; acquire tools and materials. Somehow, whatever needed to be done, there was always someone who knew how to do it or who was willing to find out how. But with each person having some particular responsibility upon himself, there wasn't time to work on group projects.

Well, we had a farm, didn't we? All we had to do was go there when it got nice and warm, plow the land, plant our seed, and wait for the vegetables to come. We didn't even have to pay any rent! It was so simple. No rush to get out there while it was still so cold.

Consequently, the farm was completely deserted until the end of April. Then news got out fast (we couldn't help but brag a little), and we found we had hundreds of friends who wanted to "come to the country." So we had to bite our tongues and violate all the laws of lower east side hospitality to avoid creating a youth hostel or a country resort. We lost a lot of friends that way.

Meanwhile, in NYC, an infinite number of conflicts existed growing out of two difficult years of co-existence, trying to work out an ideology based on anarchism-community-ecology-technology in an environment which presented a constant contradiction to it.

We had discouraged the city people. No one came. The land cried out to be tended, but people were preoccupied with their own personal grievances. The farm was all but deserted. The work fell entirely on the shoulders of a few people. Without telephone and often without car, we waited daily for friends and supplies to show up; waiting for reinforcements. Finally three friends arrived from Conway, reassuringly bringing all their worldly goods. The man started out at once, hooking up running water in the house, pruning some apple trees, then driving to a nearby town without a license or proper registration, and spending three days in jail. Soon he bought us a much-needed tractor. It was precisely this tractor (to this day still only half payed for) which shuttled up and down the one-mile dirt road, hauling cow shit (from neighboring farms, who proved surprisingly friendly) and transporting little children to the nearby town in lieu of Hershey bars—and then, as the time to plow grew nigh, flatly refused to budge.

There was absolutely nothing anyone could do. We had to wait for our friend from Florida to return. He was our only mechanic. Days passed and finally a few people started digging their own gardens—such a pathetic task for a farm that hoped to support some thirty people and then give out free food in the city.

But all this time there were small compensations. We had an opportunity now to explore this incredible land, watch the seasons change, see the snow melt and trees slowly push forth buds, see birds moving in and laying eggs; spy on porcupines each night loudly chomping on the house, make friends with cows and four wild horses grazing on neighboring fields, start to know one another in that unique way that only comes from living together.

TRIBAL FEELINGS

Now a few more old friends began to arrive. There was an incredible feeling of warmth, of family. We were becoming a tribe. There were long, good discussions, around the fire, into the night. Slowly, things were beginning to take shape. In those days I loved to look into the "community room," and see a bunch of people sprawled out on cushions around the floor, all so brown, their bodies so well-developed, their faces relaxed, naked or wearing clothes often of their own making. You could always spot someone from the city—by the whiteness of their flesh, the tenseness of their body.

It was my dream—and certainly no one openly disagreed with me— to become a tribe, a family of "incestuous brothers and sisters." Unfortunately, living so close, we probably made love less than when we lived in separate apartments in the city. And there was so much fear and tension in the air about *potential* affairs, that actual love-making all too seldom took place, and even physical contact became a rare thing. Even though we created our own environment at the farm, we still carried with us the repressions of the old environment, in our bodies and our minds.

While others were not actually opposed to these ideas, most people didn't feel quite ready for them, and certainly no one else bespoke the same vision. If we could find a form by which our visions could be shared. . . .

INCREDIBLE TRACTOR

Waiting for the tractor to be fixed (it took about a week and a half of hard labor), living our usual lives, making our own bread and yogurt, etc., we spoke to a nearby farmer and learned of a barn full of manure which he paid men to haul away for him. We offered to do it for him free, in exchange for manure to use as compost. He was so overjoyed that he offered to come up and plow our land in exchange for our labor. We thought he was joking, but a couple of days later, we heard a loud and unfamiliar motor coming up the hill, and there was that huge, incredible tractor. "Well, where do you want it?" And that's how we got six acres of land plowed and harrowed (later, we would plow a couple of acres ourselves). A couple of days later, we got our own tractor fixed in order to start hauling manure and planting at a furious pace, trying to get the crops in before it was too late. We were already at least a week behind most everyone else in the area . . . in a place with a *very short* growing season.

These people were so overwhelmingly happy to finally have the tractor, after weeks of frustrated waiting and digging by hand, that one person actually planted some forty mounds of zucchini and eighty mounds of acorn squash and several rows of corn in one day, by hand! Then he devised a method whereby he could dig five furrows at a time by building a drag with teeth for the tractor, and installing the three women as weights on the drag, where they could drop onion sets into the rows. That last part didn't work so well (all the onion sets had to be spaced again, by hand), but nonetheless, by the time the other folks got home about a week later, close to an acre of land had been planted.

Now that there were more of us, we were not so close. There was no real sense of community between us. There was good feeling, but no center, no clear-cut purpose. Some of the men felt an unfulfilled need to fight. The women felt an unfulfilled need to love.

About this time we undertook—or were overtaken by—what I consider one of our most challenging feats: trying to assimilate a young lawyer and his family, including two girls, aged four and six. Many a group meeting centered around the problem of "the kids." Because they were breaking out of a sick environment, their parents felt they needed a maximum of patience and love and understanding. Others felt they needed simply to be treated as human beings and that their mother should not repress the anger and frustration which she obviously felt.

Most of us felt we should in fact try to let them work *through* their hangups and hopefully eventually come out the other side. Let them yell "penis" and "vagina" at the top of their lungs. Let them throw Raggedy Anne into the cellar and elaborate upon her tortures while chanting, "No, you *can't* come out of the cellar!" all day long. But what no one seemed to be able to endure were the howls and wails which rose from the lungs of one sister after the other, time after time, all day long, and particularly on rainy days, of which there were many, locked up with them in the house all day long.

Apparently we just weren't strong enough nor healthy enough ourselves to be able to cope with these children. And their parents, who had had such great hopes of finding in us a healthy environment, soon had to build their own shelter in order to remove themselves from our environment.

By this time the house had become so generally unbearable that everyone else as well had decided to move out. Just before then, there had been twenty adults and ten children—with only three or four adults and one child sleeping outside—living so close together in that house. It seemed absurd to try to keep the house clean (anarchism does not necessarily mean chaos). And the flies were so bad that if we hung five strips of flypaper fresh each day in each room, by evening they were dripping with puddles of gooey flies. It was just barely possible to exist in the midst of all these copulating multitudes. (We didn't like the idea of using poison sprays, with all the cats and babies.)

And so, in a burst of desperation to escape the noise, children, chaos, flies, tension . . . everybody dropped everything and for a few days did nothing but work on their own shelters. The house was almost deserted.

People who get into community too often forget about the importance of solitude. And we were lucky enough to have plenty of land so that everyone could have their own shelter. But personal possessions (especially kitchen stuff), which had originally been pooled with a great sense of communal enthusiasm, were righteously carted off to their owners' shelters.

HOSTILE OUTSIDERS

About this time we started coming into conflict with the outside world. Ever since it got warm, we had all been walking around more or less nude most of the time. Unfortunately, we had to discontinue this most pleasant practice when neighbors started to mention casually that they could "see everything" from their property on the hill, and that "people were talking." Our local reputation was getting progressively worse. There were too many articles in the mass media about hippies, often loosely connected with legalizing marijuana. The local people, who had originally just thought of us as "strange," and had then begun to accept us as old-fashioned organic farmers, could now call us "hippies" and forbid their kids to have anything to do with us.

The local sheriff began to take an interest in us. Whenever we went into town, we were stopped by the cops. And a friendly gas station attendant told us the highway patrol had been told to watch us. It was easy to be paranoid, to imagine their trying to take our kids away for nudity. It was terrible to compromise, but most of us began to wear clothes again. That was a great loss.

ECONOMIC ARGUMENT

I suppose our first and worst economic argument was whether or not to buy chickens. At first, it was incredible how little a problem money had been. Whoever came just threw in whatever they had—$100 or $200 perhaps—and we'd live off that until someone got a tax return, a welfare check, or whatever. We never did spend more than $25 a week on food—even when there were thirty people. But the chicken crisis involved all sorts of things. Did we need eggs (wasn't wheat germ good enough)? Was it morally right to take eggs from chickens; wasn't it cruel to keep chickens caged?—but if we didn't cage them how would we keep them out of the garden? Were we really saving money on eggs, if we had to spend money on the chickens, chicken wire, and all kinds of feed? Who was going to plant an acre of millet and an acre of corn to feed them? Who would build the chicken coop? This was the first time I remember hearing anyone say, "Well, *I* won't give any money for chickens"—using money as a weapon, a personal source of power. And it wasn't long before money again became a personal possession.

BAD TIMES

I liked the young lawyer and his wife because they often spoke at meetings on a personal level, about how they *felt* about things, while most of our people maintained a kind of cold objectivity, only discussing things external to themselves. It was this lack of "feeling" which brought the lawyer to say that *Cold* Mountain was certainly an apt name for the place. And his wife complained, not unjustly, that there was not enough making of music, not enough dancing, and she felt her joy was being stifled here.

We seemed to have reached an all-time low. We had passed the summer solstice. Our money was all but depleted. We could work at haying for local farmers, but $1/hr. wasn't a hell of a lot. Until now we seemed to have been subsisting mostly on enthusiasm. Now it was hot and even our enthusiasm was gone. There was a general feeling of emptiness. Times were very bad, but we tried to hold on until the times were more favorable. We decided to limit ourselves to just a few staples (rice, oil, powdered milk, soy sauce, flour, salt, soy beans, brewers yeast, molasses, grass—always purchased in huge quantities to save money) and whatever we could get from our environment—at this time of year, dandelion greens, wintergreen and burdock root and, in a little while, fresh strawberries, rhubarb and wild leeks. And we'd soon be getting edible weeds from the garden: milkweed, sorrel, lamb's quarters. And then we would discover violet leaves, for salads. Still later, there would be mushrooms, raspberries, currants and blackberries; wild mint, thyme and oregano; green apples, pears and plums—and by then we would be getting at least zucchini, peas and baby onions from the garden.

Then, one morning someone took the shotgun and killed a groundhog. We'd been talking about hunting for a long time, but most of us were vegetarians and meat was a rare sight in these parts (the hunter himself hadn't eaten meat for the last two years!). But that night he cooked up a fine groundhog stew. Which he ate. And that big pot of stew sat on the stove and people thought about it and talked about it and went to bed without dinner. In the middle of the night a couple of us woke up and had a little. Next day some of us had some for lunch. Only four people remained staunch in their vegetarianism, and mostly they didn't condemn the rest. Each of us worked it out in our own way.

Still, the diet wasn't satisfying. Subsistence living was one thing, but we all felt damned hungry. We called a meeting and decided this had a great deal to do with the cooking—which, until then, had been just a matter of chance impulse, so that the task usually fell into the hands of the same people every day. Their boredom with cooking showed up in the quality of their meals. It seemed reasonable enough that if two different people were responsible for the kitchen each day, there would be more interest and variety in cooking, the house would be kept neater and more organized, and it would leave the other people free to concentrate completely on the garden or whatever. At that time we had fourteen adults, so it was pleasant enough to know you only had to cook and clean one day/week.

It's amazing how much this helped. We'd all begun to grow so discouraged with each other and the mess we were living in. We all felt like pigs and everyone blamed the next person. Our morale was sinking fast, the kids were screaming, and we were at each other's throats. Now suddenly the house was clean—spick and span, almost. People smiled at each other again. The meals were delicious. We felt we had been reborn. We'd stuck it out through hard times, and now virtue had its reward.

At that time, four Puerto Rican friends from the city joined us. They emanated new energy and worked hard. And they had a certain revolutionary spirit which none of us quite had. One would say, "Communism and capitalism—they are both no good. But if I had something like this farm to fight for—why, I would give my life for it." At night you could hear the guitars and there were big fires, and dancing, and singing. The hardest work was over. All we had to do now was weed and mulch. Now we had time to make music.

PUBLICITY

About this time, an article appeared about us in the *East Village OTHER*—without our knowledge or consent—claiming we needed people to help out on the farm (as if we hadn't had enough trouble discouraging people we knew from coming up!). And we were soon flooded with letters, and every two or three days a new visitor would arrive. It created terrible tensions to have to ask them to leave, to tell them it was all a mistake. And then a couple of people we *did* know arrived and announced their intention to move in. Some of us didn't want to live with these people, while others either wanted them to stay or felt we didn't have any right to ask them to leave. We had decided a long time ago that if this happened, each person in the community would just do as he felt best, and there would be no group decisions.

But how can you ask someone that you know to leave—particularly when they've brought all their things and say they have no place else to go? I think this must be a dilemma suffered by all communities. Certainly my way of dealing with it (absolute frank honesty) was far from effective. They just stayed. And stayed. And gradually, for this reason and others, the warmth and trust and sharing between us began to die. Whatever tribal or family feelings we had had were gone.

We weren't ready to define who we were; we certainly weren't prepared to define who we weren't—it was still just a matter of intuition. We had come together for various reasons—not overtly for a common idea or ideal, but primarily because there was land and there was supposed to be a "community." Even in the original community, there were people who thought of themselves (and their reason for being here) as being primarily communitarians, or primarily farmers and back-to-the-soil revolutionaries, or primarily political revolutionaries (anarchists) or "tao-archists" for whom farming and community was just one integral part of the totality, or just plain hermits who wanted to live in the woods. All of these different people managed to work together side-by-side for a while, but the fact was that there was really no shared vision.

And then still more people arrived—people we had all been looking forward to seeing. And the house was very full. And there was a lot of confusion. And it was very difficult to cook for that many people. Again, tensions began to mount. There was so little money, and now there were three or four pregnant women here, and one or two nursing mothers. Their dietary needs were very specific, and important, and the community was unable to fulfill them. They were forced to fall back on their own resources. In similar ways, one began to feel they couldn't trust the community to meet their needs, to take care of them in an emergency. There was a feeling of general malaise. The garden wasn't being weeded. The grass was growing higher and higher. Everyone felt as if everyone else was irresponsible.

In a community, things happen on such a large scale that you need the cooperation of other people in order to accomplish almost anything. But now one began to feel as if it was easier to do a thing by oneself. It was hot. Laziness had set in, very firmly. The word "failure" was being tossed around a lot. People began to just look after themselves, and to talk as if the only reason they were here was the land. The City suddenly seemed to hold a great attraction, and whenever there was a car going in, it would be filled to capacity. The young lawyer and his family finally left, quietly.

There was one ray of light in these somber times. A new couple arrived, to stay. Nobody knew them when they came, but everyone liked them at once. They brought new energies with them, and they lifted our spirits. Slowly, all the stragglers had left—empty people who had come to fill themselves, sapping our energies, needing to be taken care of and giving nothing at all—and now there were only between four and six couples and a few single people left.

WINTER APPROACHES

So we all lived together, peaceably enough, until one night it was very cold and wet and windy, and we could smell the coming of autumn. Then it was time to begin thinking about what we'd be doing in the winter—staying here, or moving on—and making plans accordingly. Mostly we had to consider the hardship of a very cold winter, no gas or electricity, a one-mile dirt road which would probably be inaccessible because of heavy snow (even during the summer, only jeeps and 4-wheel-drive cars and trucks could climb that road).

There were five couples, three of the women were pregnant, and a fourth was nursing. The babies were due in October, November and February. The first two couples wanted to deliver their own but not take the chance of doing it here. A single girl was already building a small stone house for the winter. Another man intended to live in the big house for the winter. Almost all hoped to be here early next Spring. By this time, two couples and a girl had moved entirely into their own shelters.

The communal garden was a monstrous failure. After the original enthusiasm of planting, hardly anyone cared enough to weed the rows. (Of course, the huge amount of rain this year retarded the growth of the crops and caused the weeds to grow like crazy! and six acres is a hell of a lot of land to weed by hand. If we try again next year, we'll certainly have to get a cultivator.) At least two acres of garden were lost, either because they weren't weeded adequately, or because they were planted too late and the growing season was too short, or because there wasn't enough sun and there was too much rain, or because of the aphids, or the potato blight. . . .

We didn't become *new* people—we just became physically healthy people. We didn't find a way of sharing our visions (in fact, we didn't even have a conscious understanding of the *need* for such a thing) and we didn't have a shared vision to bring us and hold us together.

We had plowed and begun to plant the earth, but we had not pierced our own ego skins. Decay, stagnation had already set in. I went into the woods to meditate. The woods explained: it was high time we plowed the earth of this community. We must apply the blade to ourselves and cut back the outer skin to expose the pulsating flesh. And then we must harrow and pulverize the outer skin and use our egos for compost. Then, in the new flesh, we must plant the seeds of the people we wish to become.

AREA 6

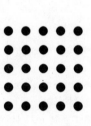

ENCOUNTER IN
MARITAL FAILURE

THE SCOPE OF SUCCESSFUL MARRIAGE

Judson T. Landis and Mary G. Landis

Where does successful marriage begin? Not with the wedding. Rather it begins somewhere in an unending circle made up of many parts— childhood experiences and feelings, parents who knew cooperation, learning experiences in youth and adulthood, and attitudes in every area of living.

A backward look at the many topics discussed in this book brings the realization that to build a successful marriage is an accomplishment unlimited in its implications. It goes far beyond the horizons of the two who marry. A good marriage becomes a force having an impact on the lives of other people encountered by either member of the pair in daily living and it reaches into the lives of future generations. It includes romance and responsibility, sacrifice, drudgery, and disappointments, as well as fundamentally rewarding fulfillments—emotional, social, sexual, psychic, and even material.

People who build successful marriages live creatively at each stage of life. During the dating years they seek to understand themselves and others. As lovers and as newly married people they try to learn to perceive the needs and feelings of those they love. They learn to bend and adjust in order to develop relationships that give meaning to life. When children come, they are able to grow up to the challenges and responsibilities of parenthood, and yet cherish and nurture the relationship with their mates in such a way that the experience of parenthood enriches the marriage. Always an essential condition for successful marriage is growth in the two who marry, a continually expanding perception of the needs and feelings of others and an increasing ability and willingness to give acceptance, respect, and cooperation. Those who build successful marriages reject any conception of life or relationships as static; they perceive that people change and that the quality of a relationship is never absolutely set. They discover with the years of living that their interaction has the potential either for growth and improvement or for deterioration and destructiveness. They are aware of the choice in their own hands of determining the direction of their relationship.

From Judson T. Landis and Mary G. Landis, *Building a Successful Marriage*, fifth edition (Englewood Cliffs, New Jersey: Prentice-Hall, Inc., © 1968), pages 531-532. Reprinted by permission.

People who build successful marriages comprehend that life always offers a balance of compensations and disappointments. They accept in the mate weaknesses and the failure to be all that might seem totally desirable, with a measure of philosophical equanimity. Each one's confidence that his own deficiencies will be overlooked and forgotten and love freely given to him anyway arises in part from his willingness to accept and forget the mate's corresponding imperfections. With their acceptance of the contradictions that are inevitably a part of marriage, and their awareness of the balance of joy and pain that life offers, they find that the bonds between them become a settled, irrevocable reality.

As such couples advance in years, they continue to reach new levels of understanding of their mates and themselves. The wisdom gained through the years and the security of a firmly based affection enables them to cope with the new and potentially frustrating physical and emotional conditions in themselves and their mates that come with aging.

In sum, two people who build a successful marriage make the most of their attributes at each stage of life. They live together in such a way that the direction of their dynamic relationship is toward excellence.

PROFESSIONALS VIEW THEIR FAILING MARRIAGE

HERBERT A. OTTO

There is much agreement today that American society is in transition, and considerable disagreement as to where this process may or should lead. Among the social frameworks seemingly caught on the crest of this wave of transition are the institutions of marriage and the family.

This is never more clear than when we examine our divorce statistics. It is safe to say that most men, women, and children in the United States have been touched by this experience, either in their own families or among friends and close acquaintances. One analyst has predicted that one-third to one-half of all marriages occurring this year are destined to end in a divorce court. I am reminded of a cartoon which recently appeared in the *New Yorker*: a young couple is shown leaving what is identified by a sign as the home of a justice of the peace. The bride, dressed in the latest "far-out" fashion, turns brightly to her young man and says, "Darling! Our first marriage!"

In part, this book is a result of my own experience with divorce. Throughout this painful process, I was struck by the fact that a large percentage of my colleagues (psychologists, psychiatrists, and social workers) either had undergone or were then undergoing a divorce. In the course of informal conversations, it became clear that even those professionals who considered themselves happily married were increasingly inclined to question the contemporary institutions of marriage and the family. I began to take informal notes, and in the course of two and a half years had more than sixty conversations with members of the helping professions concerning their marriages and divorces. Reviewing these notes, some main themes or threads could be distinguished:

1. With very few exceptions, divorce was as painful and as confusing an experience for these professionals as for any of their clientele. Many psychotherapists reported remarks from their patients such as, "Doctor, if you can't make it, how can we?"

2. There was universal dissatisfaction with the divorce process, the legal complications and procedures, which were seen to be in great need

of simplification and reform. Divorce, as an institution, was clearly recognized as being in need of regeneration. Many questioned alimony payments for wives able to support themselves or having private means.

3. Joking reference was often made to the fact that, not too long ago, man was thought to be naturally monogamous. The extensive divorce rate and the widespread practice of extra-marital affairs, in addition to the Kinsey Report and a host of contemporary studies, call into question the appropriateness of a monogamous relationship in which husband and wife depend exclusively upon each other for sexual satisfaction.

4. Many of the professionals interviewed noted that choices of mate are often made when the individual does not have the maturity and wisdom to make a good choice. Recognition of this fact has accelerated the acceptance of, and trend toward, plural marriages.

5. It was generally agreed that this society's expectations of marriage are such that they militate against the very existence of the institution in its present form. (See Hobbs, pages 30-31, for a succinct summary of these expectations.) Partners expect too much, and then are disappointed because their needs cannot be met. It was a common observation that people often seem to outgrow each other, or to grow apart despite their best efforts to the contrary.

6. There was a varied reaction to recent research which, in Reuben Hill's words, "Suggests that the advent of a child is not necessarily the fulfillment of marriage, but possibly the first point of cleavage that separates husband and wife—and that this cleavage widens with each additional child, disrupting the marriage relationship to such an extent that when the children are adolescents, the parents are so far apart that instead of being bereft at their leaving, they are, in fact, reunited, happy to pick up where they left off in the wonderful days before they had children."[1] Some professionals saw this process at work in their own marriage, others did not.

7. There were similarly varied reactions to Cuber's recent volume, *The Significant Americans*,[2] a study which sought to examine whether men and women of achievement also tended to have outstanding sexual and emotional lives. (Cuber concluded that a large majority of these successful Americans tended to develop cool, detached, almost loveless marriages, possibly because this kind of relationship is so well adapted to the pursuit of a career.) While many professionals saw themselves as

1. For a popular summary of this recent research, see "The Most Unexpected Threat to a Good Marriage," *McCall's* (July, 1967), pp. 94 ff.
2. Dr. John F. Cuber and Peggy B. Harroff (Mrs. Cuber), *The Significant Americans* (New York, Appleton-Century-Crofts, 1965).

"family-oriented" rather than "career-oriented," there was some recognition that a demanding clinical practice or other career demands had interfered with a marriage.

8. Roughly 30 to 40 percent of the persons interviewed would agree with Cadwallader that, "Contemporary marriage is a wretched institution. It spells the end of voluntary affection, of love freely given and joyously received. Beautiful romances are transmuted into dull marriages; eventually the relationship becomes constricting, corrosive, grinding and destructive. The beautiful love affair becomes a bitter contract."[3] Surprisingly, however, more than 80 percent expected to remarry "within a reasonable time."

In questioning the institution of marriage, we question indirectly the whole area of man-woman relatedness and the nature and quality of contemporary relationships between the sexes. Perhaps one of the clearest indications of the deep separation between the sexes is evidenced by the pattern of seating arrangements at most lay and professional meetings. Women tend to sit together, as do men. What appears to be in operation here is a combination of estrangement, mild anxiety, and hostility; sex stereotypes[4] are clearly in full bloom. These elements are characteristic of most man-woman relationships today.

3. Mervyn Cadwallader, "Changing Social Mores," Current (February, 1967), p. 48.
4. Herbert A. Otto, Group Methods Designed to Actualize Human Potential (Chicago, Ill., Achievement Motivation Systems, 1968), pp. 52-59.

A CHILD'S EYE VIEW OF A FAILING MARRIAGE

J. LOUISE DESPERT, M.D.

How did these events in the adult world appear to Mary?

Mary is a child of superior gifts. She has greater than average intelligence and greater than average vitality, and she can tell us more about herself and other children than the average child is able to do.

Her tantrums—those tempestuous demonstrations which a psychologist blandly termed "motor expression of hostile feelings"—reveal an intensity of protest which many another child in a divorce situation would give vent to if he could.

Her dreams and fantasies, her outspoken play activities trace clearly the orbit around which a child's emotional disturbances revolve.

Let us not be misled by the extravagant form which marriage failure has taken in Mary's case, her "three daddies and three mommies." Multiple divorce is not average, but neither is it rare. This is an extreme case, but not an exceptional one; no new phases of human behavior are exhibited here, but rather the familiar ones raised to their *nth* power. Whether she had two daddies or four or six, this child would suffer the same hurt and use it as a whip against the world. Mary speaks for all children of unsuccessful marriage who have been left to find their own explanation of what is happening and to form their own defenses against it.

So plainly does she speak that we can watch the effects of her parents' discord on Mary step by step, almost day by day. We can trace the change in Mary from a rosy, happy baby to a bundle of fierce hostilities and desperate defenses at six.

On the surface it was a swift and sudden change. Mary was not quite three years old when her mother divorced and remarried within a few weeks. Those who knew Mary at that time witnessed a spectacular transformation in her personality, and did not hesitate to relate it to the breaking up of the home. But a perceptive observer of children would have picked up the danger signals which flickered on and off for many months before.

Mary began to stall a little over her food; she began to hang back from playmates she once ran eagerly to join. At the words, "time for bed," a keen watcher would have seen her pupils widen in fear; rest-less nights, bad dreams were beginning. The tempo of Mary's day, once so quick and joyous, was slowing. The gaily colored, steadily spinning top was losing its momentum, was wavering.

It was natural that these first signs of faltering should pass unnoticed by Mary's parents. So faint, so evanescent were they that Catherine and Peter would have had to be far more alert than they could possibly be now, enmeshed as they were in the tightening web of their own conflict.

Catherine wondered once or twice whether Mary was not going to begin biting her nails; little tense gestures, fingers to mouth, had come to her, as it were, out of the corner of her eye. But nail-biting was out of character with her bright happy Mary, and Catherine dismissed the thought.

Catherine and Peter were also lulled by that little knowledge which is sometimes dangerous. In discussing children from broken homes it is customary to date the maladjustment from the point of the break. Statistics painstakingly compiled, stamped, and passed through a tabulating machine are quoted with the weight of vast numbers to demonstrate that such children stand a good chance to go to rack and ruin—*after* their parents have dissolved the marriage contract and dispersed the home.

Tags and labels, classifications, inflexible demarcation lines are tools of some technical convenience, but they do not reveal the individual drama tucked away inside each pigeonhole. The drama begins long before a separation is even thought of. Divorce is not the beginning of the child's troubles. Divorce is the end result of a conflict which has already engulfed the whole family.

The child is warned of his parents' difficulties long before they broach the subject to him, if they do. He has his own means of detection, efficient though inarticulate. He knows that something is amiss and he feels threatened by some indefinite yet powerful source of danger.

He reveals this knowledge in unmistakable ways. To be sure, he does not come and say, "You know what? My parents are going to get a divorce!" But even from the outside some signs can be observed. He may become apprehensive, irritable, restless, aggressive, or, on the contrary quieter, less attentive, less interested in his usual activities. These changes, too small perhaps to be boldly revealing, yet say unequivocally, "Danger! Someone, do something!"

The real revelation, however, is not there. It makes itself legible and audible beyond doubt in another language, the language of the child's dreams and the child's play.

Here the child develops his new themes, expressive of what he fears may be going on between his parents. Here is enacted the drama of being abandoned, left to fight for himself in a friendless world. Here he sees his parents (or the king and queen or prince and princess of the story) going each his way, either childless or disputing over the child. Animals may be substituted for the human cast of characters, but the pattern and the message are the same. The child is attuned to the internal conflict of his parents, a conflict which they themselves may not yet have voiced or may have taken great pains to conceal.

WHAT THE CHILD SEES

So Catherine and Peter, anticipating no trouble from that quarter, saw no signs of trouble. They had no warning of the child's receptiveness to the emotional state of her parents. They felt secure that the secret of their conflict was well concealed.

After all, it should not be difficult to keep a secret from a three-year-old. Her parents may be suffering an upheaval, but the ordered routine of her life goes on as usual. And her understanding is surely very limited.

But let Mary tell it as she saw it—as countless children have experienced it and later revealed it in the course of treatment. Here we have the child's first inner reaction to something unusual:

Last night I woke up and I heard Daddy yelling and Mommy was crying. I never heard that before.

And again:

Today when Daddy came home he didn't pick me up, but he and Mommy started to whisper about something. They were too busy to play with me.

Catherine and Peter were trying their best to shield the children. They checked their quarrels in mid-torrent, to tiptoe down the hall and make sure the children were asleep. They smiled at each other and talked of everyday things in the children's presence. But a young child lives by feelings, not words, and is sensitive to the subtle expressions of feeling to which a grownup, dependent on words, has become dulled:

Mommy and Daddy are not the same as they used to be. When Mommy kisses me good night she's always in a hurry. When Daddy is telling me a story he stops in the middle and looks at me as if I wasn't there. Sometimes he squeezes me too hard when he says good-by. I get scared.

Mommy is always on the telephone. When I come in she starts to whisper.

Why doesn't Nanny like it here any more? Nanny was crying and she said she was going away.

I'm scared. Maybe I've been a bad girl.

These are some of the thoughts which assailed Mary's mind. She could not have said them in words; as "thoughts" they were barely formed. She gathered such bits and pieces of information over a period of months.

Through these months her security in her parents was being undermined. By the time Catherine brought herself to the point of telling her children the hard news, Mary was already shaken. Inwardly she quivered with fears; outwardly she had begun to bristle with childishly inadequate defenses against the situation which, without explanation and reassurance from her parents, could only be felt by the child as a threat of total destruction.

To Mary as to all young children, her parents were no ordinary human beings. They could do no wrong; they always knew the answers; they had the magic to dispel every fear, ward off every danger. They were all love, all help and protection; all power. They were God and more than God, because God is someone far away whom you never see, but parents are there and they are real to the touch, the sight, the hearing.

In so absolute an attitude there is no room for complexities and shadings, no ifs, buts, or maybes. At the same time, what Mary was witnessing during those months was in fact a situation gone out of control. Things were wrong for the first time in her short life, and apparently her parents could do nothing to set them right.

Worse than this, her parents themselves were *making* things wrong; they themselves were changing in inexplicable ways. But her mother and father could not be wrong. They were the very essence and substance of rightness, the final authority, the unshakable strength and support of her world. So it must be she herself who was wrong, who was bad. She was bad, and something terrible was going to happen to her. Inwardly the helpless protest had begun: *No, no, no, it must not happen to me!*

"DADDY CAN NOT GO!"

Like most adults, Mary's mother believed that a child so young cannot understand anyway, so why explain? When circumstances forced her to an explanation at last, she remembered reading in a magazine article that ideas can be communicated to children by way of fantasy. So one evening she began telling a bedtime story: A daddy bear went on a long journey and got lost, and another daddy bear came to look after the mother bear and the little baby bears—

She did not get far. Mary put both hands over her ears and demanded, "The other story, the one you always tell—YES, YOU KNOW!— about the little girl and the good fairy."

Catherine gave up the daddy-bear version, but the failure of this little excursion into modern psychology added to her feelings of inadequacy and tension—which, of course, were passed on to the children.

Her next attempt was the direct approach, one frequently used by parents in similar straits. To the beleaguered parents it appears, at least, to be direct, but so confused and inhibited are they by their conflicting emotions that even their most forthright effort comes out in the end as not direct enough.

A few days after the fairy-tale fiasco Catherine called the children from play into her room. She was going to tell them calmly and frankly that there was going to be a change in their lives. Their father must go to work in a faraway city and the family could not go with him.

The unhappy Peter had in fact decamped a week before. Powerless to cope with the crisis in his marriage, he had abruptly requested his transfer to the Chicago branch of his firm.

If this seems like an unfeeling way to deal a blow to children, we must consider that the action takes place in a setting of general confusion. The adult actors in the drama are deeply shaken, unclear about their own reactions, unable to face the stark realities of today and of the days which will follow.

It is an ancient protective device, as old as man, to run away as Peter did, and an equally time-honored method was Catherine's when she evaded the real issue. People have always tried to spare themselves and, they hoped, others by retreating from or denying a too painful contingency. More needs to be said, and will be elsewhere, about these protective devices, the function they serve and the scars they leave behind.

At this acute moment Catherine, besieged by conflicting impulses, seized upon Peter's removal to Chicago as the readiest explanation to give the children, one they would understand, one which would not hurt them too much. How frighteningly inadequate it must be, to the young who live not by intellect but by feeling and whose sharp perceptions have caught the deeper emotional undercurrents of the situation, she very quickly discovered.

As she heard herself say, "Daddy has gone away," these few words, openly spoken for the first time, threw her into a panic. Gone was her resolution to speak calmly and frankly. The rest of her message was delivered in a noticeably shaky voice as she became increasingly frightened at revealing her secret and aware at the same time that she was not telling the real truth of the situation. She watched the children's reaction with an apprehension which she was too deeply troubled to conceal.

Mary wriggled and fretted inarticulately; her mother's words carried little meaning to her, but her mother's mood was perfectly communicated. Jane, however, rebounded with the ingenuous enthusiasm of a child who for once has been able to beat a grownup to the draw: they would all go to Chicago! By car, by train, maybe they would even fly! She waited, breathless, certain that her wonderful solution would set them all packing trunks on the instant.

At this moment Mary, taking courage from her big sister, found her voice. "Daddy CAN NOT GO!" she screamed. Or if he went she was going with him, but he was not to go anyway, and that's all!

Catherine, trapped by the unforeseen inadequacy of her explanation, tried to improve on it. It was wartime; travel was difficult; they could not find a place to live in Chicago. Weaker and weaker, her excuses trailed lamely on. No one, certainly not the children and by now not even Catherine, had the faintest illusion that these diffuse apologies cleared the air or soothed the heart.

The issue fundamental to children, the question of whether their parents love and will take care of them, still remained unspoken and unresolved. A housing shortage in Chicago could scarcely explain the threatened end of the world.

THE UNSPOKEN QUESTIONS

Mary struggled to understand. No one had told her the truth about what was happening, so she sought the truth in her own terms.

Why has Mommy let Daddy go away? Maybe she sent him away. Can this be a punishment for being bad? Maybe Daddy was bad. But what could he have done?

Maybe—this was a terrible possibility—maybe Daddy went away because he didn't love Mary any more?

And if Daddy, why not Mommy too?

This was unbearable, unthinkable. Yet Daddy was gone; that, she knew, was really true.

The anguished questions buzzed in and out, giving her no peace, and meanwhile her outer world changed with dizzying swiftness. Daddy is gone. Mother leaves, but she is coming back (six weeks in Reno). Mary and Jane are left alone with a new nurse who doesn't believe in giving in to children's whims. Mother comes back and in a few days there is a new strange man in the house whom one is supposed to call "Daddy."

But he isn't my Daddy. My real Daddy's gone away. If I'm good maybe he'll come back and stay with us. Why can't I have two daddies? But will this new Daddy let him come back? Maybe he'll stop him!

Now the changes in Mary's behavior become dramatic and obvious. She is sullen and dreamy, absorbed in her own inner dialogue. She no longer asks questions. When her mother tries to draw her out, she is either unresponsive or actively belligerent. To every approach Mary's answer is, "Leave me alone!" or even, "Shut up!"

This "changed" mother can't help any more; why should Mary tell her anything? She has spoiled the chance of Daddy coming back by bringing this new daddy into the house. And many times it seems to Mary that her mother does not love her either.

Is Mary so very wrong about this? Catherine has just gone through the painful experience of divorce. All her efforts to protect the children from this upheaval, though often misdirected, have been nonetheless sincere, and have additionally taxed her already overtaxed emotions. Now she is trying to make a new start with Andrew.

Andrew is a kind, intelligent man. He is doing his best to pull things together for all of them.

And here is Mary, sulking, rejecting every advance. Mary is making things very difficult, and it is to be expected that Catherine is occasionally sharp and impatient with her. Catherine is groping for emotional stability; the failure of her first marriage hangs heavy over her and she is doubly tense in her effort to make a success of her second. Is it surprising that she sometimes resents this little girl who sharpens her own guilt feelings, and who by her troublesome behavior endangers the precious relationship with her new husband? Mary and her mother clash like two pendulums swinging between the extremes of love and hate.

Mary both loves and hates her mother, but toward her mother's new husband Mary suffers no conflict of emotions. For her new daddy she has simple, unconfused hatred. Jane has been able to accept him to a degree, but not Mary. She sneers at his attempts to woo her, mocks his baby talk and corrects his language. His almost daily gifts she spurns or destroys. And when she sees her mother kissing him her sullen façade is torn by an explosion of the fears, the hatreds, the anguish pent within her. She screams, scratches, kicks; her child face is contorted and her child mouth spits filth and violence. She is an erupting volcano of boiling emotions.

During the first year of this second marriage Mary took no comfort; on the contrary, her agony and her protest sharpened. She dawdled endlessly at meals, cramming food into her mouth only to spew it at last over the table, the floor, the walls. Almost any small frustration could become the trigger for a temper tantrum; if she was unable to fasten the belt of her dress she became a raging demon of fury. She had sudden headaches, sudden spells of nausea.

In each of these episodes Mary was attempting to do the impossible: to reconcile her overwhelming feelings of love and hate.

"Mommy, I have a headache." *Mommy will come and hold me, stroke my head, love me.* "Mommy, I have a headache." *Mommy wants to go out, and I am spoiling her fun and annoying her.*

At the end of the year Jackie was born, in Mary's eyes another rival. One way to compete with a baby is to become as helpless and babyish as he is. Mary, who had never sucked her thumb, now had it constantly in her mouth. She could not walk upstairs; she had to be carried.

She was deathly afraid of the dark, afraid to go to sleep and confront the terrors awaiting her in her nightmares. In the morning she was a tired, cranky little girl, fussing, crying, refusing to perform the smallest tasks.

MARY AT SCHOOL

At four and a half Mary was sent to nursery school. Catherine, still trying to do her best for her little girl, chose the school with care, and Mary's teacher was sensitive and soon became aware of the depth of Mary's trouble. For the first month Mary hung onto her skirt, and this warm and sympathetic woman encouraged the frightened child to stay close to her. For a time an assistant teacher took over the rest of the group because of Mary's incessant demand for her teacher's attention.

Every aspect of living had become an ordeal for Mary. For her afternoon nap she had to be placed in a separate room so that the other children might not be disturbed, and the teacher had to remain with her. There was an elaborate ritual: Mary would kiss the teacher and demand to be kissed in return; then she would lie down and sing a song to her doll; then she must have a song from the teacher. A moment later she was up, kissing the teacher, beginning the whole ritual over again.

The toilet was a problem: she would watch the other children, but would not go to the toilet until they had left. Then she went in alone, and remained so long she had to be coaxed to come out.

She took things surreptitiously, a toy from a child, a pencil or coin from the teacher's desk.

In the course of the school year the affection and warmth of her teachers began to bring results. Mary rested better and made less of the toilet problem. She ceased to take things. She was able to detach herself from her teacher for short periods. But usually she fixed on one other child, a younger or smaller one whom she could dominate or make the victim of her aggressive attacks, a substitute for Jackie at home. She pulled this child from the others, disrupting their play, and excited her chosen companion with wild fantasies. Here is one from the teacher's record:

> Mary goes to the group which is building a city out of blocks. She gets hold of shy, timid Jimmy, her current bosom companion, and drags him to the bottom of the stairs leading to the roof.

Mary: You know what's up there?

Jimmy: What?

Mary: There's a big witch and it will kill you.

Jimmy: Yes, I can see her too.

Mary: See its black eyes. Now she's coming down. She shooted you and you're all dead.

Jimmy: She shooted you and you're all dead too.

Mary: No she didn't, but she bited me and she's going to bite you too. She's got big yellow teeth and she'll make you bleed.

Jimmy: Ooh! I'm all bleeding and you're bleeding too. She bited you on the leg.

Mary: Now he's sleeping and he won't hear us. Let's run away before he wakes up.

> The children join hands and run off to hide under the teacher's desk, whispering excitedly.

This byplay was revealing in many ways, but for our purpose we need point out only one. It showed strikingly the fears that seethed inside Mary, and one of her methods of ridding herself of them—or at least diminishing their unbearable intensity—was by living them dramatically and sharing them with another child, scaring him too, and being at least temporarily the destructive witch.

THE THIRD DADDY

In the very last months of the school year, when Mary had actually become able to sleep several times during nap and had shown other promising signs, there was a second drastic change at home. Catherine's second marriage was even shorter-lived than her first. Again there was a divorce and again a quick remarriage, this time to John.

Catherine's handling this time was more adept, and Mary's reaction less violent, but the child slipped backward into her familiar tortured patterns. The patterns now followed old grooves. The fountainhead of Mary's anguished, protesting behavior was still and would always be that period of unexplained, uncomprehended conflict which came to its climax in the first divorce: the time when her "real daddy" went away, the time when her gods first failed her. That had been the first crack in Mary's world. From then on, she could only expect further crumbling.

Mary spent part of that summer with her father and his new family in Chicago, the rest with his parents—and still another new nurse—at their summer home. When she came home her mother was pregnant again.

Back at school in the fall, a new teacher had to win Mary's confidence and soothe her fears, a task like the labors of Sisyphus; no sooner had the school pushed her part way up the hill toward recovery than events at home pulled her down again. Christmas brought presents to Mary from all her daddies and their wives, and from her own mother, among other gifts, came a new baby brother, Brucie.

Shortly after that New Year's, Catherine brought her troubled little girl for psychiatric help.

WHAT CAN BE DONE FOR THE MARYS?

At first, when her mother left the room, Mary would not sit down, nor would she take off her coat and hat. Under the jauntily tilted, bright beret her small drawn face was closed and suspicious. Yet almost her first words were revealing:

"Mommy made me come here because I'm bad."

As she dared to show a little interest in the small dolls and doll furniture on the shelves, she allowed her coat to be removed. A bright new dime fell from her fist and she swooped to retrieve it.

"My daddy gave this to me," she said defensively, and snapped on a bright smile as she went on: "My daddy is the richest man in the world. He brings me a new present every day. I have a doll bigger than me. She weewees and she shuts her eyes. She's a good baby. Not like Jackie —Jackie's bad. Daddy gave her to me and he's got a thousand hundred zillion dimes."

With this boastful description of her daddy, the kind of bravado many children display who are unsure of their parents' love, Mary picked up one of the dolls and seated it in a chair. The suggestion was made that the little girl—the doll—was in school.

Mary pushed another doll across the table.

"That's the mommy. She's coming to take her home. She's going to kiss her and kiss her and kiss her and then her nurse is going to read to her before she makes her take her rest."

She illustrated by banging the dolls together, a most violent version of kissing. A comment was made that these two, the mother and daughter dolls, were kissing pretty roughly, as if they really were not so loving to each other. A look of understanding and recognition was enough to establish that Mary caught a glimpse of her own feelings.

Then she began to build a scene at home, taking dolls from the shelf, and now naming each one literally: Mary and Mommy and Nurse, Sister Jane and Brother Jackie. But the fabulous daddy failed to appear. Where was Daddy?

"Oh, Daddy's not home. He's too busy. He's at his factory. Daddy has the biggest factory in the world. It's a thousand million feet high and it's very far away in a big woods. It's full of giants and Daddy tells them all what to do."

"I wonder why this daddy has to be so strong and powerful."

Again Mary did not answer the comment directly. She tossed her head and added, too gaily, "I don't care whether Daddy comes home. It doesn't make any difference."

And now she stepped directly into the reality of her problems. She picked up the doll Jackie and began to spank and scold him.

Jackie, she explained, was bad. He jumped into her bed and woke her up at night. He was a scairdy cat. He had bad dreams "about witches with yellow teeth and big shiny knives. They're going to take him to their dark cave and cut him up into little pieces and eat him."

At first the bad dreams were all Jackie's. The repression of her own dreams she explained by saying, "I am not a good rememberer." But imperceptibly the defense went down and Mary slipped into the dreams: "Jackie dreamed about a beautiful fairy who took him to her house and then she changed into a big ugly witch. The house was all full of tigers and snakes and they started chasing me and I ran and I ran and I ran!"

Her face flushed, her eyes glittered with excitement, and the dreams poured out in a torrent. Mary had no time now for disguising their ownership: "One time I dreamed about a big witch that was going to eat me up and just before she was going to bite me she turned into Mommy. And it was Mommy and she was standing by my bed and I kicked her in the stomach and she squealed," Mary ended, triumphant. (Internally the wheels are spinning: *I love Mommy—I hate Mommy; I want Mommy to come and comfort me—I want Mommy to come so I can punish her.*)

When Mary went to the blackboard and took up a piece of chalk, she drew, again, her family. In its directness this was helpful; indeed, child psychiatrists know that a conflict does not often flow into an expression so free of symbolism.

Here was she, with Mommy. She went to the other end of the board, leaving a wide space between, and drew two more figures. "These are my daddies." She erased one, announcing that she had decided to have only one Daddy. But after a moment of painful hesitation she lifted her hand and scrawled the second male figure in again.

"Daddy went away because I'm a bad girl. Mommy made him go." (*This all happened because I'm bad. No, because Daddy's bad.*)

"He's my real daddy." (*I have a daddy who belongs to me—I must have one!*)

"He's not going to be away all the time." (*He will come back because he does love me—he must love me!*)

"Mommy told me." (*There! If Mommy says it, it must be so.*)

"What did Mommy tell you, Mary?"

"I don't remember." (*Did she tell me? And even if Mommy told me, is it true? Mommy has told me other things . . .*) "I don't remember," said Mary, closing the subject with finality.

But the subject would not remain closed. She had to talk about it, and with gentle encouragement she began again.

"My real Daddy is in Chicago. He has another wife. I love my Daddy."

"Who is the other daddy, there on the blackboard?"

To that, with the aggressiveness which covers defeat, she hurled her challenge:

"I have three daddies and three mommies!"

But three of each were too many; Mary wanted only one. She longed to go back to the time when she had only one daddy, a "real" daddy.

"I'm going to visit my real daddy after school stops. If I'm not a bad girl I can stay there all summer."

Thus Mary told her own confused, painful version of what had happened to her. If she could only be good enough, her real daddy would love her again and let her stay with him.

Meanwhile she loved her father and longed for him, boasted about his strength because she wished him to be strong and he had not been strong when she had needed his strength.

And she loved her mother and longed to have her, as she had had her briefly in babyhood, all to herself in a safe and comfortable world. She wanted her mother apart from all the new fathers and the baby brothers who were always coming between. But she did not want the mother who sent her father away and brought in these other fathers. She did not want the mother on whom she could not rely. She did not want the mother who, witchlike, threatened her with destruction for some "badness" which she did not understand.

THE ACCEPTANCE OF HARD REALITY

Can anything be done to help Mary?

Yes, a great deal.

Mary can be relieved of her anxieties, those inexplicable churning fears which make her nights and half her days a horror of dreadful fantasies. She can be helped to talk them out, to play them out, to see them in daylight and to get at what is behind them, and thus to free herself of the tug and pull of these anxieties.

Mary can be relieved of her guilt. She can come to accept it as a fact that her father does not think she is bad, that he did not leave because she was bad, that his leaving had nothing to do with her, that he was sorry to leave her and would like to have her with him.

She can come to understand that her father loves her and has always loved her, that he does not always expect her to be "good," that even when she is "bad," she is not so bad as she thinks, and he still loves her.

She can come to accept her father as he is, not a god, but a man, who can make mistakes and who is sorry if his mistakes hurt his little girl, who wants his little girl to be happy even though his search for his own happiness takes him far away from her.

Mary can come to accept and love her mother; though she can never again rely on her as all-knowing and all-powerful, she would in time be obliged to recognize her mother's human fallibility anyway. Now, for her own sake, she must only recognize it sooner, and grow strong enough within herself to accept her mother's weakness.

All this is hard, and it takes time. Mary cannot undo in a day the elaborate defenses she has been months and years in building against her fate, and then in another day build a set of new, realistic, and healthy protections against hurt.

But it can be done. It has been done. Many children even more troubled than Mary have done it, when they have been helped through the tangle of their confusions and slowly led back toward reality, perhaps not an ideal reality but an acceptable one. Some children have made dramatic recoveries. Parents have even indulged in such words as "phenomenal." By such oversize descriptions they are in fact only giving the measure of their own relief.

These recoveries are not phenomenal. When parents can follow with warmth and sympathy the same path which the child is trying to follow, then these "phenomenal" recoveries become understandable.

At six Mary stands before us, emotionally maimed. She is ridden by fears and hatreds; her only defense is to attack. As we have come to know her, the chances for her future happiness look bleak indeed.

But they need not remain so. She longs to love and be loved. She can learn again that which, as a happy infant, she instinctively knew, but she will learn it on a more mature level. As with other children, the therapeutic process can in a sense help Mary develop a kind of maturity to deal with her parents' immaturity. She will have to accept realities which more fortunate children need not learn so painfully, nor so young. But she can learn to accept them.

Can we prevent what happened to Mary?

In one way we can prevent the damage which she has suffered.

We cannot undo the past. Catherine and Peter did not want or choose to fail at marriage; their failure was in the cards they were dealt at birth. They have married and divorced, not to harm their children, but because they could not help themselves. Parents like Catherine and Peter may, however, become troubled enough about themselves to seek the kind of help which could change their destiny. As part of Mary's treatment, both parents were brought in to participate, and they developed enough insight eventually to accept the suggestion of treatment for themselves.

BEFORE THE DAMAGE IS DONE

So far in this story we have been concerned with the aftermath of divorce, in a situation which required momentous changes.

But the Catherines and Peters can be helped to understand in advance what is happening to their children before the divorce stage is reached. Even what may appear small points in handling may have big consequences.

If Peter, for example, had perceived what his precipitate departure would do to his little girl, would he have gone in quite the same reckless way? If Catherine had known how her lame, shaking, inadequate explanations did not explain, but only reinforced the fears which had already begun to form in the child's mind, would she have plunged ahead into the morass of confusion?

And if either had realized, during the first crucial period of conflict between them, how badly their secret was actually being kept, would they not have stopped to take thought, to take counsel with each other, perhaps to seek advice?

Most parents would. Many parents have. When they have felt themselves inadequate, or when they have come to realize what the child has at stake, they have sought advice where they could find it.

Their very understanding of the child's need has guided them in better ways, often without outside advice. They have found ways to help their children even while they themselves have been caught in the débris of their shattered marriage.

CHILDREN WHO HATE

FRITZ REDL AND DAVID WINEMAN

THE CHILDREN: THIS IS WHAT HAPPENED
TO THEM BEFORE THEY CAME

We think that it is important for the reader to have some perspective into the past of the children who came to live with us. Yet we do not intend to go into such details as one would expect to find in a case history analysis since, if we attempted to do this for each Pioneer, we would require a whole new volume to present our material. What is intended is to introduce the reader to some of the important experiences with which these children came to us and which loom behind their behavioral productions as they emerge in the recorded material in succeeding chapters.

The Adults in Their Lives

If prevailing criteria for what constitutes an adequate child-adult relationship pattern are used as a basis for reaching conclusions, we can see very little in the case history profiles of our children that would satisfy even the most naive clinician or educator that they had had anything even approaching an "even break." In very few instances were we able to gather any evidence that there had been even continuity of relationship with original parent images. Broken homes through divorce and desertion, the chain-reaction style of foster home placements and institutional storage, were conspicuous events in their lives. Aside from continuity, the quality of the tie between child and adult world was marred by rejection ranging from open brutality, cruelty, and neglect to affect barrenness on the part of some parents and narcissistic absorption in their own interests which exiled the child emotionally from them. Certainly there were also operative heavy mixtures of both styles of rejec-

From *Children Who Hate* by Fritz Redl and David Wineman (New York: The Macmillan Company, © 1951 by The Free Press, a Corporation; Free Press paperback edition 1966), pages 60-61. Reprinted by permission.

The experiences and observations which formed the basis of this book came from three social work projects in Detroit. One included a treatment house, called Pioneer House, for extremely aggressive children who could no longer be helped or handled successfully in any other facility for disturbed children.

tion, overt and unconscious. One of the things that constantly amazed us when we would observe the parents and children together was how much like strangers they were to one another. In this connection, we were impressed by how little interest the parents took in what was happening to the children in treatment. Contrary to our expectations that they might become competitive with the treatment milieu on the basis of feelings of guilt for placing the child and for their own inadequacy, they never became involved on any level at all. Their main, unconcealed reaction was: "We're glad you've got them, not us. Life is so peaceful without them."

This phenomenon of casual surrender of their own children marks these parents off decisively from the parents of the typical neurotic child who has had to go into institutional placement. The parents of the neurotic child who cannot live with the child also begin to feel in his absence that they cannot live without him either. He is somehow necessary to their neurotic design. This difference in the parental style of involvement with one's own child between the two groups is of very basic etiological significance in determining their contrasting symptom structures, since it is really the difference between little or no relationship at all, as we saw in our group, and an ambivalent but strong love-hate-ridden relationship. Further, we could gather no impression, either from case histories or subsequent material productions by the children, once they were in treatment, that they had known even one adult with whom they had built up a warm relationship on an occasional friendly visit basis to which they could look back and say, "Gee, it was fun when I was with so-and-so once." There were no uncles, aunts, cousins, or friends who seemed to take any interest in them which was enough to provide significant gratifications. This whole vacuum in adult relationship potentialities cannot possibly be overestimated in terms of how impoverished these children felt or how much hatred and suspicion they had toward the adult world.

THOUSANDS FINDING MARITAL RELIEF IN 'NO FAULT' DIVORCE

Jack V. Fox

Los Angeles (UPI)—Mr. Leon, a gray haired man in his forties who works for an electronics firm, was on the witness stand for less than 20 seconds.

"Have irreconcilable differences developed in your marriage?" his lawyer asked.

"Yes."

"Have those differences brought a breakdown of your marriage?"

"Yes."

"Is there any chance of a reconciliation?"

"No."

"Do you wish to avail yourself of marriage counseling services?"

"No."

That was it. The judge ruled that the marriage was dissolved and a union that had lasted 19 years was broken. Mrs. Leon didn't say a word. The couple had stipulated the division of their property and the husband agreed to pay $30 a month alimony plus support of the two children whose custody was awarded to Mrs. Leon.

It sounds cold and callous but the chief judge of the domestic relations courts in Los Angeles hails California's "no fault" dissolution of marriage system as one of the most sensible approaches to the ceaseless battle between the sexes that could have been legislated.

Superior Court Justice William Hogoboom said that fears that such a relatively easy means of dissolving marriages, with no reason except incompatibility, might lead to an avalanche of broken homes have proved unfounded.

Applications for dissolution of marriage went up 8.8 per cent in Los Angeles County in the year of 1970 when the new law went into effect, compared with suits for divorce in 1969, he said. But this year the rate has dropped to only 4-5 per cent above 1969.

Hogoboom said he feels the most important thing is that husbands and wives who have lived together in bitterness and even hatred rather than go through the trauma of public accusations can start new lives.

Reprinted from the Ontario-Upland *Daily Report* by permission of the editor and UPI.

"They don't have to prove that the other has done something terrible," he said.

"And they can go their ways before rigid divorce laws force the man to start sleeping with another woman or his wife to hit him on the head with a frying pan."

California was the first state to put such "no fault" divorce into effect. Iowa followed suit with a similar law and Texas has such legislation approved. New York, which until only a few years ago had adultery as the only grounds for divorce, is studying the same approach.

Hogoboom said, in fact, that the California experiment is unique in the whole Western world culture.

The question of fault in a broken marriage enters into the California system only in the case where there is a dispute over custody of the children. Usually the mother is granted custody but there are exceptions when testimony is produced that she is unfit.

Community property is split right down the middle regardless of why the marriage broke up. Alimony and support are based on the two criteria of need and ability to pay. Battles between wealthy couples still lead to long, drawn out court fights.

It is now so simple to get a dissolution of marriage in California that one mate can go to the county clerk's office and get three forms, fill them out and institute suit without ever consulting a lawyer.

There is a standard questionnaire which asks for vital statistics and then leaves four lines open to answer the question: "What do you feel is wrong with this marriage?"

Hogoboom said one of the more encouraging trends under the new law is that the number of couples seeking reconciliation rose by 12½ per cent during 1970. He said 33 per cent did reconcile and followups showed that a year later 75 per cent were still maintaining a home.

Hogoboom also said the new law has enabled the domestic courts to cut down on the backlog of cases since dissolutions now are being handled twice as fast as previously.

The judge acknowledges that the relatively more easy endings to marriage may lead some young couples to break up before really putting themselves to the test of adjusting to the marital status, but he does not believe that is often the case and that, at any rate, it is far overbalanced by the cases of couples who should have ended unhappy liaisons years ago.

It still takes six months for the dissolution to become final. Under the previous divorce law, that term was one year.

THE DOUBLE CROSS

GEORGE ROLEDER

Why do many of those beautiful courtships go sour in marriage? One answer is that they run into a "double cross." That is, some of the wonderful traits which attract mates to each other actually become the source of marital problems!

It seems incredible (and unfair) that this should be, that attractions before marriage could lead to stress after marriage. That's why they are called a "double cross." It is terribly ironic. Which may explain why many couples can't pin down the true source of their conflict even when they try. Who would suspect attractions?

The questionnaires which follow are an attempt to help you predict whether you and your mate (or future mate) are in danger of experiencing one or more "double crosses." Follow the directions in filling them out. Then study the discussion of the scoring which follows. Sample solutions are also offered. Of course, the application to each marriage must be much more specific. In fact it will be necessary for some couples to enlist the help of a marriage counselor to explore their needed adjustments more carefully. The survey is intended merely to alert you to potential areas of conflict, not to guarantee success or failure in your marriage.

PART 1—WHAT YOU LIKE

DIRECTIONS: Circle one of the three adjectives in parentheses (*very, somewhat, not at all*) which best describes your preferred *date* or *mate*, in each of the six items listed below.

I am attracted to a date (or mate) who is:

1. (very, somewhat, not at all)   cute, good-looking, attractive to most members of the opposite sex.

Adapted from the author's *FAMLAB—Family Laboratory* (Dubuque, Ia.: Kendall/ Hunt Publishing Co., 1970).

2. (very, somewhat, not at all)   independent of the advice or
                                               help of others.

3. (very, somewhat, not at all)   careful with money.

4. Males answer here:
   (very much, somewhat, not at all)   the typical feminine female,
                                               clothes-conscious, concerned
                                               about manners, etiquette, and
                                               home life.

4. Females answer here:
   (very much, somewhat, not at all)   the typical masculine male, he-
                                               man, outdoor type.

5. (very, somewhat, not at all)   fond of social life and social
                                               functions.

6. (very, somewhat, not at all)   ambitious and interested in a
                                               career outside the home.

PART 2—WHAT YOU'RE LIKE

Listed below are six samples of personality and behavior. Rate *yourself*
by circling one of the three appropriate adjectives in parentheses (*very,
somewhat, not at all*) to describe what you're like. Then see page 219 and
study the results.

1. I am (very much, somewhat, not at all)   the jealous type.

2. I am (very, somewhat, not at all)   desirous of helping others,
                                               pleased to be needed for advice
                                               or helpful tasks.

3. I am (very, somewhat, not at all)   impulsive in the use of money,
                                               hesitant to save it up.

4. I am (very, somewhat, not at all)   desirous to have my mate accept
                                               and appreciate my outlook on
                                               life, my idea of fun and what is
                                               essential for me to spend money
                                               on.

5. I am (very much, somewhat, not at all)   the stay-at-home type who can
                                               do without crowds and parties.

6. I am (very, somewhat, not at all)   desirous of having my mate put
                                               me and our marriage first, before
                                               a successful career.

   Now let's put the two surveys together and see if you are destined
for marital bliss or a marital "double cross."

ITEM 1

Suppose you circled *very* for item #1 on both parts of the survey. In other words, you really go for a cute partner (Part 1). But you are also the jealous type (Part 2). You want your date or mate all to yourself. You expect exclusiveness. You worry when you hear that things are getting cozy at the office. In fact you worry even before you hear it! You simmer with anger (fear?) when there's an office party for your mate but you're not invited. Why worry? Well, you tell yourself, you were attracted to that cute number, so why shouldn't others fall the same way you did? That's why your worry seems realistic to you. If your fear spills over into your conversations, you may even resort to false accusations and thus ruin some of the mutual trust on which marriages depend.

Before that happens confront your mate with your worry-dilemma. This will give your (probably surprised) mate a chance to reassure you directly and often. Ask your mate to stay in touch more than would be expected by a non-jealous partner. Telephone calls when the other is away, brief notes and explanations will help keep your imagination under control.

If you marked *somewhat* for either part, the risk of a "double cross" is still present, just not as great. If you marked *not at all* on either of the two parts, this item is not a potential problem area for you.

ITEM 2

A *very* or *somewhat* in either Part 1 or Part 2 on this trait spells trouble. In Part 1, for example, it means that you are attracted to the independent type. That's the type who is self-reliant and gets along quite well without the advice or help of others. Nice American ideal, wouldn't you say? Of course. No wonder you and many others are attracted to that sort. However, a *very* or *somewhat* on Part 2 would suggest that you enjoy being helpful to others. But, unfortunately, your independent mate won't need much help! You enjoy the feeling of being needed. Sorry, you'll have to do your helping somewhere else. Your mate is self-sufficient, remember. And save your advice. Your mate may have tolerated it during courtship (when romance dictated polite manners). In marriage, however, the truth comes out. Your pearls of wisdom fall on bored ears. You'll say, "My mate doesn't seem to need me anymore." You may begin to wonder if it means a loss of love. Useless to your competent mate, you may also feel resentment about the inferior position in which this places and keeps you.

Solutions for this "double cross" include the reminder that your mate hasn't changed since you met. Fact is, your help was never needed as much as you thought. So remember you must have been desired by your mate for other reasons. You must have other attributes. Explore those and concentrate on them. Keep yourself attractive that way and forget the big helper routine. On the other hand, no mate is competent in all areas. Discover the gaps in that independence. Make your help more selective. The increased responsibilities of marriage and family life should provide some new needs in which your help could count.

A *not at all* for either survey means no trouble; the proper combination exists between what attracts you and what you are like.

ITEM 3

A *very* or *somewhat* on either or both parts of Item #3 calls attention to the contrast between your thrifty, penny-saving date or mate, and your own carefree attitude toward money. During courtship you may have liked that in your date because it suggested a secure, bills-paid future. But in marriage that same penny-*saver* comes across as a penny-*pincher.* Especially if that mate controls most of the spending and doesn't agree with your idea of "essential" spending.

If you get caught in this "double cross," you may have to engineer a budget which allows you spending money of your own, a personal allowance. You can squander it as you like without answering to your tight-fisted partner, and without ruining the family finances. Or consider earning money of your own. You may need a "his" and "hers" budget system to keep money squabbles out of your romance.

Suppose you are an impulsive *male* matched to a thrifty wife. You're lucky. Your "double cross" is not as threatening to your happiness. You can more easily indulge your whims in the good ole' double-standard, male-chauvinistic U.S.A. After all, it's your money. You'll have no problems until the income gets shorter than the bills. Or until your worried mate explodes in self-pity over her enormous role (she feels) of budget-saver. In the interest of marital peace, do some compromising as recommended above. Agree to a monthly amount which each of you can "blow" or "save" to suit your unique life styles. Make the amount large enough to satisfy your marriage-compromised need, but not so great as to endanger the family budget or the sanity of your mate, whichever is closer to the breaking point!

Relax! There's no future "double cross" if you marked a *not at all* on either survey.

ITEM 4

This item alerts you to the problems created by mixing the sexes in marriage. Not that I believe, as some do, that the sexes must inevitably be at odds. I believe that friendship and companionship are most responsible for the pleasures of married life. And yet this item unnerves me. Take any combination of *very's* or *somewhat's* and you have a potentially go-nowhere marriage. That would be the matching of the typical male and female. The stereotypes. That was fine in a traditional America when men had to be tough, outdoor he-men. That's what it took to cope with the work and danger. Transportation, for example, required manual taming of wind, wave, or wild horse. Brawn made sense. Wives were busy enough with an indoor world of sewing and baking to leave the man's world to him. It is true that in public they were expected to act refined, quiet, and submissive. However, understanding of each other's worlds was kept alive, because much of the planting, raising, harvesting, and preserving of crops was a partnership venture. Family members watched each other at work and at play, more than many moderns realize.

In today's money-economy approach to family life, a wedge has unintentionally been driven between the sexes. Money comes from some foreign, mysterious source—through Dad or Mom. It is spent by the younger males for their world; by females for theirs. Unfortunately, each sex knows little about the personal money-world of the other—not until their two worlds collide in marriage. Thus "feminine" females are good to look at, but they have difficulty accepting the importance of male essentials: tires for cars, costs of baseball tickets, gun club magazines, beer, liquor, and nude centerfolds. "Won't he ever grow up and do without his *toys?*" complains the surprised wife.

Likewise, "masculine" males of Marlboro fame may keep alive an American dream, but there are few cattle to rope in suburban backyards. The muscled, outdoor type is fun to admire on the beach and football field, but he has generally learned little about the high cost of carrots, cosmetics, and baby diapers. When he is asked to *pay* for them, he'll have no sympathy for such "unnecessary" items. When he starts saying things like, "Spending our money for such foolishness" or "All women seem to think about are the latest styles and hair colors," then his "double cross" has begun.

Misunderstanding, harsh words, and the resulting shaky marriage must be saved by deliberate male-female appreciation. Identify your first rumbles for what they really are: symptoms of mixed sexes. Not selfishness or stupidity, just the result of living in single sex compartments for eighteen years. You might try the following: Males, repeat after me, "Her things are as important to her as mine are to me. My things are as silly to her as hers are to me." Gals, repeat after me, "His things are as important to him as mine are to me. My essentials are as silly to him as his are to me."

Until the differences make sense to both, you could ease the spending strain by splitting the budget into "sex" compartments, agree to a general price tag for each and thus maintain a temporary armed truce.

Not at all appearing in either survey saves these traits from becoming future irritants.

ITEM 5

How did you fare on Item #5? Are you strangely attracted to the type who is fond of social life, even though you prefer to find your own entertainment at home? If your *very* or *somewhat* appeared on either part, the conflict will be obvious to you. Or will it? For many this difference doesn't become a source of irritation until after marriage. Why not? Why isn't this "double cross" exposed during dating and courtship?

Several reasons account for the surprising conflict remaining hidden before marriage. For one thing, until you are actually married you can each visit your same-sex friends as much as you like. Neither of you feels trapped. So you don't *feel* the difference between you. Secondly, during courtship each may curb his natural trait and stretch himself toward the other's life style. Thus the introvert will endure enough social life to hang on to the beloved. Likewise, the social bug will consent (and act content) when kept in. The payoff for the grounded partner may be in the form of intimate necking, petting, and whatnot. So who'd complain? Not even the extrovert!

There's a third reason. Let's imagine that you are the stay-at-home type. During courtship you enjoy your socially experienced friend because of the "social security" provided. You can go places you've always been curious about but afraid to tackle alone. Your date keeps an eye on you. That is also what makes dating fun—being the center of your companion's attention. So you like it. It's not until after marriage that you discover how much your partner's social pace is not your own. You're getting enough marital companionship at home. Why go out? You settle back into your introvert pattern.

What does your crowd-loving mate do after marriage? Chafes under the confinement. Itches to get out. Can't understand what happened to you. So you are asked: "Is it okay to go out without you? To evening activities? At the church? At a nightclub? To parties where couples will be present?"

Do you get the picture? At the stay-at-home end of this relationship you might very well become upset over your mate's desire and ability to achieve public recognition through (too many!) social, church, or civic "duties." Such a mate won't easily say "No" to requests for club work. You will spend time alone with the children. It will be hard to complain about that because your mate invited you to go along (you'll be reminded). Furthermore, those social activities are all "worthwhile." So you'll probably suffer in silence, sleep alone, and have dreams of setting dynamite under enemy bridges.

What might ease the strain? Showing your true self earlier during courtship would alert your partner to the need for adjustment. That would create less future shock. After marriage, your half of the compromise style would include pushing yourself out more often with your mate. Encourage participation without you. Invite friends in more than you really prefer, especially if you wonder what goes on when you're not around. Does this sound like hard work? Compromise usually is.

Notice that on Item #5 you can pick up the "double cross" in reverse. That is, if your preferred date is *not at all* fond of social activities (Part 1), but you are *not at all* the stay-at-home type (Part 2), that's the same problem but with you grounded instead. Work toward the compromise described above. And remember that your home-body mate will respond better to social *invitations* than to *bullying* or *threatening*.

A *not at all* in combination with a *very* or *somewhat* will not produce the "double cross."

ITEM 6

This final item seems ridiculous! What could possibly be dangerous about falling in love with someone who is ambitious? Isn't this what a majority of females list as very important in their choice of mate? In a male, isn't this the trait which makes him a steady provider? Doesn't ambition in a female give her incentive to develop as a person, find a career, keep her brain active, and make her an interesting companion (not to mention the money her career adds to the family finances)? Right! It is a wonderful attribute. And it won't cause irritation in your marriage unless you also happen to expect that ambitious mate to put you and the marriage first. In other words, if you also circled that you are *very* or *somewhat* desirous of having your mate put you and the marriage before a successful career, you are inviting a "double cross."

Think about it! Getting to the top is almost impossible in a competitive society like ours unless it is placed first in one's efforts. That also takes time—time away from home. So if by "first" you mean where and on what your mate spends the most time and effort, you're creating a conflict in which you can't win.

So you will wait at home with cold food, or in vain at the department store meeting place when your ambitious mate forgets to call about working late. You will be expected to forgive the forgetfulness because of the "importance" of the work. How can you object when the extra effort is "for the future of the marriage"? If you also suffer from jealousy (see Item #1, p. 219) you will even add suspicion to your festering resentment.

Solutions? Remember, first of all, that your mate was already like this when you married. It wasn't *because* of you or the marriage that this type became ambitious. It was already part of the personality. Marriage only supplied an additional reason to stay absorbed in work. Remind yourself, secondly, that your mate knows you were attracted by that ambitious streak. Now it's a matter of holding your attraction. You may have to convince your mate that you can settle for a little less ambition, that you're willing to wait a few years for a new home. Try to turn the ambition away from economic success and toward projects within the family.

Perhaps you're also trying to feel successful through your mate. In that case you ought to try working toward a career yourself. As you try to hold home and career together, you will also understand your mate's conflict better.

A *not at all* in either Part 1 or Part 2 means there is no potential conflict on this item.

A FINAL WORD

It may be that your choices fit the categories of a "double cross," but you haven't noticed any problems in your marriage adjustment. Fine! Let's not create problems where none exist. Perhaps you made the switch quickly and maturely. Or perhaps the degree of the traits is milder in reality than the labels of this questionnaire indicated for you. On the other hand, the events which create tensions may still lie in a future stage of your family life cycle.

The aim of the survey is not to condemn you to an irreversible mismatch but to alert you to possibilities and likelihoods of conflict. That's so you can identify your problem and start your switch in thinking early in the marital game. If you uncover very much of, or even somewhat of, a "double cross" while you're still in the dating stage, great! The fewer surprises after marriage, the better.

abortion, 58, 170
age for marriage, 5
age of mates, learned custom, 5
ambition, conflict over, 196, 223
American Association of Sex Educa-
    tors and Counselors, 70
American Civil Liberties Union, 79
American Institute of Family Rela-
    tions, 160
American Medical Association, 72
American Psychiatric Association, 72
Armour, Richard, 3

bachelorhood, end of, 49
Bartel, Gilbert D., 60
Beatles, 36
behavior modification, 142-146
Bell, Robert R., 29
Benson, Leonard, 113
Bettelheim, Bruno, Dr., 108, 147
Bible, 28, 44
Blood, Robert O., Jr., 93
Braun, Saul, 14
budget. *See* money

Cadwallader, Mervyn, 197
Calderone, Mary, 48
Canadian family life, 117
career, and family, 93, 99, 108, 196,
    224
chastity, 23, 43, 133
children
    age for entering school, 118
    and development of hate, 213
    in divorce, 198-212
    effects of working mothers on, 108
    freedom of choice by, 147-152
    need for extended family, 177-180
    and prejudice, 123, 125
    in Russian family life, 117
    sex education of, 132-141

training by behavior modification,
    142-146
in unlicensed marriage, 164
Christian ethics, 27, 43
cohabitation, 38, 160
Coleman, James, 118
college education, choice of, 151
commitment
    in successful marriage, 193
    in unlicensed marriage, 173, 175
communes, 181-190
companionship, 221
compensation, motive in marrying, 16
compromise, in marriage, 219-225
Congdon, Tom, 49
contraception, 28, 41, 58
courtship
    of liberated women, 155-157
    polite behavior in, 219
Cox, Frank D., 7
crush, 3, 16

dating, 7-14, 15-21
day-care centers, 112, 157
de Beauvoir, Simone, 157
Denmark, sex in, 67, 77
Despert, J. Louise, Dr., 198
divorce
    and age of mates, 18
    and children, 198-212
    effect of, 166
    experience of, 195-197
    new laws, in California, 215
double standard, 24, 33, 44
draft, 151
Durkheim, Emile, 119

Ehrlich, Paul R., 57
Ehrmann, Winston W., 31
Eller, Vermard, 14
Ellis, Albert, 30

emotions, learned, 5
equal opportunity. *See* welfare
escalation, in sex, 11
exploitation, 23-25
extended family
  modern, 177-180
  rural commune, 183-190
extramarital sex, 52, 60-62, 168
extrovert, 16, 222

family
  extended, 177-180
  See also marriage
  as social unit, 113
father
  influence on daughter, 16
  role as breadwinner, 113
  role in divorce, 198-212
femininity, 34, 100, 133, 155, 221
fertility, 50
Fort, Joel, Dr., 48
Fraser, Ian M., 22
Friedan, Betty, 157
frigidity, 25
Furlong, Monica, 23

Gallup poll, 88
game of sex, 11-13
Gardener, Joyce, 181
Gay World, 60
genocide, 58
Gibb, J. R., 139
Goffman, E., 177
Graham, Billy, 43
group sex, 60-62

Hacker, Helen, 120
Halpern, Howard, 117
Harrad Experiment, 38, 60
Harris poll, 88
hedonism, 29
heterosexual stage, 7-14
Hill, Reuben, 113, 196
Himes, Norman, 40
Hobart, Charles, 114
Hochstein, Rollie, 15
Hoffman, Martin, 60
Holdren, John P., 57

homosexual, 60-61, 82
Hunt, Morton M., 29, 48

illegitimacy, 9, 25, 134
independence, 19, 219
infertility, 23
inheritance, of wealth, 119
intercourse, 7, 12, 23, 40, 51, 81, 84
introvert, 16, 222
Israeli kibbutzim, 117, 119

jealousy, 71

Kinsey, Alfred, 14, 32, 88

Landis, Judson T., 193
Landis, Mary G., 193
Lerner, Max, 33
Lewinsohn, Richard, 34
love
  attitudes of, male and female, 168
  as basis for marriage, 16
  development of, 3, 18
  falling in love, 15, 18
  and personality problems, 17
  romantic, 15, 18, 166, 197
Luckey, Eleanore Braun, 132
lust, 48, 160

Mace, David, 117
machismo, 157
McIntire, Roger W., 142
McLuhan, Marshall, 14
marital roles
  in child discipline, 143-146
  conflict in, 97, 217-225
  division of labor, 93, 99
  father-as-breadwinner, 113-120
  in Israeli kibbutzim, 117
  in the new marriage, 158, 161-162
  in pregnancy, 49
  and sex education, 132-139
  switching roles, 99-107
  traditional, 99-101
  and women's liberation, 155-157
  working mothers, 99, 108-112
marriage
  and community attitudes, 172, 185,
    188

as dynamic relationship, 194
failure, 195, 198-212
as institution, 16, 18, 113
inter-racial, 125-131
without license, 160-176, 183
personality adjustment in, 217-225
preparation for, 174, 217-225
readiness for, testing, 19-21
and romantic love, 16
successful, 193
surprises in, 49, 225
masculinity, 11, 23, 50, 103, 116, 120, 133, 157, 221
Masters, William, Dr., 47, 50
masturbation, 50
mate selection
attractions in, 217
and backgrounds, similar, 17
proper choice, 19-21
mature love, 16-18
micro-bopper, 8
Millet, Kate, 157
Mogey, John, 120
money
family-budget ethic, 114
sex compartments, 222
as source of conflict, 220
in unlicensed marriage, 167, 171, 186
Montagu, Ashley, 101
Moore, Barrington, 114
Morison, Robert, 118
Motz, Annabelle B., 177
movie idols, as ideal, 17
Murdock, George, 8, 14

National Congress of Parents and Teachers, 72
National Council of Churches, 72
National Education Association, 72
National Institute of Mental Health, 79
new marriage, defined, 159
"No Fault" divorce, 215
non-sex, 12, 43
nudism, 42, 47

Otto, Herbert A., 158, 195, 197
overpopulation, 57

parents
effect on children, 16, 213
See also marital rules
peer group, 11, 17
personal development, 20, 133, 147-152
personality adjustment
of children in divorce, 198-212
in communes, 183-190
in successful marriage, 193
Piaget, Jean, 112
Playboy, 47, 61
population growth, 57
pornography
and aggression, 84
Commission Report on, 63-89
criticism of Commission Report, 77-89
delinquent behavior, and, 67, 80-87
effects of, 63-68, 80-87
recommendations of Commission, 73-77
satiation through, 65
and sex education, 23, 69
pregnancy, husband's reaction to, 49
premarital sex
with affection, 34, 41
and Christian ethics, 27, 43
and double standard, 24, 33, 44
effect on marriage, 31
experiments with, 38
frequency of, 31
infatuation in. See crush
medical opinion about, 26
among star-worshippers, 36
puberty, 7

rape, 9, 85
Redl, Fritz, 213
Reiss, Ira L., 29, 32-34
religion
and premarital sex, 27, 35, 43
and sex knowledge, 25-27, 43, 137
and "swinging," 61
and unlicensed marriage, 160, 173
remarriage, 197, 198
reproduction. See overpopulation
Rimmer, Robert, 38, 60
Roleder, George, 217

roles. *See* marital roles
Ruch, Floyd, 7
Rue, James, Dr., 160, 173
Russian family life, 117

sex
  in Britain, 22, 36
  and Christian ethics, 27, 43
  and drugs, 36
  and emotions, 24
  and groupies, 36
  without guilt, 161
  knowledge of, 6, 22-27, 47, 132-141
  and love, 18, 41
  in marriage, 47, 49
  during pregnancy, 51
  and social class, 52
  and social mores, 8
  statistics on, 26, 31
sex behavior, defined, 12
sex education
  from adults, 8, 22, 70
  in Britain, 22-27
  experimental, 38
  goals of, 134
  in medical schools, 71
  from peers, 3-6, 22
  and pornography, 23, 69
  results of, 71
  sources of, 70
  in theological schools, 71
  and values, 137
sex roles, compared, 23, 168, 221
sexual
  arousal, 11, 23, 25
  desire, and love, 15, 18
  experimentation, 7-11, 13, 38
  maturity, 134

potency, 7
  pressure, source of, 7
Shevey, Sandra, 155
SIECUS, 48
Simon, William, Dr., 48
social class and reproduction, 57-59
social mores and sex, 8
Sorokin, Pitirim A., 29
steady dating, 13-14
Stoller, Frederick H., 177
Sugarman, Daniel A., 15
swapping mates. *See* swinging
swinging, 61

Talmon, Yonina, 113
Terman, Lewis, 13
T-Group Theory, 139
traditional marriage
  characteristics, 158
  criticism of, 196

unlicensed marriage
  goals of, 161-162, 175
  implications of, 171
Updike, John, 52

value system and sex, 11
venereal disease, 23, 25, 134
virginity. *See* chastity
virility, male, 7, 50. *See also* masculinity

Wallace, George, 61
Watts, Alan, 47
Welfare ethic, 115
Whitman, Howard, 30
Wineman, David, 213
women's liberation, 33, 48, 101, 155, 164